Yashka

Maria Botchareva (Yashka)

Yashka

My Life as Peasant, Officer and Exile

The Recollections of the Founder and Commander
of the Russian Women's Battalion of Death during
the First World War

ILLUSTRATED

Maria Botchkareva

LEONAUR

Yashka
My Life as Peasant, Officer and Exile
The Recollections of the Founder and Commander of the Russian Women's Battalion of
Death during the First World War
by Maria Botchkareva

ILLUSTRATED

First published under the title
Yashka My Life as Peasant, Officer and Exile

Leonaur is an imprint of Oakpast Ltd

Copyright in this form © 2019 Oakpast Ltd

ISBN: 978-1-78282-790-0 (hardcover)
ISBN: 978-1-78282-791-7 (softcover)

http://www.leonaur.com

Publisher's Notes

Contents

Introduction

In the early summer of 1917 the world was thrilled by a news item from Petrograd announcing the formation by one Maria Botchkareva of a women's fighting unit under the name of "The Battalion of Death." With this announcement an obscure Russian peasant girl made her debut in the international hall of fame. From the depths of dark Russia Maria Botchkareva suddenly emerged into the limelight of modern publicity. Foreign correspondents sought her, photographers followed her, distinguished visitors paid their respects to her. All tried to interpret this arresting personality. The result was a riot of misinformation and misunderstanding.

Of the numerous published tales about, and interviews with, Botchkareva that have come under my observation, there is hardly one which does not contain some false or misleading statement. This is partly due to the deplorable fact that the foreign journalists who interpreted Russian men and affairs to the world during the momentous year of 1917 were, with very few exceptions, ignorant of the Russian language; and partly to Botchkareva's reluctance to take every adventurous stranger into her confidence. It was her cherished dream to have a complete record of her life incorporated in a book someday. This work is the realisation of that dream.

To a very considerable extent, therefore, the narrative here unfolded is of the nature of a confession. When in the United States in the summer of 1918, Botchkareva determined to prepare her autobiography. Had she been educated enough to be able to write a letter fluently, she would probably have written her own life-story in Russian and then had it translated into English. Being semi-illiterate, she found it necessary to secure the services of a writer commanding a knowledge of her native language, which is the only tongue she speaks. The procedure followed in the writing of this book was this: Botchkareva recited to me in Russian the story of her life, and I recorded it in English in longhand, making every effort to set down her narrative *verbatim*. Not infrequently I would interrupt her with a question intended to draw out some forgotten experiences. However, one of Botchkareva's natural gifts is an extraordinary memory. It took nearly a hundred hours, distributed over a period of three weeks, for her to tell me every detail of her romantic life.

At our first session Botchkareva made it clear that what she was going to tell me would be very different from the yarns credited to her in the press. She would reveal her innermost self and break open for the first time the sealed book of her past. This she did, and in doing so ruined completely several widely circulated tales about her. Perhaps the chief of these is the statement that Botchkareva had enlisted as a soldier and gone to war to avenge her fallen husband. Whether this invention was the product of her own mind or was attributed to her originally by some prolific correspondent, I do not know. In any event it was a handy answer to the eternal question of the pestiferous journalists as to how she came to be a soldier. Unable to explain to the conventional world that profound impulse which really drove her to her remarkable destiny, she adopted this excuse until she had an opportunity to record the full story of her daring life.

This book will also remove that distrustful attitude based on misunderstanding that has been manifested toward Botchkareva in radical circles. When she arrived in the United States she was immediately hailed as a "counter-revolutionary," royalist and sinister intriguer by the extremists. That was a grave injustice to her. She is ignorant of politics, contemptuous of intrigue, and spiritually far and above party strife. Her mission in life was to free Russia from the German yoke.

Being placed virtually in the position of a father confessor, it was my privilege to commune with the spirit of this phenomenal rustic, a privilege I shall ever esteem as priceless. She not only laid bare before me every detail of her amazing life that memory could resurrect, but also allowed me to explore the nooks and corners of her heart to a degree that no friend of hers ever did. Maintaining a critical attitude from the beginning of our association, I was gradually overwhelmed by the largeness of her soul.

Wherein does the greatness of Botchkareva lie? Mrs. Emmeline Pankhurst called her the greatest woman of the century. A correspondent in July, 1917 wrote:

The woman that saved France was Joan of Arc—a peasant girl, Maria Botchkareva is her modern parallel.

Indeed, in the annals of history since the days of the Maid of

Orleans we encounter no feminine figure equal to Botchkareva.

Like Joan of Arc, this Russian peasant girl dedicated her life to her country's cause. If Botchkareva failed—and this is yet problematical, for who will dare forecast the future of Russia?—it would not lessen her greatness. Success in our materialistic age is no measure of true genius. Like Joan of Arc, Botchkareva is the symbol of her country. Can there be a more striking incarnation of France than that conveyed by the image of Joan of Arc? Botchkareva is an astounding typification of peasant Russia, with all her virtues and vices. Educated to the extent of being able to scribble her own name with difficulty, she is endowed with the genius of logic. Ignorant of history and literature, the natural lucidity of her mind is such as to lead her directly to the very few fundamental truths of life. Religious with all the fervour of her primitive soul, she is tolerant in a fashion behoving a philosopher.

Devoted to her country with every fibre of her being, she is free of impassioned partisanship and selfish patriotism. Overflowing with gentility and kindness, she is yet capable of savage outbursts and brutal acts. Credulous and trustful as a child, she can be easily incited against people and things. Intrepid and rash as a fighter, her desire to live on occasions was indescribably pathetic. In a word, Botchkareva embodies all those paradoxical characteristics of Russian nature that have made Russia a puzzle to the world. These traits are illustrated almost in every page of this book. Take away from Russia the veneer of western civilization and you behold her incarnation in Botchkareva. Know Botchkareva and you shall know Russia, that inchoate, invincible, agonized, striving, rising colossus in all its depth and breadth.

It must be made unmistakably clear here that the motives responsible for this book were purely personal. In its origin this work is exclusively a human document, a record of an exuberant life. It was the purpose of Botchkareva and the writer to keep the narrative down to a strict recital of facts. It is really incidental that this record is valuable not only as a biography of a startling personality, but as a revelation of certain phases of a momentous period in human history; not only as a human document, but as a historical document as well. Because Botchkareva always has been and still is strictly non-partisan and because she does not pretend to pass judgment upon events and men, her revelations are of prime importance. The reader gets a picture of Kerensky in action that completely effaces all that has hitherto been said of this tragic but typical product of the Russian *intelligentsia*. Kornilov, Rodzianko, Lenine and Trotzky and some other outstanding personalities of the Russian revolution appear in these pages exactly as they are in reality.

Not a single book, as far as I know, has appeared yet giving an account of how the Russian Army at the front reacted to the Revolution. What was the state of mind of the Russian soldier in the trenches, which was after all the decisive factor in the developments that followed, during the first eight months of 1917? No history of unshackled Russia will be complete without an answer to this vital question. This book is the first to disclose the reactions and emotions of the vast Russian Army at the front to the tremendous issues of the revolution, and is of especial value coming from a veteran peasant soldier of the rank and file.

Perhaps surpassing all else in interest is the horrible picture we get of Bolshevism in action. With the claims of theoretical Bolshevism to establish an order of social equality on earth Botchkareva has no quarrel. She said so to Lenine and Trotzky personally. But then come her experiences with Bolshevism in practice, and there follows a blood-freezing narrative of the rule of mobocracy that will live forever in the memory of the reader.

Botchkareva left the United States towards the end of July, 1918, after having attained the purpose of her visit—an interview with President Wilson. She went to England and thence to Archangel, where she arrived early in September. According to a newspaper despatch, she caused the following proclamation to be posted in village squares and country churches:

I am a Russian peasant and soldier. At the request of the soldiers and peasants I went to America and Great Britain to ask these countries for military help for Russia.

The Allies understand our own misfortunes and I return with the Allied armies, which came only for the purpose of helping to drive out our deadly enemies, the Germans, and not to interfere with our internal affairs. After the war is over the Allied troops will leave Russian soil.

I, on my own part, request all loyal free sons of Russia, without reference to party, to come together, acting as one with the Allied forces, who, under the Russian flag, come to free Russia from the German yoke and in order to help the new free Russian Army with all forces, including Russia, to beat the enemy. Soldiers and peasants! Remember that only a full, clean sweep of the Germans from our soil can give you the free Russia you long for.

New York City,
November, 1918.

CHAPTER 1

My Childhood of Toil

My father, Leonti Semenovitch Frolkov, was born into serfdom at Nikolsko, a village in the province of Novgorod, some three hundred *versts* (a *verst* is about two-thirds of a mile) north of Moscow. He was fifteen when Alexander II emancipated the serfs in 1861, and remembers that historic event vividly, being fond even now of telling of the days of his boyhood. Impressed into the army in the early seventies, he served during the Russo-Turkish War of 1877-78, and distinguished himself for bravery, receiving several medals. When a soldier he learned to read and write, and was promoted to the rank of sergeant.

Returning home at the end of the war, he passed through Tcharanda, a fishermen's settlement on the shore of a lake, in the county of Kirilov, within forty *versts* of Nikolsko. No longer dressed as a moujik, military in gait and bearing, with coins jingling in his pocket, he cut quite a figure in the poor hamlet of Tcharanda. There he met my mother, Olga, the eldest daughter of Elizar Nazarev, perhaps the most destitute dweller of the place.

Elizar, with his wife and three daughters, occupied a shabby hut on the sandy shore of the lake. So poor was he that he could not afford to buy a horse to carry his catch to the city, and was compelled to sell it, far below the market price, to a traveling buyer. The income thus derived was not sufficient to keep the family from hunger. Bread was always a luxury in the little cabin. The soil was not tillable. Elizar's wife would hire herself to the more prosperous peasants in the vicinity for ten *kopecks* a day to labour from sunrise to sunset. (A *kopeck* is normally half a cent.) But even this additional money was not always to be had. Then Olga would be sent out to beg for bread in the neighbouring villages.

Once, when scarcely ten years old, little Olga underwent a harrowing experience, which she could never later recall without horror. Starting home with a basketful of bread, collected from several villages, she was fatigued but happy at the success of her errand, and hurried as fast as she could. Her path lay through a forest. Suddenly she heard the howling of a pack of wolves. Olga's heart almost stopped beating. The dreadful sounds drew nearer. Overcome by fright, she fell unconscious to the ground.

When she regained her senses, she found herself alone. The wolves apparently had sniffed her prostrate body and gone their way. Her basket of bread was scattered in all directions, trampled in the mud. Out of breath, and without her precious burden, she arrived home.

It was in such circumstances that my mother grew to be nineteen, when she attracted the attention of Leonti Frolkov, who was then stopping in Tcharanda on his way home from the war. She was immensely flattered when he courted her. He even bought her a pair of shoes for a present, the first shoes she had ever worn. This captivated the humble Olga completely. She joyously accepted his marriage proposal.

After the wedding the young couple moved to Nikolsko, my father's birthplace, where he had inherited a small tract of land. They tilled it together, and with great difficulty managed to make ends meet. My two elder sisters, Arina and Shura, were born here, increasing the poverty of my parents. My father, about this time, took to drinking, and began to maltreat and beat his wife. He was by nature morose and egotistic. Want was now making him cruel. My mother's life with him became one of misery. She was constantly in tears, always pleading for mercy and praying to God.

I was born in July, 1889, the third girl in the family. At that time many railroads were being built throughout the country. When I was a year old, my father, who had once been stationed at Tsarskoye Selo, the *Tsar's* residence town near the capital, decided to go to Petrograd to seek work. We were left without money. He wrote no letters. On the brink of starvation, my mother somehow contrived, with the aid of kind neighbours, to keep herself and her children alive.

When I was nearly six years old a letter came from father, the first he had written us during the five years of his absence. He had broken his right leg and, as soon as he was able to travel, had started home. My mother wept bitterly at the news, but was glad to hear from father whom she had almost given up for dead. In spite of his harshness toward her, she still loved him. I remember how happy my mother was when father arrived, but this happiness did not last long. Poverty and misery cut it short. My father's rigid nature asserted itself again.

12

Hardly had a year gone by when a fourth child, also a girl, arrived in our family. And there was no bread in the house.

From all parts of our section of the country peasants were migrating that year to Siberia, where the government allowed them large grants of land. My father wanted to go, but mother was opposed to it. However, when our neighbour, Verevkin, who had left some time previous for Siberia, wrote glowingly of the new country, my father made up his mind to go, too.

Most of the men would go alone, obtain grants of land, till them, build homesteads, and then return for their families. Those of the peasants who took their families with them had enough money to tide them over. But we were so poor that by the time we got to Tcheliabinsk, the last terminal in European Russia, and the government distribution point, we had not a penny left. At the station my father obtained some hot water to make tea, while my two elder sisters were sent to beg for bread.

We were assigned to Kuskovo, a hundred and twenty *versts* beyond Tomsk. At every station my sisters would beg food, while father filled our tea-kettle with hot water. Thus, we got along till Tomsk was reached. Our grant of land was in the midst of the *taiga*, the virgin Siberian forest. There could be no thought of immediately settling on it, so my father remained in Tomsk, while the rest of us were sent on to Kuskovo. My sisters went to work for board and clothing. My mother, still strong and in good health, baked bread for a living, while I took care of the baby.

One day my mother was expecting visitors. She had baked some cakes and bought half a pint of vodka, which she put on the shelf. While she was at work I tried to lull the baby to sleep. But baby was restless, crying incessantly. I did not know how to calm her. Then my eyes fell on the bottle of vodka.

"It must be a very good thing," I thought, and decided to give a glass to baby. Before doing so I tasted it myself. It was bitter, but I somehow wanted more. I drank the first cup and, the bitterness having somewhat worn off, I drained another. In this manner I disposed of the entire bottle. Drowsy and weak, I took the baby into my arms and tried to rock it to sleep. But I myself began to stagger, and fell with the child to the floor.

Our mother found us there, screaming at the top of our voices. Presently the visitors arrived, and my mother reached for the bottle, only to discover that it had been emptied. It did not take her long to

13

find the culprit. I shall always remember the whipping I got on that occasion.

Toward winter father arrived from Tomsk. He brought little money with him. The winter was severe, and epidemics were raging in the country. We fell sick one by one, father, mother, then all the girls. As there was no bread in the house, and no money to buy anything, the community took care of us till spring, housing and feeding us. By some miracle all of us escaped death, but our clothes had become rags. Our shoes fell to pieces. My parents decided to move to Tomsk, where we arrived barefoot and tattered, finding shelter at a poor inn on the outskirts of the town.

My father would work only a couple of days a week. He was lazy. The remainder of the week he idled away and drank. My sisters served as nurse-maids, while mother worked in a bakery, keeping the baby and me with her. We slept in the loft of a stable, with the horses stamping below us. Our bed was of straw, laid on the floor, which consisted of unshaven planks thrown across logs. Soon the baker's wife began to object to feeding an extra mouth, which belonged to me. I was then over eight years old.

"Why don't you send her to work? She can earn her own bread," she argued.

My mother would draw me to her breast, weep and beg for mercy. But the proprietress became impatient, threatening to throw us all out.

Finally, father came to see us, with the good tidings that he had found a place for me. I was to care for a five-year-old boy, in return for my board and eighty-five *kopecks* a month.

"If you do well," my father added, "you will by and by receive a *ruble*."

Such was the beginning of my career in life. I was eight and a half years old, small and very thin. I had never before left my mother's side, and both of us wept bitterly at parting. It was a grey, painful, incomprehensible world into which I was being led by my father. My view of it was further blurred by a stream of tears.

I took care of the little boy for several days. One afternoon, while amusing him by making figures in the sand, I myself became so engrossed in the game that I quarrelled with my charge, which led to a fight. I remember feeling keenly that I was in the right. But the child's mother did not inquire into the matter. She heard his screams and spanked me for it.

I was deeply hurt by the undeserved spanking administered by a strange woman.

"Where was my mother? Why did not she come to avenge me?"

My mother did not answer my cries. Nobody did. I felt miserable. How wrong was the world, how unjust! It was not worth while living in such a world.

My feet were bare. My dress was all in rags. Nobody seemed to care for me. I was all alone, without friends, and nobody knew of the yearning in my heart. I would drown myself, I thought. Yes, I would run to the river and drown myself. Then I would go up, free of all pain, into the arms of God.

I resolved to slip out at the first chance and jump into the river, but before the opportunity presented itself my father called. He found me all in tears.

"What's the matter, Manka?" he asked.

"I am going to drown myself, papa," I answered sadly.

"Great Heavens! What's happened, you foolish child?"

I then poured my heart out to him, begging to be taken to mother. He caressed me and talked of mother's distress if I left my place. He promised to buy me a pair of shoes, and I remained.

But I did not stay long. The little boy, having seen his mother punish me, began to take advantage of me, making my life quite unbearable. Finally, I ran away and wandered about town till dark, looking for my mother. It was late when a policeman picked me up crying in the street and carried me to the police-station. The officer in charge of the station took me to his home for the night.

His house was rather large. I had never been in such a house before. When I awoke in the morning it seemed to me that there were a great many doors in it and all of them aroused my curiosity. I desired to know what was behind them. As I opened one of the doors, I beheld the police-officer asleep on a bed, with a pistol alongside of him. I wanted to beat a hasty retreat, but he awoke. He seized the pistol and, still dazed from sleep, threatened me with it. Frightened, I ran out of the room.

My father, meanwhile, had been informed of my flight and had gone to the police-station in search of me. He was referred to the police-officer's home. There he found me, weeping on the porch, and took me to my mother.

My parents then decided to establish a home. All their capital amounted to six *rubles*. They rented a basement for three *rubles* a month. Two *rubles* my father invested in some second-hand furniture, consisting of a lame table and benches, and a few kitchen utensils. With a few *kopecks* from the last *ruble* in her purse my mother prepared some food for us. She sent me to buy a *kopeck's* worth of salt.

The grocery store of the street was owned by a Jewess, named Nastasia Leontievna Fuchsman. She looked at me closely when I entered her store, recognising that I was a stranger in the street, and asked me:

"Whose are you?"

"I am of the Frolkovs. We just moved into the basement in the next block."

"I need a little girl to help me out. Would you like to work for me?" she asked. "I'll give you a *ruble* a month, and board."

I was overjoyed and started for home at such speed that by the time I got to my mother I was quite breathless. I told her of the offer from the grocery-woman.

"But," I added, "she is a Jewess."

I had heard so many things of Jews that I was rather afraid, on second thought, to live under the same roof with a Jewess. My mother calmed my fears on that score and went to the grocery to have a talk with the proprietress. She came back satisfied, and I entered upon my apprenticeship to Nastasia Leontievna.

It was not an easy life. I learned to wait on customers, to run errands, to do everything in the house, from cooking and sewing to scrubbing floors. All day I slaved without rest, and at night I slept on a box in the passageway between the store and house. My monthly earnings went to my mother, but they never sufficed to drive the spectre of starvation away from my home. My father earned little but drank much, and developed his severe temper even more.

In time I got a raise to two *rubles* a month. But as I grew I required more clothes, which my mother had to supply me from my allowance. Nastasia Leontievna was exacting and not infrequently punished me. But she also loved me as though I had been her own daughter, and always tried to make up for harsh treatment. I owe a great deal to her, as she taught me to do almost everything, both in her business and in housework.

I must have been about eleven when, in a fit of temper, I quarrelled with Nastasia Leontievna. Her brother frequented the theatre and constantly talked of it. I never quite understood what a theatre was like, but it allured me, and I resolved one evening to get acquainted with that place of wonders. I asked Nastasia Leontievna for money to go there. She refused.

"You little *moujitchka* (peasant woman) what do you want with the theatre?" she asked derisively.

"You d——d Jewess!" I threw into her face fitfully, and ran out of the store. I went to my mother and told her of the incident. She was horrified.

"But now she won't take you back. What will we do without your wages, Marusia? How will we pay the rent? We will have to go begging again." And she cried.

After some time, my employer came after me, rebuking me for my quick temper.

"How could I have known that you were so anxious to go to the theatre?" she asked. "All right, I'll give you fifteen *kopecks* every Sunday so that you can go."

I became a steady Sunday attendant of the gallery, watching with intense interest the players, their strange gestures and manners of speech.

Five years I worked for Nastasia Leontievna, assuming greater duties with the advance of my years. Early in the morning I would rise, open the shutters, knead the dough, and sweep or scrub the floors. I finally grew weary of this daily grind and began to think of finding other work. But my mother was sick and father worked less and less, drinking most of the time. He grew more brutal, beating us all unmercifully. My sisters were forced to stay away from home. Shura married at sixteen, and I, fourteen years old, became the mainstay of the family. It was often necessary to get my pay in advance in order to keep the family from starving.

The temptation to steal came to me suddenly one day. I had never stolen anything before, and Nastasia Leontievna repeatedly pointed out this virtue in me to her friends.

"Here is a *moujitchka* who doesn't steal," she would say. But one time, on unpacking a barrel of sugar delivered at the store, I found, instead of the usual six sugarloaves, seven. The impulse to take the extra loaf of sugar was irresistible. At night I smuggled it stealthily out of the store and took it home. My father was astonished.

"What have you done, Marusia? Take it back immediately," he ordered. I began to cry and said that the sugar was not really Nastasia Leontievna's, that the error had been made at the refinery. Then my father consented to keep it.

I returned to my place at the grocery and went to bed, but my eyes would not close; my conscience troubled me. "What if she suspected

17

that a loaf of sugar was missing? What if she discovers that I have stolen it?" And a feeling of shame came over me. The following day I could not look straight into Nastasia Leontievna's eyes. I felt guilty. My face burned. At every motion of hers my heart quivered in anticipation of the terrible disclosure. Finally, she noticed that there was something the matter with me.

"What's wrong with you Marusia?" she questioned drawing me close to her. "Are you not well?"

This hurt even more. The burden of the sin I had committed weighed heavier and heavier. It rapidly became unbearable. My conscience would not be quieted. At the end of a couple of restless days and sleepless nights I decided to confess. I went into Nastasia Leontievna's bedroom when she was asleep. Rushing to her bed, I fell on my knees and broke into sobs. She awoke in alarm.

"What's happened, child? What is it?"

Weeping, I proceeded to tell the story of my theft, begging forgiveness and promising never to steal again. Nastasia Leontievna calmed me and sent me back to bed, but she could not forgive my parents. Next morning, she visited our home, remonstrating with my father for his failure to return the sugar and punish me. The shame and humiliation of my parents knew no bounds.

Sundays I spent at home, helping my mother in the house. I would go to the well, which was a considerable distance away, for water. My mother baked bread all week and father carried it to the market, selling it at ten *kopecks* a loaf. His temper was steadily getting worse, and it was not unusual for me to find mother in the yard in tears after father's return in an intoxicated state.

I reached the age of fifteen and began to grow dissatisfied with my lot. Life was awakening within me and quickening my imagination. Everything that passed by and beyond the confined little realm in which I lived and laboured called me, beckoned to me, lured me. The impressions of that foreign world which I had caught in the theatre implanted themselves in my soul deeply and gave birth there to love-stirring forces. I wanted to dress nicely, to go out, to enjoy life's pleasures. I wanted to be educated. I wanted to have enough money to secure my parents forever from starvation and to be able to lead for a time, for a day even, an idle life, without having to rise with the sun, to scrub the floor or to wash clothes.

Ah! what would I not have given to taste the sweetness, the joy, that life held. But there seemed to be none for me. All day long I slaved in the little store and kitchen. I never had a spare *ruble*. Something revolted within me against this bleak, purposeless, futureless existence.

CHAPTER 2

Married at Fifteen

Came the Russo-Japanese War. And with it, Siberia, from Tomsk to Manchuria, teemed with a new life. It reached even our street, hitherto so lifeless and uneventful. Two officers, the brothers Lazov, one of them married, rented the quarters opposite Nastasia Leontievna's grocery. The young Madame Lazov knew nothing of housekeeping. She observed me at work in the grocery store, and offered me service in her home at seven *rubles* a month.

Seven *rubles* a month was so attractive a sum that I immediately accepted the offer. What could one not do with so much money? Why, that would leave four *rubles* for me, after the payment of mother's rent. Four *rubles*! Enough to buy a new dress, a coat, or a pair of those modish shoes. Besides, it gave me an opportunity to release myself from the bondage of Nastasia Leontievna.

I took entire charge of the housekeeping at the Lazovs. They were kind and courteous, and took an interest in me. They taught me table and social etiquette, and took care that I appeared neat and clean.

The younger Lazov, Lieutenant Vasili, began to notice me, and one evening invited me to take a walk with him. In time Vasili's interest in me deepened. We went out together many times. He made love to me, caressing and kissing me. Did I realise clearly the meaning of it all? Hardly. It was all so new, so wonderful, so alluring. It made my pulse throb at his approach. It made my cheeks flame with the heat of my young blood.

Vasili said he loved me. Did I love him? If I did, it was more because of the marvellous world into which he was to lead me than on account of himself. He promised to marry me. Did I particularly want to marry him? Scarcely. The prospect of marriage was more enticing to me because of the end it would put to my life of drudgery and misery than on account of anything else. To become free, independent, possessed of means, was the attractive prospect that marriage held for me.

I was fifteen and a half when Vasili seduced me by the promise of marriage. We lived together for a short while, when orders came to the Lazovs to leave for a different post. Vasili informed me of the order.

"Then we will have to get married quickly, before you go," I declared. But Vasili did not think so.

"That's quite impossible, Marusia," he said.

"Why?" I inquired sharply, something rising in my throat, like a tide, with suffocating force.

"Because I am an officer, and you are only a plain *moujitchka*. You understand, yourself, that at present we can't marry. Marusenka, I love you just as much as ever. Come, I'll take you home with me; you'll stay with my parents. I'll give you an education, then we will get married."

I became hysterical, and throwing myself at him like a ferocious animal, I screamed at the top of my voice:

"You villain. You deceived me. You never did love me. You are a scoundrel. May God curse you."

Vasili tried to calm me. He drew near, but I repulsed him. He cried, he begged, he implored that I believe that he loved me, and that he would marry me. But I would not listen to him. I trembled with rage, seized by a fit of uncontrollable temper. He left me in tears.

I did not see Vasili for two days. Neither did his brother nor sister-in-law. He had disappeared. When he returned, he presented a pitiable sight. His haggard face, the appearance of his clothes, and the odour of vodka told the story of his two days' debauch.

"Ah, Marusia, Marusia," he lamented, gripping my arms. "What have you done, what have you done? I loved you so much. And you did not want to understand me. You have ruined my life and your own."

My heart was wrung with pity for Vasili. Life to me then was a labyrinth of blind alleys, tangled, bewildering. It is now clear to me that Vasili did love me genuinely, and that he had indulged in the wild orgy to forget himself and drown the pain I had caused him. But I did not understand it then. Had I loved him truly, it might all have been different. But a single thought dominated my mind: "He had promised to marry me and failed." Marriage had become to me the symbol of a life of independence and freedom.

The Lazovs left. They gave me money and gifts. But my heart was like a deserted ruin in the winter, echoing with the whine of wild beasts. Instead of a life of freedom, my parents' basement awaited me. And deep in my bosom lurked a dread of the unknown. . . .

I stealthily returned home. My sisters had already noticed a different air about me. Perhaps they had seen me with Vasili at one time or another. Whatever the cause, they had their suspicions, and did not fail to communicate them to mother. It required little scrutiny for her to observe that from a shy little girl I had blossomed forth into a young woman. And then there began days and nights of torture for me.

My father quickly got wind of what had happened at the Lazovs. He was merciless and threw himself upon me with a whip, nearly lashing me to death, accompanying each blow with epithets that burned into me more than the lashes of the whip. He also beat my mother when she attempted to intervene for me.

My father would return home drunk almost every day, and immediately take to lashing me. Often, he would drive me and mother barefoot out of the house, and for hours, at times, we shivered in the snow, hugging the icy walls. Life became an actual inferno. Day and night, I prayed to God that I fall ill or die. But God remained deaf. And still I felt that only sickness could save me from the daily punishment. "I must get sick," I said to myself. And so, I lay on the oven at night to heat my body, and then went out and rolled in the snow. I did it several times, but without avail. I could not fall sick.

Amid these insufferable conditions, I met the new year of 1905. My married sister had invited me to participate in a masquerade. My father would not hear, at first, of my going out for an evening, but consented after repeated entreaties. I dressed as a boy, which was the first time I ever wore a man's clothes. After the dancing we visited some friends of my sister's, where I met a soldier, just returned from the front. He was a common *moujik*, of rough appearance and vulgar speech, and at least ten years older than myself. He immediately began to court me. His name was Afanasi Botchkarev.

It was not long afterward that I met Botchkarev again in the house of a married sister of his. He invited me to go out for a walk, and then suddenly proposed that I marry him. It caught me so unexpectedly that I had no time for consideration. Anything seemed preferable to the daily torments of home. If I had sought death to escape my father, why not marry this boorish *moujik*? And I consented thoughtlessly.

My father objected to my marrying since I was not yet sixteen, but without avail. As Botchkarev was penniless, and I had no money, we decided to work together and save. Our marriage was a hasty affair. The only impression that I retain is my feeling of relief at escaping from my father's brutal hands. Alas! Little did I then suspect that I was exchanging one form of torture for another.

On the day following our marriage, which took place in the early spring, Afanasi and I went down to the river to hire ourselves as day laborers. We helped to load and unload lumber barges. Hard labour

21

never daunted me, and I would have been satisfied, had it only been possible for me to get along with Afanasi otherwise. But he also drank, while I didn't, and intoxication invariably brutalised him. He knew of my affair with Lazov, and would use it as a pretext for punishing me.

"That officer is still in your head!" he would shout. "Wait, I'll knock him out of there." And he would proceed to do so.

Summer came. Afanasi and I found work with an asphalt firm. We made floors at the prison, university and other public buildings. We paved some streets with asphalt. Our work with the firm lasted about two years. Both of us started at seventy *kopeks* a day, but I rose to the position of assistant foreman in a few months, receiving a *ruble* and fifty *kopecks* a day. Afanasi continued as a common labourer. My duties required considerable knowledge in the mixing of the various elements in the making of concrete and asphalt.

Afanasi's low intelligence was a sufficient torment. But his heavy drinking was a greater source of suffering to me. He made a habit of beating me, and grew to be unendurable. I was less than eighteen years old, and nothing but misery seemed to be in store for me. The thought of escape dug itself deeper and deeper into my mind. I finally resolved to run away from Afanasi.

My married sister had moved to Barnaul, where she and her husband served as domestics on a river steamer. I saved some twenty *rubles*, and determined to go to my sister, but I needed a passport. Without a passport one could not move in Russia, so I took my mother's.

On the way, at a small railway station, I was held up by an officer of the *gendarmes*.

"Where are you going, girl?" he asked brusquely, eyeing me with suspicion.

"To Barnaul," I replied, with sinking heart.

"Have you a passport?" he demanded.

"Yes," I said, drawing it out of my bag.

"What's your name?" was the next question.

"Maria Botchkareva."

In my confusion I had forgotten that the passport was my mother's, and that it bore the name of Olga Frolkova. When the officer unfolded it and glanced at the name, he turned on me fiercely:

"Botchkareva, ah, so that is your name?"

It dawned upon me then that I had committed a fatal mistake. Visions of prison, torture and eventual return to Afanasi flashed before me. "I am lost," I thought, falling upon my knees before the officer to beg for mercy, as he ordered me to follow him to headquarters. In an outburst of tears and sobs, I told him that I had escaped from a brutal husband, and since I could not possibly obtain a passport of my own, I was forced to make use of my mother's. I implored him not to send me back to Afanasi, for he would surely kill me.

My simple peasant speech convinced the officer that I was not a dangerous political, but he would not let me go. He decided that I should go with him. "Come along; you will stay with me, and tomorrow I will send you to Barnaul. If you don't, I'll have you arrested and sent by *étape* (under convoy from prison to prison) back to Tomsk."

I was as docile as a sheep. This was my first contact with the authorities, and I dared not protest. If I had any power of will it must have been dormant. Wasn't the world full of wrong since my childhood? Wasn't this one of Life's ordinary events? We *moujiks* were created to suffer and endure. They, the officials, were made to punish and maltreat. And so I was led away by the guardian of peace and law, and made to suffer shame and humiliation. . . .

I was then free to go to Barnaul, and I resumed my journey. When I arrived there, my sister quickly found employment for me on the steamship. The work was comparatively easy, and my life rapidly took a happier turn. It was such a relief to be away from that drunken, brutal, savage husband.

But the relief was short-lived. Afanasi came to my mother after my disappearance to inquire for my whereabouts. She evinced surprise upon hearing of my flight, denying all knowledge of my destination. He returned to our house again and again. One day in his presence the mail-carrier delivered a letter from Shura. He seized it, and through it learned that I was in Barnaul.

One morning, as I was standing on the deck of the ship, which was anchored in the harbour, my eyes suddenly fell on a figure approaching the wharf. It was a familiar figure. In another moment I recognised it as that of Afanasi. My blood froze and my flesh crept as I sensed what was coming.

"Once fallen into his hands, my existence would become one of continuous torture," I thought. "I must save myself."

But how could I escape? If I were on land I might still have a chance. Here all avenues are closed. There, he is already approaching the gate to the wharf. He is stopping to ask a question of a guard, who nods affirmatively. Now, he is walking a little faster. His face wears a grin that strikes terror into my heart. I am trapped. . . . But no, just wait a moment, Afanasi. Don't celebrate yet. I rush to the edge of the deck, cross myself and jump into the deep waters of the Ob. Ah, what a thrill it is to die! So, I have outwitted Afanasi, after all. It's cold, the water is cold. And I am going down, down. . . . I am glad. I am triumphant. I escaped from the trap . . . into the arms of death.

I awoke, not in Heaven, but in the hospital. I was observed jumping into the river, dragged out unconscious, and revived. The authorities questioned me as to the cause of my attempted suicide, and drew up a protocol. I told them of my husband, of his brutality, and of the utter impossibility of living with him.

Afanasi was waiting in the anteroom, to see me. My attempt at drowning had upset him tremendously. It aroused a sense of shame in him. Touched by my story, the authorities went out and angrily rebuked him for his maltreatment of me. He pleaded guilty, and swore that he would be gentle to me in the future.

He was then admitted to the ward in which I lay. Falling on his knees, he begged my forgiveness, repeating his oath to me and professing his love for me in the most endearing terms. His pleas were so compelling that I finally consented to return home with him.

For a while Afanasi was truly a different man. In spite of his coarse habits, I was deeply moved by his efforts at tenderness. However, that did not last long. We resumed our life of drudging toil. And vodka resumed its grip on him. Once drunk, he would turn savage again.

Gradually life with Afanasi grew as insufferable as before my escape. That summer I turned nineteen, and I saw ahead of me nothing but an infinite cycle of dreary years. Afanasi wanted me to take to drink. I resisted, and that infuriated him. He made it a habit to torment me daily, holding a bottle of vodka to my face. Deriding me for my efforts to lift myself above my environment, he resorted to blows and tricks to force the bitter drink down my throat. One day he even stood over me with a bottle of vodka for three whole hours, pinning me down to the ground so that I was unable to move a muscle. I remained unconquerable.

Winter came. I baked bread for a living. Sundays I went to church to pray God to release me from my bondage. Again, the thought of escaping wormed itself into my mind. The first requisite was, of course, a passport, so I went secretly to a lawyer for advice, and he undertook to obtain one for me legally. But hard luck attended me. When the police constable called to deliver the passport to me, Afanasi was at home. My scheme was discovered, and I, trapped. Afanasi jumped at me and bound me hand and foot, deaf to my entreaties and cries. I thought my end had arrived. In silence he carried me out of the house and tied me to a post.

It was cold, very cold. He flogged me, drank, and flogged me again, cursing me in the vilest terms. "That's what you get for trying to escape," he bawled, holding the bottle to my mouth. "You won't escape any more. You will drink or you will die!"

I was obdurate and implored him to leave me alone. He continued his flogging, however, keeping me for four hours at the post, till I finally broke down and drank the alcohol. I became intoxicated, staggered out into the street, and fell to the pavement in front of the house. Afanasi ran after me, cursing and kicking me. We were quickly surrounded by a crowd. My neighbours, who knew of his cruelty to me, came to my defence. Afanasi was roughly handled by the people, so roughly, indeed, that he left me in peace for some time afterwards.

Christmas was fast approaching. I had saved, little by little, fifty *rubles*. Every *kopeck* of that money was earned by extra toil during the night. It was all the earthly possession that I had, and I guarded it jealously. Somehow, Afanasi got wind of its hiding place and stole it. He spent it all on drink.

I was crazed with fury upon discovering the loss. What the money meant to me in the circumstances is difficult to describe. It was my blood, my sweat, a year of my youth. And he, the beast, squandered it in one orgy. The least I could do to my torturer was to kill him.

Frantically, I ran to my mother, who was struck by the expression of my face.

"Marusia, what ails you?"

"Mother," I gasped, "let me have an axe. I am going to kill Afanasi."

"Holy Mother, have mercy!" she exclaimed, raising her hands to Heaven and falling on her knees, exhorting me to come to my senses. But I was too frantic with rage. I seized an axe and ran home.

Afanasi returned, drunk, and began to taunt me with the loss of my precious savings. I was white with wrath and cursed him from the depth of my heart. He gripped a stool and threw it at me. I caught up the axe.

"I will kill you, you blood-sucker!" I screamed.

Afanasi was stupefied. He had not expected that from me. The desire to kill was irresistible. Mentally, I already gloated over his dead body and the freedom that it would bring me. I was ready to swing the axe at him. . . .

Suddenly the door flew open and my father rushed in. He had been sent by my mother.

"Marusia, what are you doing?" he cried out, gripping my arm. The break was too abrupt, my nerves collapsed, and I fell unconscious to the floor. Upon awakening I found police authorities in the house, and I told them everything. Afanasi was taken to the police-station, while the police officer, a very humane person, advised me to leave town to get away from him.

I got my passport, but my money was gone. I could not afford to buy a ticket to Irkutsk, where Shura had moved from Barnaul. Determined to go at all cost, I boarded a train without a ticket. The conductor discovered me on the way, and I cried and begged him to allow me to proceed. He proposed to hide me in the baggage car and take me to Irkutsk, on condition that I . . . Enraged, I pushed him violently from me.

"I will put you off at the next station," he shot at me, running out of the car. And he kept his word.

Nearly all the distance to Irkutsk was yet before me, and I wanted to get there without selling myself for the price of a ticket. There could be no thought of going back. I had to get to Irkutsk. I boarded the next train, stealthily crouched under a bench, as it moved out of the station.

Ultimately, I was discovered, but this conductor was an elderly man and responded to my tears and implorations. I told him of my experience with the first conductor and of my total lack of money. He allowed me to proceed, but as soon as an inspector would board the train, the conductor would signal to me to hide under the bench. Sometimes I would spend several hours at a stretch there, concealed by the legs of some kind passengers. In such a manner I journeyed for four days, finally reaching my destination—Irkutsk.

Chapter 3

A Little Happiness

I arrived in Irkutsk without money. All I had was what I wore. I went to look for my sister, who was in poor circumstances and sick. Her husband was out of work. One could not expect an enthusiastic welcome under such conditions. I lost little time in seeking employment, and quickly found a place as a dishwasher at nine *rubles* a month. It was an unbearable task, in a filthy hole patronized by drunkards. The treatment I received at the hands of the clients was so revolting that I left at the end of the first day.

On the third day I found work in a laundry, where I had to wash hundreds of pieces daily. From five in the morning till eight in the evening I was bent over the washtub. It was rough labour, but I was forced to stay at it for several weeks. I lived with my sister in one small room, paying her rent. Presently I began to feel pains in my back. The hard work was telling on me. I resolved to leave the laundry, although my sister opposed it. I had no money saved.

Having had experience in concrete work, I applied for employment to an asphalt contractor. He was kind enough to give me a trial as an assistant foreman on a job he was doing at the Irkutsk prison. I was to take charge of ten men and women laborers.

When I began I was met by an outburst of mirth on all sides. "Ha, ha," they laughed, "a *baba* (woman in popular terminology) assuming a foreman's place!"

I paid no heed to the ridicule and proceeded about my business quietly and gently. The men obeyed, and as they perceived that I knew what I was about, began even to gain respect for me. I was given for that first test the preparing of a floor. Stretching myself on the ground with the rest of the party, planning and working, I managed to finish my task a couple of hours ahead of my schedule, and marched the men triumphantly out of the building, to the utter amazement of the other foremen.

My boss was all merriment. "Look at this *baba!*" he said. "She will have us men learning from her pretty soon. She should wear trousers."

The following day I was put in charge of twenty-five men. As they still regarded me as a queer novelty, I addressed a little speech to them, telling them that I was a plain peasant worker, only seeking to earn my bread. I appealed to their sense of fairness to cooperate with me. Sending for some vodka and sausages I entertained them and won their good will completely. My men called me "Manka" affectionately, and we got along splendidly. I was such a phenomenon that the contractor himself invited me to his home for tea. His wife, who was a very kind soul, told me that her husband had been praising me to her very much.

The great test, however, came several days later. I had to prove my ability in preparing asphalt and applying it. We were all at work at four o'clock in the morning. As the quality of asphalt depends on the proportions of the elements used, the men were waiting rather amusedly for my orders. But I gave them without hesitation, and when the boss arrived at six o'clock he found the kettles boiling and the laborers hard at work, pouring the asphalt on the gravel.

This work must be done without relaxation, in awful heat and suffocating odours. For a whole year I stayed at it, labouring incessantly, with no holidays and no other rest. Like a pendulum, always in motion, I would begin my daily cycle before dawn, returning home after sunset, only to eat and go to bed to gain strength for another bleak day's round.

At the end I broke down. I caught cold while working in a basement, and became so weak that I was taken to the Kuznetzov Hospital, where I was confined to bed for two months. When I recovered and rested for about a week, I returned to my job, but found it occupied by a man who had been especially brought from European Russia. Besides, there wasn't much work left for the firm in Irkutsk.

My sister and her husband moved back to Tomsk about this time, and my situation grew desperate. I looked for a place as a domestic servant, but having no reference, I found it impossible to obtain one. The little money I had finally gave out. My only friends in town were the Sementovskys, neighbours to my sister. I lived with them, but they were poor themselves, and so, for days at times, I would go hungry, my only sustenance consisting of tea.

One day I applied at an employment agency and was informed, after being asked if I would agree to leave town, that a woman had been there looking for a servant, and offered to pay twenty-five *rubles* a month. I instantly expressed my willingness to go with her. She appeared in the afternoon, young, beautiful, elegantly dressed, her fingers and neck adorned with dazzling jewels. She was so tender to me, eyed me carefully, asking if I was married.

"I have been," I replied, "but I escaped from my husband about two years ago. He was such a brutal drunkard." I was then in my twenty-first year.

The lady, whose name was Anna Petrovna, gave me ten *rubles* to pay the rent I owed. I met her at the station, where she was accompanied by several men friends, and we started together for Stretinsk, in a second-class coach. I had never been in one before in my life. Nothing occurred on the way. I was well fed and nicely treated by her. She spoke to me of their business, and I got the idea that her husband kept a store. Upon our arrival at Stretinsk we were met by a man and two young women. The man was introduced to me as her husband and the two women as her foster daughters. We drove home, where I was

28

assigned to a neat little room.

I was getting uneasy. Things looked suspicious. "Where is the store?" I inquired.

"In the market," was the answer. Anna Petrovna took me by the arm and caressingly suggested:

"Marusenka, won't you dress up nicely? We will have guests tonight." And she handed me some very dainty and light garments, not at all befitting a servant. I was amazed, and objected strenuously.

"I never wore such bizarre clothes, Anna Petrovna. I am a plain working girl," and I blushed deeply. I was both ashamed and afraid. I had a premonition of evil. And when she handed me a very *décolleté* gown I became thoroughly frightened.

But Anna Petrovna was persuasive and persistent, and I was finally induced into putting it on. It was so transparent that my cheeks flamed with shame. I refused to leave my room, but was forced by Anna Petrovna's coaxing to follow her. As I stepped on the threshold I saw several girls seated freely with men, drinking beer. A young man was standing aside, evidently anticipating our appearance. He moved toward us. Anna Petrovna had apparently promised me to him.

Stars were shooting before my eyes. "A house of shame!" The thought pierced my mind and made me furious. I lost all my submissiveness and meekness. Seizing my clothes, I tore them wildly into shreds, stamping with my feet, cursing, shrieking and breaking everything that I could get hold of. I caught up several bottles of beer and shattered them into fragments on the floor.

This outbreak lasted but a moment. Everybody in the room was too stupefied to move before I ran out of the house, wrapped only in a shawl. I hastened to the police-station at a pace that made people in the streets think that I must be mad. Arriving there, I made my complaint to the officer in charge.

To all appearances he was little touched by my story. While I prayed for mercy and relief, on my knees before him, he was regarding me with amusement. He drew me near him and proposed that I go to live with him! I was shocked and overwhelmed. He, whose duty it was to protect me, was clearly in alliance with the white slavers.

"You are all scoundrels and murderers!" I cried out in anguish. "You ought to be ashamed to take advantage of a defenceless girl."

He grew angry and ordered me locked up for the night. The policeman who took me down also made advances to me, and I had to slap him to keep him away. The cell was cold, dark and dirty. I had left my shawl upstairs. Enraged against the authorities, I broke all the windows and hammered continuously at the doors and walls, till I was set free in the morning.

But my troubles had only begun. I had no place to go. For two days I wandered about town day and night. I was starved and worn out. Then I knelt on the bank of the river and prayed for half an hour. I prayed devoutly, pouring out my whole soul. It seemed to me that the Lord had heard my plea, and I felt relieved.

I resolved to return to Anna Petrovna after my prayer. I thought she had been so kind at first that if I begged her to let me work for her as a servant she would agree. Before entering her house, I went into the little grocery store nearby, and posing as the new servant of Anna Petrovna, who was a customer of the place, got a small bottle of essence of vinegar. I then entered the house and was well received. However, the solicitude for my safety angered me, and I resented Anna Petrovna's caresses. I locked myself up in my room, getting ready to poison myself with the essence.

As I was saying my last prayers there was a knock at the door.

"Who is it?" I asked sharply. The reply was:

"I am that young man whom you saw two days ago in the parlour. I want to help you. I realise that you are not a girl of that sort. Pray, open the door and let me talk to you."

I naturally thought that this was another trap and answered wrathfully: "You are a villain! You are all villains! What do you want with me? What have I done to deserve torture and starvation? If I fall into your hands it will be only when I am dead. I am going to drink this poison here and let you gloat over my corpse."

The man got excited. He ran out into the yard, raised an alarm, and dragging several people with him, shouted of my threat to take poison. A large crowd had collected around the house, and he forced the window of my room from the outside and jumped in. Seizing the glass of essence, he threw it out of the window, cursing Anna Petrovna and her house. He made every effort to calm me, expressing his admiration for my courage and virtue. His professions of sincerity and friendship were so convincing that I yielded to his invitation to go with him to the home of his parents.

My saviour, who was a handsome young man of about twenty-four, was Yakov Buk. He was a man of education, having studied at high school for some time. His father was a butcher. I was well received by his family, fed, dressed and given a rest. They were kind and hospitable people. Yakov, or Yasha, as he was called intimately, took especial care of me. He loved me, and it was not long before he declared that he could not live without me.

I was also attracted toward him. He knew of my previous marriage and proposed that we live together by civil agreement, without the sanction of the Church, a very common mode of marriage in Russia of late years, because of the difficulty in obtaining a divorce. I consented to his proposal, on condition that he tell me the reason for his living in a small barn in the back yard, apart from the family. He agreed.

"When I was twenty," he began, "my father was in the business of supplying meat to several army regiments. He was a partner in a firm, and was assisted by my brothers and myself. Considering me the most industrious and reliable of his sons, he entrusted me once with ten thousand *rubles* to go to buy cattle. Most of the money did not belong to him.

"On the train I was drawn into a game of cards, staged for innocent passengers, such as I was, by a group of adventurers. I lost all my money and my clothes to boot. Dressed in rags, with two *rubles*, presented to me by the gamblers, in my pocket, I alighted at the Chinese border in a mood for suicide. There I became acquainted, at an inn, with some Chinese brigands who were members of a band operating in the neighbourhood. One of them was the chief of the band.

"I told him my story, adding that I would do anything to save my father from disgrace and bankruptcy. He proposed that I join his band in a raid on an incoming train which was carrying fifty thousand *rubles*. The invitation nearly petrified me. But then I had a vision of my parents thrown out of their house, of their property sold at auction, and of them forced to go begging. It rent my heart. There was nothing to do but accept the offer. Led by the chieftain into the field, I was there introduced to most of the robbers. I was the only white man in the band.

"In the evening we armed ourselves with daggers, pistols and rifles and started for the railroad line, where we lay in wait for the train. It nearly congealed my blood to think that I had turned highwayman. It was so unlike myself.

"The train was to pass at one in the morning. I prayed to God that he save me somehow from this experience. Suddenly a body of Cossacks appeared in the distance, racing in our direction. The authorities had been on the track of this band for a long time. Every man in the gang threw down his weapons and ran into the forest. I, too, ran for all I was worth.

"The Cossacks pursued us, and I was caught. As I was a Russian and a new member of the organisation, I succeeded by persistent denials of any knowledge of the band in creating doubt in the minds of my captors as to my participation in the projected raid. But I was arrested and sent to the Irkutsk prison, where I was kept for a whole year. There I came in contact with many politicals and was converted to their ideas. Finally, for lack of evidence I was set free.

"Disgraced, I returned home. My father had arrived at an understanding with his partner whereby he was to pay in monthly instalments the sum I had gambled away. He would not let me enter the house, but my mother defended me. There was a quarrel, which ended in an agreement that I be allowed to occupy this barn. But father swore that he would disinherit me, giving my share of his estate to his other sons."

I soon had occasion to discover that Yasha was considered a suspicious character by the local police, because of his imprisonment. His kindness, too, was his misfortune. Freed or escaped prisoners would sometimes visit him secretly and he would give them his last penny, piece of bread or shirt. But I liked him all the more for that, for it was this warm heart in him that had rescued me from death. We vowed to be faithful to each other forever. And I entered upon my duties as a housewife.

The barn in which we were going to live was filled with rubbish, and had never been cleaned. I applied myself studiously to make it habitable. It was not an easy task, but I finally succeeded. We received a gift of one hundred *rubles* from Yasha's parents, and decided to establish a butcher shop of our own. We got some lumber and built a small store. Then Yasha bought three cows and the two of us led them to the slaughter house, where I learned how to butcher. Yasha ran the shop. I was the first woman butcher in that locality.

One summer day, while walking in the street, I saw some boys peddling ice-cream. I had learned how to make ice-cream during my apprenticeship with Nastasia Leontievna. It occurred to me that I could make ice-cream to sell. Finding out from the boys how much they paid for it, I offered them a lesser price and a better cream and asked them to come for it the next day. I immediately returned home and bought milk from Yasha's mother, who offered to give it free to me upon learning the purpose for which it was intended. The ice-cream I prepared was, happily, very good, and it sold quickly. During the summer I earned two or three *rubles* daily from this source.

I led a life of toil and peace with Yasha for about three years. Every morning I would get up at six o'clock and go with him to the slaughter-house. Then all day I would spend at home. There were always many poor people, mostly women and children, stranded in our town, which was the junction of a railway and river line. They would wander about the streets, begging for bread and shelter. The larger part of them would land in our barn-home. At times they would fill the cabin completely, sleeping in rows on the floor. Frequently they were sick. I fed them, washed them, tended to their children.

Yasha would often remonstrate with me for labouring so incessantly and so hard. But I had my reward in the gratitude and blessings those women bestowed upon me. There was joy in being able to serve. In addition, I sent regularly to my mother ten *rubles* a month. Yasha taught me in leisure moments how to read.

My name became a household word in the neighbourhood. Wherever I went I was blessed. "There goes Buk-Botchkareva!" people would point at me, whispering. Yasha's parents also grew very attached to me.

It all ended one evening in May, 1912. There was a peculiar knock at the door, and Yasha went out to admit a man of about thirty, well dressed, with a beard and *pince-nez*, of distinguished appearance. He was pale and apparently agitated. He stood with Yasha in the passageway for ten minutes, conferring inaudibly. He was then introduced to me as an old friend of Yasha's. He had escaped from prison and it was up to us to hide him, as his capture would mean his death. The unexpected guest was no less a person than the revolutionary slayer of a notorious Siberian Governor.

Yasha proceeded to remove our bed from its corner. He next removed a board in the lower part of the wall, revealing, to my great astonishment, a deep cavity in the ground underneath. Our visitor was invited to make himself comfortable there. The board was replaced and the bed restored to its former position. Yasha and I went to bed.

We had barely put out the light when there was heard a thumping of many feet around the house, followed by loud knocks at the door. The police were there! My heart was in my mouth, but I feigned sleep while Yasha opened the door. He had previously given me his revolver to hide and I concealed it in my bosom. The search continued for nearly two hours. I was dragged out of bed, and everything in the house was turned upside down.

We denied any knowledge of a political fugitive, but the sheriff took Yasha along with him. However, he was released a couple of hours later. Upon his return Yasha let the man out of the secret hole, supplied him with peasant clothes and food, harnessed our horse and drove away with him before dawn, instructing me to answer to all inquiries by saying that he had gone to buy cattle.

On the outskirts of the town a policeman, emerging from some dive in a semi-intoxicated state, observed Yasha driving by. He attached little significance to the fact at the time, but when he reported for duty in the morning and learned of the fugitive, he told that he had seen Yasha leave town with a stranger. I was doing some washing when the house was again surrounded by police.

"Where is your husband?" the sheriff inquired, fiercely.

"Gone to buy cattle," I replied.

"*Odievaisya!*" (Dress!) he rang out angrily. I pleaded innocence, but in a terrible voice he informed me that I was under arrest.

I was taken to the detective bureau, where a middle-aged man, who talked very gently, and seemed very mindful of my comfort, entered into a conversation with me and even invited me to tea, which invitation I refused. He went about his work very subtly, and I was nearly caught when he asked me if I had also met the young man who had arrived at our house at nine o'clock the night before.

His information was quite correct, but I obdurately refused to admit his implications. I knew nothing of the young man he spoke of, but my examiner was patient. He was generous in his praise of my help and devotion to the poor. Promising me immunity, he urged me to tell the truth.

I would not yield, and his patience finally wore out. Furious, he struck me with a rubber whip a couple of times. I was enraged and addressed him by some epithets that led to my being locked up in a cell where two drunken street women were confined. They were of the most abominable sort, cursing everybody. They persecuted me unceasingly. It was a horrible night that I passed there. The stench alone was sufficient to drive one mad. I was greatly relieved when morning arrived, and I was taken to the office for another examination.

I continued denying. There were threats of long imprisonment, coaxings, rebukes and attempts to extort a confession from me, from which I learned that Yasha had been arrested on his way back, before reaching home, so that he did not know of my arrest. I was detained for seven days, at the end of which the authorities, having been unable to obtain anything from me, set me free.

Yasha was still in jail, and I started out to visit various officials and bureaus in his behalf. The chief of police of the province was then in town, stopping in the house of a friend of ours. I invoked the aid of the latter in obtaining an interview for me. I was finally admitted before a largely built man wearing the uniform of a colonel. I fell on my knees before him and pleaded my husband's innocence, praying for mercy. I was so unnerved that he helped me to rise and ordered some water for me, promising to investigate the case and do justice.

I went next to the jail, hoping to see Yasha. But there I was informed that he had been sent to Nertchinsk, about eighty *versts* from Stretinsk. I did not tarry long in an effort to catch up with him. Taking along a hundred *rubles*, I took the next train to Nertchinsk, just as I was, and, immediately upon my arrival there, sought an audience with the governor, and was told to await my turn in the line. When my turn came the governor, reading my name from the list, asked:

"Well, what's your case?"

"My husband, your Excellency, Yasha Buk," I replied.

"Your husband, eh? How is he your husband if your name is Botchkareva?"

"By civil agreement, your Excellency."

"We know these civil marriages," he remarked derisively. "There are many like you in the streets," and dismissed my case. He said it in the hearing of a room full of people. My blood rushed to my face, and I was painfully hurt. It was with difficulty that I got a card of admission to the prison, but how profound was my grief upon being informed that Yasha had spent there only one night and had been sent on to Irkutsk.

I had barely enough money with me to buy a fourth-class ticket to Irkutsk, and almost no belongings, but I did not hesitate to take the next train westward. It took two days to reach the Siberian capital. I stopped again with the Sementovskys, who were glad to welcome me. I wended my way to the Irkutsk prison, only to discover that Yasha had been taken to the Central Distribution Prison at Alexandrovsk, thirty *versts* from the near railway station of Usolye. There was little time to lose. I left the same day for Usolye, whence I had to walk to Alexandrovsk.

It was late in the autumn of 1912. I started out with little food, and was soon exhausted. It was not an easy task to get to Alexandrovsk. The road lay across a river and through an island, connected by ferries.

On the way I made the acquaintance of a woman, Avdotia Ivanovna Kitova, who was also bound for the prison. Her husband was there too, and she told me why. He was drunk when the dog-catcher came to take away his favourite dog, and he shot the dog-catcher; now he was sentenced to exile, and she had decided to go along with him, with her two children, who were in Irkutsk.

At the Central Prison I received another shock. I wouldn't be admitted without a pass. I did not know that it was necessary to have a pass, I argued. But the warden in charge, a dried-up old man, with a flowing white beard, angrily shouted "No! No!" at me. "Get out of here. It's against the law; you can't be admitted. Go to Irkutsk and come back with a pass, and we will let you in."

"But I travelled a thousand *versts* to see him," I pleaded, in tears. "I am worn out and hungry. Allow me to see him just for five minutes—only five short minutes. Is there no mercy in your heart for a weak woman?"

With this I broke down and became hysterical. The harsh little warden, and his assistants in the office, became frightened. Yasha was brought in for a brief reunion. The few minutes that we were allowed to pass in each other's presence gave us new strength. He told me of his experiences, and I of mine to him, and we decided that I go to the Governor-General, Kniazev, to entreat his mercy.

The day was on the decline when I started back to the railway station. I reached the river by twilight and managed to catch a ferry to the island. But it was dark when I landed there, and I lost my way trying to cross the island to the other ferry.

I was cold, hungry, exhausted. My feet were swollen from wandering for several hours in a frantic effort to find the right path. When at last I got to the other side it must have been about midnight. I saw the lights across the water and called with all my remaining strength for the ferry. But there was no response. Only the wind, shrieking through the woods back of me, echoed my cries. I kept calling all night, but in vain.

When it dawned, I gathered my last energies, stood up and called out again. This time I was observed, and a canoe was sent after me. Unfortunately, it was in charge of a boy. I was too sick to move, and he could not carry me to it. I had to creep on all fours to the boat. With the boy's aid, I finally found myself in the canoe. It took him a long time to ferry me across, and I was in a state of collapse by the time we reached the other side. I was taken to the Kuznetzov Hospital in Irkutsk again, where I lay dangerously ill for several weeks. During this time, I lost all of my hair and half of my weight.

After my visit to Yasha he naturally told his prison mates of it, being proud of my loyalty to him, but when days and weeks passed by, and I did not return, his comrades began to tease him about me.

"A fine *baba* is yours. You may indeed be proud of her," they would torment him. "She found some other husband. A lot does she need you, a prisoner. They are all alike, yours and ours." Yasha took such drolleries very much to heart. He was in complete ignorance of my whereabouts and finally made up his mind that I had betrayed him.

As soon as I was released from the hospital, I went to the governor-general, in whose office I was told that Yasha had been sentenced to four years' exile. Obtaining a pass, I went to Alexandrovsk to see him. But Yasha would not see me. Believing his comrades' taunts, confirmed by my two months' absence, he resolved that he was through with me. I was naturally at a loss to account for this abrupt change, and wept bitterly. Some of his acquaintances, who had been brought downstairs, saw me cry and reported to him my emaciated appearance. Then he came down.

Visitors were not allowed to come in contact with the prisoners at Alexandrovsk. There were two steel gratings in the office, separated by a distance of a couple of feet. The prisoner was kept behind one grating, while the persons who came to see him were placed behind the other. They could not touch each other.

This was the setting in which I was permitted to meet Yasha. We both cried like children, he, at the sight of my thinness, realising that he had wronged me in suspecting me of faithlessness. It was a pathetic scene, this meeting behind bars. Yasha told me that he would not be exiled before May. As I offered to accompany him into exile, it was necessary for me to spend the several intervening months at some work. I also had to get permission to join Yasha in exile.

I found work with the same asphalt firm, but now as a common labourer, earning only fifty *kopecks* a day. At intervals I would go to Alexandrovsk to see Yasha. One time I was working at a job in the Irkutsk prison, and it was not long before the prisoners knew that I had a husband in Alexandrovsk, for there was a complete underground system of communication between the two prisons. On the whole, I was well treated by convicts.

One evening, however, while at work in the hall, a trusty, catching me in a corner, attacked me. I fought hard as he knocked me down.

My cries were heard by the laborers of my party and several prisoners. Soon we were surrounded by a crowd, and a quarrel ensued between those who defended me and the friends of the trusty. An assistant warden and some guards put an end to it, drawing up a protocol of my complaint to have the trusty tried in court for assault.

As the day of the trial drew near Yasha was urged by his fellow prisoners to influence me to withdraw my charge. He told me that the law of prison communal life demanded that I comply with the request to drop my complaint. I knew that my refusal might mean Yasha's death, and when I was called in court to testify against the trusty, I declared that there had been no assault and that I had no complaints to make. The case was dismissed, and my act enhanced Yasha's reputation among the inmates of both prisons.

The winter passed. Toward Easter of 1913 I succeeded in obtaining permission to have myself arrested and sent to Alexandrovsk, in anticipation of my exile with Yasha. I was put in the women's building, in which were detained a number of women criminals. What I endured at their hands is almost beyond description. They beat me, but I knew that complaining would make my lot more bitter. When supper was served to us the matron asked me if I had been maltreated. I answered negatively, but she must have known better, for, turning to the women, she instructed them not to punish me.

My reply to the matron somewhat improved my status with my prison-mates, but they forced me, nevertheless, to wait on them and do their dirty work. In addition to these sufferings, the food was putrid. The bunks in which we slept were unclean. Eight of us were in one tiny cell. I saw Yasha only once a week, every Sunday. I spent two months in this voluntary imprisonment, but it seemed like two years to me, and I looked forward eagerly and impatiently to the day of our starting on the open road to exile.

CHAPTER 4

Snared by a Libertine Governor

May had come. The Lena had opened and become navigable. The heavy iron doors of the prison were unlocked and hundreds of inmates, including Yasha and me, were mustered out in the yard to prepare for exile.

Every winter the huge prison at Alexandrovsk would gather into its walls thousands of wrecked human beings, murderers, forgers, thieves, students, officers, peasants and professional persons, who had transgressed against the tyrannical *régime*. Every spring the gloomy jail would open its doors and pour out a stream of half-benumbed men and women into the wild Siberian *taiga* and the uninhabited regions bordering on the Arctic.

All spring and summer this river of exasperated humanity would flow through Alexandrovsk into the snowbound north, where they languished in unendurable climatic conditions and succumbed in large numbers in the land of the six months' night. Tens of thousands of them lie scattered from the Ural Mountains to Alaska in unmarked graves. . . .

So finally, we were to breathe some fresh air. There was bustle and hustle before our party was formed. There were about a thousand persons in it, including twenty women. Our guard consisted of five hundred soldiers. We were to go on foot to Katchugo, near the source of the Lena, a distance of about two hundred *versts*. Our baggage was loaded on wagons.

We made thirty-five *versts* in the first day, according to schedule, stopping for the night at an exile-station on the edge of a village. The Siberian roads are criss-crossed by such stations—large wooden buildings of barn-like construction, with iron doors and grated windows. Empty inside, but for double tiers of bunks, they are surrounded by high fences, with a sentry-box at every corner. They offer no opportunity for escape.

We supped on food we had brought from the prison, and turned in for the night. Our party was divided into groups of ten, each group choosing a trusty charged with the purchasing of food. Beginning with the second day, each of us received an allowance of twenty *kopecks*.

There were about one hundred politicals in the party, the remainder being a conglomeration of criminals. The two sections did not get along well, and there was a continuous feud. Men and women were packed together, and some of the latter conducted themselves outrageously. The filth, the vermin-eaten bunks, the unimaginable stench, the frequent brawls, made our trip insufferably hideous.

Besides, there was a privileged group with us. It consisted of the long-sentence convicts, in chains, who were always given priority by the unwritten law of the criminal world. They would be first to use the kettles to prepare their food. Until they were through none of us dared approach the fire. Their word was law. They were always given the right-of-way. Even the soldiers and officers respected their privileges. One of them was the chieftain of the party, and if he pledged himself, in return for more freedom for all of us, to guarantee that there would be no escapes, his word would be taken without question by the commander of the Guard, and it never was broken.

The weather was fine the first three days. We made thirty *versts* the second day and the same distance the third day, but then it began to pour, and the roads became almost impassable. The mire was frightful, but we had to walk our scheduled thirty *versts*. Many in our party fell sick. We looked forward to the next exile-station with keen hope, so soaked were we and so fatigued. We longed for a roof and a dry floor, and nothing else. We forgot our hunger, we did not feel the vermin that night, for as soon as we reached the station we dropped like dead in deep slumber.

We had a two days' rest upon our arrival at Katchugo, and were allowed to bathe in the Lena when our chieftain made himself responsible for our conduct. We found a small party waiting to join us at Katchugo.

A member of this new group was recognised by some of the exiles as an alleged betrayer of his comrade in a raid, and was dragged for trial before the entire body. Here I witnessed a remarkable scene, the trial of a criminal by criminals. There was as rigid a code of morals in the underworld as in any legitimate government, and just as relentless a prosecution. A call went out that there would be a trial and the privileged criminals in chains were chosen as judges. The accusers were called upon to state their charges, in the hearing of the whole party. They told of the accused man's betrayal of a comrade in a robbery some time before.

There went up cries, "Kill him! Kill him! The traitor! Kill him!" This was the usual punishment for one found guilty. It was the custom of the authorities to watch the proceedings and never interfere with the carrying out of a sentence. As the mob was closing in on the accused, my heart sinking within me, the judges called for order and demanded that the man be given a hearing too. All white and trembling, he got up to tell his story in detail.

"There were two of us," he began, "in the scheme to rob a banker. It was decided that I force my way into the house through a window, hide there and signal to the other fellow at the opportune moment. I found that the banker had gone for the evening to a club, and concealed myself in a closet, waiting for his return. My comrade kept guard, without hearing from me, for a couple of hours.

"When the banker returned he sent his valet for something in the closet in which I was hidden. Discovering me, the latter raised an alarm, and some servants ran out to call for help just at the moment when my comrade was about to enter the house. He was caught. I managed to escape through the window and the garden. I am innocent, comrades. I have been a criminal for many years, and I have a clean, honourable record."

He then proceeded to enumerate the major accomplishments of his career, and the chiefs under whom he had worked, and those robbers with whom he had cooperated in the past.

He must have mentioned some very important personages, as immediately a number of voices were raised in his favour. Some got up and eulogised the connections of the accused, while others quizzed him. The deliberations lasted for several hours, resulting in the acquittal of the man.

The entire party, at the conclusion of the rest at Katchugo, was taken aboard a huge roofed barge. A thousand people in one hole! The prison at Alexandrovsk, the exile-stations, were paradises in comparison with this unimaginable man-made burrow. There was no air and no light. Instead of windows there were some small openings in the roof. Many fell sick, and were left lying there without care, some dying. We were so crowded that we slept almost on top of one another, inhaling the foulest of odours. Every morning we were allowed to come out on the deck of the barge, which was towed by a tug.

In our group was the woman Kitova, with her husband and two children. We cooked and ate our food together, enduring a great deal at the hands of the criminals. There were some quiet people among the latter, and they suffered from the whims of the leaders and their lackeys. There was a case of such a man, who happened to cross the path of an old criminal. The latter did not like the way he looked at him, and the poor man was beaten and, without any ceremony, thrown overboard and drowned. We were all locked up for it inside the barge and were denied the privilege of going out on the deck. It was the most cruel of punishments, worse than a long term in prison.

We changed barges on the way, spending about two months on the water, having made about three thousand *versts* upon arriving at Yakutsk at the end of July. We were beached at night, but it was almost as light as day, though much colder.

Our joy at landing was indescribable. The local politicals all came out to welcome us. We were marched to the Yakutsk prison, where

41

our roll was called. Here the women were separated from the men, and those who voluntarily accompanied their husbands were set free.

I then went to the office to inquire about the fate of Yasha, and was told that it was probable that he would be sent farther north. I was cared for by the local politicals, who sheltered me and gave me new clothing and money with which to purchase food and cook dinners for Yasha.

Yakutsk is such a distant place that the prisoners there are allowed considerable freedom. I was nicely treated by the officials when I took the dinner-pail to Yasha, and was permitted to remain with him as long as I desired, even in privacy.

Shortly afterwards Yasha was informed that he had been assigned to Kolymsk, within a hundred *versts* of the Arctic ocean, where the snow never melts and the winter never relaxes its grip. The news struck us as a bolt from the blue. To be buried alive in some snowbound hut! What for? To live like beasts in that uninhabitable region from which only few return to this world!

There was still one ray of hope. Governor Kraft, of Yakutsk, had the reputation of being a very kind man, and he might reassign Yasha if I begged him. Yasha had been advised to appeal to the governor, and he sent me on this mission.

The governor's office was in his home. He received me very kindly, even shook my hand, and invited me to be seated. He was a tall, erect, black-bearded man of middle-age, and he showed every consideration for me as I told my story. I proposed to him to open a sanitary butcher-shop in Yakutsk if he allowed Yasha to remain there, as the local butcher-shops were impossibly filthy.

He at first refused my suggestion, but, apparently on second thought, bade me follow into his apartment, where he seated me at a table, and, filling two glasses with wine, invited me to drink with him. I declined, wondering as to the reason for this extreme friendliness. He drew nearer to me, laid his hands on my coat and removed it Before I recovered from my astonishment he seized my hand and kissed it. No man had ever before kissed my hand, and I had an idea that it was a practice signifying immoral intentions only. Startled and indignant, I jumped to my feet.

"I will give you a thousand *rubles*, room for a butcher-shop in the market, and keep your husband in Yakutsk. if you will agree to belong to me," the governor declared, trying to calm me.

I lost my self-control. "Scoundrels! beasts! you men are all alike! all!

all! all! High and low, you are all depraved." Grabbing my coat, I ran out of the house, leaving the governor speechless.

I rushed to my lodging, locked myself in a room and wept all night. My errand failed, and it was now up to me to choose between a living death for Yasha and selling myself. I had visions of Kolymsk, a settlement of several scattered huts, populated by natives, lost in the vast expanse of the ice-bound *tundra* (a *steppe* in Northern Siberia) and buried for months under mountains of snow. I could almost hear the howling of the Arctic winds and the frightful growling of the polar bears.

I pictured Yasha in the midst of it, cut off from our race, slowly languishing in the monotony of inactivity. Then my thoughts would veer about to the other alternative. Live and work with Yasha in outward happiness, and stealthily, in the night, go to this degenerate governor! And what if Yasha learned of my secret trips? How would I explain? And of what avail would any explanations be to him? No, it was impossible, impossible! Ah, what a terrible night it was! From hugging the frozen banks of the Arctic waters, my imagination would carry me to the revolting embraces of Governor Kraft, in a fruitless search for a way out.

Morning finally came and found me all worn out. When asked by friends as to the result of my call on the governor I replied that he had refused my appeal. In low spirits I went to see Yasha. He quickly noticed my downcast appearance and inquired into the cause.

"I saw the governor, and he would not change your place of exile," I informed him, gloomily.

Yasha flared up. "You appealed to the governor, eh? The governor never refused yet an appeal of this sort by a woman, I am told. He is the kindest of men. The warden here just told me that the governor has long felt the need of a first-class butcher-shop in town, and would never let us go if properly appealed to. And I hear that you did not plead sufficiently. You want to get rid of me, eh? You want to have me sent to Kolymsk to die, so that you can remain here alone and carry on with some other man."

Yasha's words pained me deeply. He always had been very jealous, but the strain of the imprisonment and journey now made him more excitable. Besides, it was evident that someone from the governor's office had communicated to him the intelligence that I had not sufficiently exerted myself in his behalf. I did not dare to tell him the truth, for that would have meant sure exile to Kolymsk, and I still hoped against hope.

"Yasha," I implored, "how can you say such things of me? You know how I love you, and if you go to Kolymsk I'll go along with you. I have been to the governor, and begged him."

"Then go again. Fall on your knees before him, and beg harder. He is said to be such a kind man that he will surely have mercy. Otherwise, we are lost. Think of our destination, a land without the sun, a colony of three or four shacks, spread over a space of ten or fifteen *versts*, this is Kolymsk. No horses, no business, no trades! A land not for the living. Go, pray to the governor, and he may take pity."

I looked at Yasha, and my heart was filled with anguish. He was only twenty-seven, but his hair was already turning grey. He looked pale and exhausted. I could not keep myself from breaking out into sobs. Yasha was touched, and, placing his arm around me, apologized for his insinuation, assuring me of his devotion and appreciation of my endeavours to sustain him in his trials. I left him, with the understanding that I would call on the governor again.

"To go or not to go," was the thought that tormented me on the way from Yasha. I learned that the governor was notorious as a libertine. He had married into a high bureaucrat's family for a career, and his wife was a hunchback, spending most of her time abroad. Plucking up courage, I went to the governor again, hoping to win his favour by a passionate plea for Yasha. As I entered the office I saw the clerks wink at one another significantly. I could scarcely keep myself together, trembling in anticipation of another meeting with the governor. As I was admitted into his study he arose, smiled benevolently, saying:

"Ah, so finally you did come, my *golubka* (little dove). Now, don't be afraid; I won't harm you. Calm yourself, and be seated," and he helped me to a chair.

"Have pity on us, sir. Permit Yasha to remain here," I sobbed.

"Now, now, don't weep," he interrupted me. "I will. He shall remain."

My heart was full of gratitude, and I threw myself on the floor at his feet, thanking and blessing him for his kindness. Then it occurred to me that Yasha would be overjoyed to hear the news, and I arose to go, telling the governor of my purpose.

"You need not exert yourself by rushing to the prison. I will have the message telephoned to the warden, with instructions to inform your husband immediately," the governor said, "and you may rest here a while."

I was overflowing with thankfulness. He poured some wine into a glass and insisted that I drink it to refresh myself. I had never tasted wine before, and this particular wine was of a very strong quality. I felt a wave of warmth creep over me. It was so sweet and languorous. The governor then filled my glass again and, also one for himself, inviting me to drink with him. I made an effort to resist, but was too weak to withstand his coaxing. After the second glass it was much easier for the governor to make me empty the third. I became drowsy and dull, unable to move. Very dimly I seemed to realise it all, and, collecting my last strength, I attempted to struggle, but felt as if I had been drugged. . . .

I awoke about four in the morning and found myself in unfamiliar, luxurious surroundings. For a few moments I could not understand where I was, and thought that I was dreaming. There was a strange man near me. He turned his face, and I recognised him as the governor. I suddenly remembered everything. He made a motion to embrace me, but I cried out, jumped up, dressed myself hastily and ran from the house as if pursued.

Day was just breaking. The town was still engulfed in slumber, and a low mist merged the city with the river. It was early autumn. There was peace everywhere but in my heart; there, the elements were raging, and life grappled with death for supremacy. "What will I say to Yasha? What will our friends think of me? A prostitute!" pierced my mind poignantly. "No, that must never happen. Death is my only saviour."

I wandered about the streets for a while, until I found a grocery store open, and I purchased there thirty *kopecks'* worth of essence of vinegar. Entering my lodging, I was met by the question:

"Where were you, Maria Leontievna, where did you sleep last night?" My appearance in itself was enough to arouse suspicion. Without answering, I rushed into my room and locked the door. After offering my last prayers, I resolutely drank all of the poison, and began writhing in terrific pain.

At the same time, about ten in the morning, Yasha was released from prison and given five hundred *rubles* for the establishment of a butcher-shop. Happily, he marched to my stopping-place, completely unaware of what had befallen me. It was only when he arrived at the house that he observed an unusual commotion. The door of my room had been broken in when my moans were heard. The poison had scorched my mouth and throat as if with a flame, and I was found unconscious on the floor, recovering my senses only in the hospital.

Around me stood Yasha, some nurses, and a physician who was pouring something into my throat. I could not speak, although I understood all that was going on in the room. I had lost so much blood, the doctor explained to Yasha, in reply to his anxious questions, that my recovery was very doubtful. "Only an unusually powerful constitution could withstand and emerge alive from such an ordeal," he added.

For two weeks I hovered between this and the other world, suffering agonising pains, writhing in breath-arresting convulsions. I was fed only on milk, introduced into my throat through a tube. For a month I remained speechless, at the end of which time I was out of danger, but had to spend another month in the hospital before I regained my normal health.

Yasha could not, at first, understand the reason for my act. The governor was so kind, so generous. He not only commuted his sentence, but gave us five hundred *rubles* for a store. Could there be anything more noble? He finally arrived at the conclusion that the trials of the last year had resulted in my temporary mental derangement, which was responsible for my attempt at suicide, I did not disillusion him, although I felt like doing it whenever he eulogised the governor.

Upon leaving the hospital, we opened the butcher-shop and immediately began to do good business. For several months we led a peaceful life. Then, one afternoon, the governor suddenly called at our store, ostensibly to inquire how we were getting along with the shop. He stretched his hand toward me, but I turned away.

The governor left, and Yasha raged at me for my inexplicable conduct. Had I gone mad? I must have, to be capable of refusing to greet our benefactor, the kindest of men! I was sullen and silent, but Yasha would not be downed. He demanded an explanation. There was nothing left for me to do but to make a clean breast of it, which I did.

The truth was too shocking and threw him into spasms. He struck me with something and felled me to the floor. His face turned chalk-white, the veins stood out on his temples, and he was all atremble. He seemed unable to grapple with this nightmare. The governor's liberality was now explained. The five hundred *rubles*, the commutation of his sentence, it was all a price dearly paid for by his beloved.

My attempted suicide now appeared to him in its true light. He would take vengeance. He would kill the governor, he swore, yes, he would murder that most despicable of villains. I hugged his feet and begged him not to attempt to carry out his threat. He paid no heed to my prayers, and talked of the hollowness of his life if he did not avenge me.

He left on his fateful errand, all my efforts to bar his way having failed. When he appeared at the governor's office, requesting an audience, giving his name, the clerks immediately suspected him of some dark motive. The secretary reported to the governor that Buk, the butcher, acting in a suspicious manner, desired an audience. The governor ordered that he be detained and searched. A long, sharp knife was found on him, and he was arrested, under instructions to have him exiled on the following day to Amga, a Yakut hamlet within two hundred *versts* of Yakutsk. I had only twenty-four hours to dispose of the shop, and was compelled to deliver it into the hands of a local political, with the understanding that he would pay us for it a few months later.

It was Easter-Eve, 1914, when we started out in a hack, driven by a Yakut, for Amga. The mud was the worst I have ever come across. The horses sank so deep, and the wheels of the vehicle stuck so often, that it frequently was necessary for us to alight and help in extricating them. We met Easter in a native's hut on the road, in which children, women and animals lived together. There is always a fire in the centre of those huts, the smoke being allowed to escape through a hole in the roof. The cows were milked right there, and the filth was beyond words. Supping on some bread and a sort of tea, which was unfit for human consumption, we went to sleep. The following day we resumed our journey to Amga.

CHAPTER 5

Escape from Exile and Yasha

We spent about six days on the road to Amga. It was a town with a mixed population. Half of its homes were tiny cabins, built by Russian exiles, many of whom had married Yakut women, as they were physically attractive and considered it a cause for pride to be the wives of white men. Their own men maltreated them and were lazy, so that the women usually laboured to sustain the families. Some of the Yakuts were very wealthy, owning as many as a thousand head of deer and cattle. Men, women and children alike dressed only in garments of fur. They made their bread of a coarse flour, ground by hand.

There were about fifteen political exiles in Amga. Five of these were university graduates, and one of them was Prince Alexander Gutemurov, who had been arrested eight years before, and had turned grey in exile.

I was the first Russian woman to come to Amga, and the joy of the small colony of politicals knew no bounds. As the Yakut women never wash clothes, the filth in which the white men lived was unspeakable, and their unkempt appearance testified eloquently to the conditions surrounding them. They were at the mercy of vermin, and offered little resistance to epidemics. Clean food, drinkable milk, could not be had at any price. Money was cheap at Amga. The prince, for instance, received a monthly allowance of one hundred *rubles*, but he could not get a bath for a thousand.

I immediately took charge of the situation, rented a small cabin at two *rubles* a month, and it soon became the social centre of the colony. I had benches and a table made, and a bed constructed. I obtained flour at the general store owned by Kariakin, who had been exiled there for a murder in 1904, and prospered through the establishing of this business. I baked real Russian bread, cooked a regular home meal, and made Russian tea, inviting all the politicals to dinner.

It was a feast fit for the Gods to them, and those of them who were single asked me to board them regularly, and I not only boarded them, but I washed and repaired their clothes as well. I had a hut turned into a bathhouse, and it was not long before the politicals looked human again. My duties in the house demanded all my time and energy, but I was happy in being able to serve. The men regarded me as their mother, and never tired of praising me.

I planted a garden, and sowed some grain, as land was given by the community for the asking, there being few settlers in spite of the natural riches of the region. The rivers in Northern Siberia are full of fish, and there is no end to the wealth of timber. Within a couple of hundred *versts* from us gold mines were being worked. On the strength of our ownership of the butcher-shop in Yakutsk we were able to buy, on credit, a horse, and also borrow some money.

My popularity with the politicals irritated Yasha. He grew jealous of their kind words, now suspecting one man of courting me and now another. As he had nothing to do, he nursed his jealousies till they expanded in his imagination. He took to playing cards, which is very popular with the Yakuts, who like to gamble. This led gradually to his becoming a professional gambler. He would leave the home for some neighbouring Yakut settlement and stay away, frequently for several days, spending all his time in gambling. It finally became a habit with him. He would disappear, and reappear suddenly, only in different moods.

When he won he would return all in smiles, with money jingling in his pockets, bringing me some presents, and displaying great generosity generally. But that was not the usual case. Most of the time he lost, and then he would come back home in gloom, depressed and dejected, nervous and irritable, picking quarrels and acting provokingly. Especially was he aroused whenever he found some political in the house. Consumed by jealousy, he would taunt me, and not infrequently resort to blows.

"Yashka, have you lost your senses?" I would say. "Do you need some money? You know I am always glad to help you out," and I would dig into my small savings, knowing that he had lost his last penny. But that would not alleviate my suffering. It was with relief that I looked forward to his departures, and with apprehension that I saw him return.

At the end of about three months, we obtained permission to visit Yakutsk for the purpose of collecting the money due to us for the butcher-shop, but the man to whom we intrusted the business now denied owing us any money, claiming to have paid fully at the time of our exile to Amga. There was a violent quarrel, but no money. As I delivered the store to him on faith, we could not substantiate our claims and oust him from his possession of the premises. There was nothing to be done but return with empty hands, with the burden of the debts we had acquired at Amga weighing heavily on our shoulders. There was the dreary prospect of toil before me, of hard and continuous toiling, to pay what we owed.

One summer day a new party of exiles arrived at Amga. One of them was a young fellow of about twenty. Yasha took a liking to him and proposed that he remain in our house to help me along. Knowing of Yasha's jealousy, I objected.

"Yasha," I argued, "what are you doing? You know how jealous you become when you find one of the colony in the house, and now you want me to keep this youngster here, with you away most of the time. You are just creating trouble for me, I don't want him, I need no help. Please don't burden me with him."

"Marusia," Yasha replied, tenderly, "I swear that I won't be jealous any more. I won't, dear. Forgive me for all the pain I have caused you."

Yasha's words did not entirely pacify me, but he overruled my objections, promising to be reasonable in the future. The same afternoon a Yakut called for him, and they left together to go to a gambling place. The young man remained with me. Nothing occurred the first day or two. Then, one night, I was awakened by the young man bending over me. I repelled him, appealing to his sense of shame, but he persisted in his advances, and I struck him violently, jumping out of bed, grabbing a chair and, shouting at the top of my voice, drove him out of the house.

It was about one o'clock in the morning. Prince Gutemurov was returning home from an evening with a friend, and saw me put the young man out into the night. The latter, however, harboured a deep feeling of vengeance against me. He resolved to await Yasha's return, on the road outside the village, and tell him a false version of the story!

"A fine wife is yours," he addressed Yasha, derisively, as soon as the latter appeared.

"What's happened?" questioned Yasha excitedly. The young man replied that the night before I had come to him, but, being a loyal friend to Yasha, he drove me off and left the house with the purpose of intercepting and informing him of the incident. Yasha only had sufficient self-control to thunder the question:

"Swear, are you telling the truth?"

The young rascal answered:

"Of course, it's the truth."

When Yasha appeared on the threshold I observed immediately with horror that he was in a ferocious mood, suppressing a storm. That made him the more dangerous. He spoke slowly, coining his words deliberately, words which struck terror to my soul.

"You are a faithless woman, a harlot! You always have been faithless, deceiving me continually, but you are caught now, and you won't escape. It's fortunate that Dmitri is a decent young fellow and repelled your advances. You can say your last prayers, you base creature."

While speaking thus Yasha proceeded in a cold, business-like, purposeful manner to make a noose to hang me. It was this calm about Yasha's actions, bespeaking his terrible earnestness, that made shivers run over me.

"Yasha, I am innocent, Yasha," I sobbed, throwing myself at his feet and kissing them. "I swear that I am innocent," I cried. "Have mercy! think what you are doing! I tell you I am innocent!"

Yasha went on with his preparations, undisturbed.

He attached the rope to a hook on the ceiling and tested the noose.

"Yasha, come to your senses," I implored, hugging his legs.

He pushed me aside, placed a stool under the rope and ordered me, in a terrifying voice, to stand up on it.

"Now, say your last prayers," he repeated.

He then placed the noose around my neck and jerked the stool from under my feet. In an instant it tightened about my throat; I wanted to cry out but could not; the pressure against the crown of my head was so terrific that it seemed about to crack open. Then I lost consciousness. . . .

As the noose was tightening around my neck Yasha came to himself and hastened to loosen it. I dropped, lifeless, to the floor. In response to his calls for help several politicals, among whom were a couple of medical students, came running to the house. They made every effort to revive me, succeeding only after long and persistent exercises. When I opened my eyes, the whole colony was at my bedside. Pressed for an explanation of his inhuman act Yasha told of Dmitri's story.

Then Prince Gutemurov revealed what he had seen the previous night, on his way home. Yasha was overwhelmed. He fell on his knees and begged my forgiveness, cursing Dmitri and promising to make short work of him. But Yasha could not find him. Dmitri learned of the disclosure and disappeared forever from Amga.

Soon afterward, another incident occurred which further embittered my life with Yasha. In his absence Vasili, a political, came and told me that the authorities were in receipt of an order to arrest and send him to Irkutsk to be tried on a new charge, which carried with it the death-sentence. It was a regular practice of the *Tsar's* government to recall exiles for second trials on some additional bit of evidence.

Vasili asked that I lend him our horse, Maltchik, to help him escape. Knowing how attached Yasha was to the horse, I refused Vasili's request. But he persisted in imploring me, claiming that Prince Gutemurov had seen the order for the arrest, and that the sheriff was already on his tracks.

"But how could the horse be returned?" I asked Vasili, touched by his continuous pleading. He replied that he would leave it with a certain Yakut friend of ours, some hundred *versts* away, and I finally yielded, although not without misgivings. As soon as he left with Maltchik my anxiety grew into alarm. I hurried to Prince Gutemurov to verify Vasili's story. How thunder-struck I was upon learning from the prince that he knew of no order to arrest Vasili, and that he had even not seen him. It was clear that I had been swindled and that I would never see the horse again.

"My God!" I thought, "what will happen upon Yasha's return and his discovery that Maltchik is gone?" The spectre of death rose up before me, the impression of my recent escape from hanging still fresh in my mind. I was all atremble in anticipation of Yasha, with the feeling of an entrapped animal seeking an escape. But there seemed to be no opening.

It was August, 1914. The rumblings of the great collision were just reaching the remote Siberian provinces. The order for mobilization came, and there was a great stirring, even in the death-bound Arctic settlements, as if suddenly a new life had been infused into that land of monotony. Upon the heels of the call to arms came the *Tsar's* manifesto, abolishing the scourge of our national life—vodka, and with it a gigantic wave of popular enthusiasm, sweeping the steppes, valleys, and forests of vast Russia, from Petrograd and Moscow, across the Ural Mountains and the Siberian *tundras* and *taiga*, to the borders of China, and the Pacific coast.

There was something holy about the nation's response. Old men, who had fought in the Crimean War, in the Turkish Campaign of 1877-78, and the Russo-Japanese War, declared that they never saw such exaltation of spirit. It was an elevating, glorious, unforgettable moment in one's life. My soul was gripped, and I had a dim realisation of a new world coming to life, a purged world, a happier and Godlier one.

And when Vasili robbed me of our horse, and the dread of Yasha's frenzy had seized me, intensified by my inability to find an escape, the thought, "WAR!" suddenly flashed into my mind.

"Go to war to help save thy country!" a voice within me called.

To leave Yasha for my personal comfort and safety was almost unthinkable. But to leave him for the field of unselfish sacrifice, that was a different matter. And the thought of going to war penetrated deeper and deeper into my whole being, giving me no rest.

When Yasha returned, Prince Gutemurov and several other friends were in the house ready to defend me. He had already learned from the natives, on his way home, that Vasili had escaped on our horse. It seemed impossible to him that I could have given his favourite horse to anybody without his permission, and he therefore suspected me of an intrigue with Vasili, whom I had despatched to make preparations for an elopement. He made a violent scene, throwing himself upon me savagely, showering blows. My friends tore him away, which only infuriated him the more. This inability to give vent to his rage made him act like one demented.

His temper was clearly becoming a menace, for which a remedy was needed. A physician came to Amga only once a month. As Yasha

52

considered himself in good health, there could be no question of suggesting to him that he consult the physician. It was, therefore, agreed among my friends that Prince Gutemurov should take a walk about the village with the doctor when he arrived, pass by our house as if by accident, and for me to greet them with an invitation to come in for tea. Everything went smoothly. The physician was introduced to Yasha and immediately remarked upon his pale appearance and his inflamed eyes.

"What ails you?" he asked Yasha, "you seem to have fever. Let me examine you."

The result of the examination was the advice to Yasha to go to a hospital for treatment, which he, of course, ridiculed. Privately, the doctor informed Prince Gutemurov that Yasha's nerves had broken down and that he was dangerous to live with, as he might kill me for some trivial cause. The physician urged that I leave him at once. But I hesitated. Another quarrel, however, was not long in coming. Yasha actually made another attempt to kill me, but was stopped by our comrades. The cup was full. I decided to escape.

Day and night my imagination carried me to the fields of battle, and my ears rang with the groans of my wounded brethren. The impact of the mighty armies was heard even in uncivilized Northern Siberia. There were rumours in the air, rumours of victory and defeat, and in low voices people talked of torrents of blood and of rivers of maimed humanity, streaming back from the front, and already overflowing into the Siberian plains. My heart yearned to be there, in the boiling caldron of war, to be baptized in its fire and scorched in its lava. The spirit of sacrifice took possession of me. My country called me. And an irresistible force from within pulled me. . . .

I only awaited the opportunity when Yasha would be gone for several days. It arrived one September day. Some Yakuts called for Yasha. As soon as he left I cut off my hair, dressed in men's clothes and provided myself with two loaves of bread. I had no money to speak of, as I took no one of the colony into my confidence.

It was evening when I stealthily hurried out of Amga and took the road to Yakutsk. There were two hundred *versts* of it before me. I ran at such a pace that night, as I could not expect to travel in the daytime without being recognised, that I covered, by dawn, fifty *versts*.

Several times I had met Yakuts, and answered their greetings in their native dialect, with which I had grown familiar. In the dark they must have taken me for a Yakut. Otherwise, the journey was uneventful. The road was dry, the weather calm, and only the stars lit my way, my fast-beating heart echoing my footsteps.

When day broke I stopped beside a limpid stream and feasted on bread and cold water. I then made a bed of twigs in a hole by the road, lay down, covered myself with branches and went to sleep for the day. I awoke when evening came, offered my prayers to God, dined on some more bread and water, and resumed my journey. It took me six nights of walking to arrive at Yakutsk, living only on bread and water, and sleeping in hidden nooks by the road during the day.

There was a new governor in Yakutsk. Baron Kraft had gone to Western Europe to join his wife at some health resort, was stranded there after the outbreak of the war, and later died a prisoner in the hands of the enemy. The new governor received me well, and granted my request to be sent home, to Tomsk, at the expense of the government. He even offered me a convoy for protection.

My escape was a success, but my heart would not rejoice. The image of Yasha, stricken with grief, frantically searching for me, calling to me, rose before my eyes, and demanded an account from my conscience. Was it right, was it just, to leave poor Yasha all alone in forlorn Amga? Had I not vowed to remain eternally faithful to him? Was it not my bounden duty to stand by him to the end? Should I not return to him, then, and give up this wild fancy of going to war?

I vacillated. Was it not true, on the other hand, that Yasha had become a professional gambler? Was not life with him a perilous adventure? Devotion to Yasha, a voice within me spoke, did not mean perishing with him, but an effort to save him. Indeed, to get Yasha out of that wilderness was an idea which suddenly gripped my imagination. And how could I ever expect to find a better opportunity to do so than by distinguishing myself in war and then petitioning the *Tsar* in his behalf?

So, there I was again in the magic circle of war. I asked an acquaintance to write a letter for me to Yasha. Apologising for my unusual departure, I informed him that I was going to Tomsk to enlist as a soldier, leave for the front and win distinction for bravery, then petition the *Tsar* to pardon him, so as to enable us to resume our peaceful life in Stretinsk.

It was a plan with which Destiny, that held no more peace for me, played havoc. The war was to continue as many years as I had expected it to last months, shrouding Russia in darkness, sowing revolution, bearing thunder and lightning in its wings, spreading famine and chaos and seeds of a new world order. In those stormy years Yasha was to retreat to the far background of my life, then vanish altogether. But my heart was all with him that autumn day of 1914, when I turned my eyes toward the bleak north for the last time, as I boarded the barge that was to carry me to Irkutsk, from there to Tomsk, and thence to war.

CHAPTER 6

I Enlist by the Grace of the Tsar

Nearly two months I travelled homeward from Yakutsk, by water, rail and foot. The war was everywhere. The barge on the Lena was filled with recruits. In Irkutsk the uniform was much in evidence, and every now and then a regiment of soldiers would march through the streets on the way to the station, arousing one's martial spirit. My convoy left me upon my arrival there, and I had to appeal to the authorities for funds to continue my journey.

My heart was hammering when I reached Tomsk, after an absence of about six years. Tears dimmed my eyes as I walked the familiar streets. Here, in this two-storeyed house, I had first learned the fickleness of man's love. That was ten years ago, during the Russo-Japanese War, and I was only fifteen years old. There, in that dilapidated little store, where I can see the figure of Nastasia Leontievna bent over the counter, I spent five years of my early youth, waiting on customers, scrubbing floors, cooking, washing and sewing. That long apprenticeship, under the severe eyes of Nastasia Leontievna, served me in good stead in later years, I must admit. The smoking chimney yonder belongs to the house in which I was married, some eight years ago, only to experience at first hand the brutality of man. And here, in this basement, my father and mother have been dwelling for seventeen years.

I swung open the door. My mother was baking bread and did not turn immediately. How old she had grown! How bent her shoulders, how white her hair! She veered her head about and stared at me for a fraction of an instant. A lump rose in my throat, rendering me speechless.

"Mania!" she exclaimed, rushing toward me and locking me in her arms.

We wept, kissed each other, and wept again. My mother offered prayers to the Holy Mother and swore that she would never let me leave her side again. The bread was almost burned to charcoal, having been forgotten in the oven in the excitement of my return. Father came in, and he also was greatly aged. He greeted me tenderly, the years having softened the harshness of his nature.

I paid some visits to old friends. Nastasia Leontievna was overjoyed to see me. The sister of Afanasi Botchkarev, my first husband, also welcomed me cordially, in spite of the fact that I had escaped from her brother. She realised well enough how brutal and rough he was. She told me that Afanasi had been called in the first draft, and that it was reported that he was among the first prisoners taken by the Germans. I have never heard of him again.

I rested for about three days. The news from the front was exciting. Great battles were raging. Our soldiers were retreating in some places and advancing in others. I wished for wings to fly to their succour. My heart yearned and ached.

"Do you know what war is?" I asked myself. "It's no woman's job. You must make sure before starting out, Marusia, that you won't disgrace yourself. Are you strong enough in spirit to face all the trials and dangers of this colossal war? Are you strong enough in body to shed blood and endure the privations of war? Are you firm enough at heart to withstand the temptations that will come to you, living among men? Search your soul for an answer of truth and courage."

And I found strength enough in me to answer "yes" to all these questions. I suppressed the hidden longing for Yasha in the depths of my being, and made the fateful decision. I would go to war and fight till death, or, if God preserved me, till the coming of peace. I would defend my country and help those unfortunates on the field of slaughter who had already made their sacrifices for the country.

It was November, 1914. With my heart steeled in the decision I had made, I resolutely approached the headquarters of the Twenty-Fifth Reserve Battalion, stationed in Tomsk. Upon entering, a clerk asked me what I wanted.

"To see the commander," I replied.

"What for?" he inquired.

"I want to enlist," I said.

The man looked at me for a moment and burst out laughing. He called to the other clerks. "Here is a *baba* who wants to enlist!" he announced jokingly, pointing at me. There followed a general uproar. "Ha! ha! ha!" they chorused, forgetting their work for the moment. When the merriment subsided a little I repeated my request to see the commander, and his adjutant came out. He must have been told that a woman had come to enlist, for he addressed me gaily:

"What is your wish?"

"I want to enlist in the army, your Excellency," I answered.

"To enlist, eh? But you are a *baba*," he laughed. "The regulations do not permit us to enlist women. It is against the law."

I insisted that I wanted to fight, and begged to see the commander. The adjutant reported me to the commander, who asked to have me shown in.

With the adjutant laughing behind me, I blushed and became confused when brought before the commander. He rebuked the adjutant and inquired what he could do for me. I repeated that I wanted to enlist and fight for the country.

"It is very noble of you to have such a desire. But women are not allowed in the army," he said. "They are too weak. What could you, for instance, do in the front line? Women are not made for war."

"Your Excellency," I insisted, "God has given me strength, and I can defend my country as well as a man. I have asked myself before coming here whether I could endure the life of a soldier and found that I could. Can't you place me in your regiment?"

"*Golubushka*," (little dove), the commander declared gently, "how can I help you? It is against the law. I have no authority to enlist a woman even if I wanted to. You can go to the rear, enlist as a Red Cross nurse or in some other auxiliary of the service."

I rejected his proposal. I had heard so many rumours about the women in the rear that I had come to despise them. I therefore reiterated my determination to go to the front as a regular soldier. The commander was deeply impressed by my obstinacy, and wanted to help me. He suggested that I send a telegram to the *Tsar*, telling him of my desire to defend the country, of my moral purpose, and pray that he grant me the special right to enlist.

The commander promised to draw up the telegram himself, with a recommendation of his own, and have it sent from his office. He warned me, however, to consider the matter again, to think of the hardships I would have to bear, of the soldiers' attitude toward me, and the universal ridicule that I would provoke. I did not change my mind, though. The telegram was sent at my expense, costing eight *rubles*, which I obtained from my mother.

When I disclosed to my folks the nature of my visit to the commander of the Twenty-Fifth Battalion they burst into tears. My poor mother cried that her Mania must have gone insane, that it was an unheard-of, impossible thing. Who ever knew of a *baba* going to war? She would allow herself to be buried alive before letting me enlist. My father sustained her. I was their only hope now, they said. They would be forced to starve and go begging, without my help. And the house was filled with sobs and wails, the two younger sisters and some neighbours joining in.

My heart was rent in twain. It was a cruel, painful choice that I was called upon to make, a choice between my mother and my country. It cost me so much to steel myself for that new life, and now, when I was seemingly near the goal, my long-suffering mother called upon me to give up this ideal that possessed me, for her sake. I was tormented and agonised by doubt. I realised that I must make a decision quickly and, with a supreme effort and the help of God, I resolved that the call of my country took precedence over the call of my mother.

Sometime later a soldier came to the house.

"Is Maria Botchkareva here?" he questioned.

He came from headquarters with the news that a telegram had arrived from the *Tsar*, authorising the commander to enlist me as a soldier, and that the commander wanted to see me.

My mother did not expect such an answer. She grew frantic. She cursed the *Tsar* with all her might, although she had always revered him as the Little Father. "What kind of a *Tsar* is he?" she cried, "if he takes women to war? He must have lost his senses. Who ever heard of a *Tsar* calling women to arms? Hasn't he enough men? Goodness knows, there are myriads of them in Mother-Russia."

She seized the *Tsar's* portrait on the wall, before which she had crossed herself every morning, and tore it to bits, stamping them on the floor, with imprecations and anathema on her lips. Never again would she pray for him, she declared. "No, never!"

The soldier's message had an opposite effect on me, and I was thrown into high spirits. Dressing in my holiday costume, I went to see the commander. Everybody at headquarters seemed to know of the *Tsar's* telegram, smiles greeting me everywhere. The Commander congratulated me and read its text in a solemn voice, explaining that it was an extraordinary honour which the August Emperor had conferred on me, and that I make myself worthy of it. I was so happy, so joyous, so transported. It was the most blissful moment of my life.

The commander called his orderly in and instructed him to obtain a full soldier's outfit for me. I received two complete undergarments made of coarse linen, two pairs of foot-rags, a laundry bag, a pair of boots, one pair of trousers, a belt, a regulation blouse, a pair of epaulets, a cap with the insignia on it, two cartridge pockets and a rifle. My hair was clipped off.

There was an outburst of laughter when I appeared in full military attire, as a regular soldier of the Fourth Company, Fifth Regiment. I was confused and somewhat bewildered, hardly being able to recognise myself. The news of a woman recruit had preceded me at the barracks, and my arrival there precipitated a riot of fun. I was surrounded on all sides by green recruits who stared at me incredulously, but some were not satisfied with mere staring, so rare a novelty was I to them. They wanted to make sure that their eyes were not deceived, so they proceeded to pinch me, jostle me and brush against me.

"Get out, she ain't no *baba*," remarked one of them.

"Sure, she is," said another, pinching me. "She'll run like the devil at the first German shot," joked a third, provoking an uproar.

"We'll make it so hot for her that she'll run before even getting to the front," threatened a fourth.

Here the commander of my company interfered, and the boys dispersed. I was granted permission to take my things home before settling permanently at the barracks, and asked to be shown how to salute. On the way home I saluted every uniform in the same manner. Opening the door of the house, I stopped on the threshold. My mother did not recognise me.

"Maria Leontievna Botchkareva here?" I asked sharply, in military fashion. Mother took me for some messenger from headquarters, and answered, "No."

I threw myself on her neck. "Holy Mother, save me!" she exclaimed. There were cries and tears which brought my father and little sister to the scene. My mother became hysterical. For the first time I saw my father weep, and again I was urged to come back to my senses and give up this crazy notion to serve in the army. The proprietress of the house and old Nastasia Leontievna were called in to help dissuade me from my purpose.

"Think what the men will do to a lone woman in their midst," they argued. "Why, they'll make a prostitute of you. They will kill you secretly, and nobody will ever find a trace of you. Only the other day they found the body of a woman along the railroad track, thrown out of a troop-train. You always have been such a level-headed girl. What has come over you? And what will become of your parents? They are old and weak, and you are their only hope. They often said that when Marusia came back they would end their lives in peace. Now you are but shortening their days, dragging them to their graves in sorrow."

For a short space of time I vacillated again. The fierce struggle in my bosom between the two elements was resurrected. But I stuck by my decision, remaining deaf to all pleas. Then my mother grew angry and, crying out at the top of her voice, she shouted:

"You are no longer my daughter! You have forfeited your mother's love."

With a heavy heart I left the house for the barracks. The commander of the company did not expect me, and I had to explain to him why I could not pass that night at home. He assigned me to a place in the general bunk, ordering the men not to molest me. On my right and on my left were soldiers, and that first night in the company of men will ever stand out in my memory. I did not close my eyes once during the night.

The men were, naturally, unaccustomed to such a phenomenon as myself and took me for a loose-moralled woman who had made her way into the ranks for the sake of carrying on her illicit trade. I was, therefore, compelled constantly to fight off intrusions from all sides. As soon as I made an effort to shut my eyes I would discover the arm of my neighbour on the left around my neck, and would restore it to its owner with a crash. Watchful of his movements, I offered an opportunity for my neighbour on the right to get too near to me, and I would savagely kick him in the side. All night long my nerves were taut and my fists busy. Toward dawn I was so exhausted that I nearly fell asleep, when I discovered a hand on my chest, and before the man realised my intention, I banged him in the face. I continued to rain blows till the bell rang at five o'clock, the rising-hour.

Ten minutes were given us to dress and wash, tardiness being punished by a rebuke. At the end of the ten minutes the ranks formed and every soldier's hands, ears and foot-rags were inspected. I was in such haste to be on time that I put my trousers on inside out, provoking a veritable storm of hilarity and paroxysms of laughter.

The day began with a prayer for the *Tsar* and country, following which every one of us received the daily allowance of two-and-a-half pounds of bread and a few cubes of sugar from our respective squad commanders. There were four squads to a company. Our breakfast consisted of bread and tea and lasted half an hour.

At the mess I had an opportunity to get acquainted with some of the more sympathetic soldiers. There were ten volunteers in my company, and they were all students. After eating, there was roll-call. When the officer reached my name, he read: "Botchkareva," to which I answered, "Aye." We were then taken out for instruction, since the entire regiment had been formed only three days previous. The first rule that the training officer tried to impress upon us was to pay attention, watch his movements and actions. Not all the recruits could do it easily. I prayed to God to enlighten me in the study of a soldier's duties.

It was slow work to establish proper relations with the men. The first few days I was such a nuisance to the company commander that he wished me to ask for dismissal. He hinted as much on a couple of occasions, but I continued to mind my own business and never reported the annoyances I endured from the men. Gradually I won their respect and confidence. The small group of volunteers always defended me. As the Russian soldiers call each other by nick-names, one of the first questions put to me by my friends was what I would like to be called.

"Call me Yashka," I said, and that name stuck to me ever after, saving my life on more than one occasion. There is so much in a name, and "Yashka" was the sort of a name that appealed to the soldiers and always worked in my favour. In time it became the pet name of the regiment, but not before I had been tested by many additional trials and found to be a comrade, and not a woman, by the men.

I was an apt student and learned almost to anticipate the orders of the instructor. When the day's labours would be completed and the soldiers gathered into knots to while away an hour or two in games or story-telling, I was always sought after to participate. I came to like the soldiers, who were good-natured boys, and to enjoy their sports. The group which Yashka joined would usually prove the most popular in the barrack, and it was sufficient to secure my cooperation in some enterprise to make it a success.

There wasn't much time for relaxation, though, as we went through an intensive training course of only three months before we were sent to the front. Once a week, every Sunday, I would leave the barracks and spend the day at home, my mother having reconciled herself to my soldiering. On holidays I would be visited by friends or relatives. On one such occasion my sister and her husband called. I had been detailed for guard duty in the barrack that day. While on such duty a soldier is forbidden to sit down or to engage in conversation. I was entertaining my visitors when the company commander passed.

"Do you know the rules, Botchkareva?" he asked.

"Yes, your Excellency," I answered.

"What are they?"

"A soldier on guard duty is not allowed to sit down or engage in conversation," I replied. He ordered me to stand for two hours at attention, at the completion of my guard duty, which took twenty-four hours. Standing at attention, in full military equipment, for two hours is a severe task, as one has to remain absolutely motionless under the eyes of a guard, and yet it was a common punishment.

During my training I was punished in this manner three times. The second time it was really not my fault. One, night I recognised my squad commander in a soldier who annoyed me, and I dealt him as hard a blow as I would have given to any other man. In the morning he placed me at attention for two hours, claiming that he had accidentally brushed against me.

At first there was some difficulty in arranging for my bathing. The bath-house was used by the men, and so I was allowed one day to visit a public bath-house. I found it a splendid opportunity for some fun. I came into the women's room, fully dressed, and there was a tremendous outbreak as soon as I appeared. I was taken for a man. However, the fun did not last long. In an instant I was under a bombardment from every corner, and only narrowly escaped serious injury by crying out that I was a woman.

In the last month of our training we engaged in almost continuous rifle practice. I applied myself zealously to the acquisition of skill in handling a rifle and won a mention of excellence for good marksmanship. This considerably enhanced my standing with the soldiers and strengthened our relations of camaraderie.

Early in 1915 our regiment received orders to prepare to proceed to the front. We received a week's freedom from duty. The soldiers passed these last days in drink and revelry and gay parties. One evening a group of boys invited me to go along with them to a house of ill repute.

"Be a soldier, Yashka," they hilariously urged me, scarcely expecting me to accept their invitation.

A thought flashed through my mind.

"I'll go along and learn the soldier's life, so that I will understand his soul better." And I expressed my willingness to go. Perhaps my curiosity had something to do with my decision. It was greeted with a storm of fun. Noisily we marched through the streets, singing and laughing, until we came to the red-light district.

My knees grew weak as the party was about to enter one of the dives. I wanted to turn back and flee. But the soldiers would not let me. The idea of Yashka going with them to such a place took a strong hold on their imagination. Soldiers, before going to the front, were always welcome in the district of vice as they spent their money freely. Our group was, therefore, promptly surrounded by the women of the place, and one of them, a very young and pretty girl, picked me as her favourite, to the boundless mirth of the boys. There were drinking, dancing and much noise-making generally. Nobody suspected my sex, not even my youthful love-maker, who seated herself in my lap and exerted all her charms to entice me. I giggled, and the boys nearly raised the roof in accompaniment. Presently I was left alone with my charmer.

Suddenly the door swung open and an officer entered. Soldiers were forbidden to leave their barracks after eight o'clock, and our party had slipped out in the dark when we were supposed to be asleep.

"Of what regiment are you?" the officer asked abruptly, as I rose to salute.

"The Fifth Reserve Regiment, your Excellency," I replied ruefully.

While this was going on the boys in the other rooms were notified of the officer's presence and made their escape through windows and all available doors, leaving me to take care of myself.

"How dare you leave your barracks?" he thundered at me, "and bum around in such places so late at night? I'll order you to the military prison for the night." And he commanded me to report there immediately.

It was my first acquaintance with the disciplinary barrack. It is not a very comfortable place to spend a night in. In the morning I was called before the prison *commandant*, who was very rigid in his questions. Finally, I could contain myself no longer and broke out into laughter.

"It was all a mistake, your Excellency," I said.

"A mistake, eh? What the devil do you mean, a mistake? I have a report here!" he cried out angrily.

"I am a woman, your Excellency," I laughed.

"A woman!" he roared, opening wide his eyes and taking me in. In an instant he recognised the truth of my words. "What the h—l!" he muttered. "A woman indeed! A woman in a soldier's uniform!"

"I am Maria Botchkareva, of the Fifth Regiment," I explained. He had heard of me. "But what did you, a woman, do in that dive?" he inquired.

"I am a soldier, your Excellency, and I went along with some of our boys to investigate for myself the places where the soldiers pass their time."

He telephoned to the commander of my regiment to inquire into my record and told him where and why I was detained. A titter ran through the offices when they learned of Yashka's adventure. The soldiers already knew from their comrades of the night's escapade, and suppressed with great difficulty their merriment, not wanting to attract the attention of the officers. But now there was a universal riot of laughter. When I arrived, it reached such a degree that men were actually rolling on the floor, holding their sides. I was punished by two hours at attention, the third and last time during my training. For a week afterward, the regiment talked about nothing but Yashka's adventure, nearly every soldier making it a point to meet me and inquire: 'Yashka, how did you like it there?"

The date of our departure was set. We received complete new outfits. I was permitted to go home to spend the last night, and it was a night of tears and sobs and yearnings. The three months I had spent in Tomsk as a soldier were, after all, remote from war. But now I felt so near to that great experience, and it awed me. I prayed to God to give me courage for the new trials that were before me, courage to live and die like a man.

There was great excitement in the barracks the following morning. It was the last that we were to spend there. In full martial equipment we marched to the cathedral where we were sworn in again. There was a solemn service. The church was filled with people, and there was an enormous crowd outside. The bishop addressed us. He spoke of how the country was attacked by an enemy who sought to destroy Russia, and appealed to us to defend gloriously the *Tsar* and the Motherland. He prayed for victory for our arms and blessed us.

There was a spiritual upheaval among the men. We were all so buoyant, so happy, so forgetful of our own lives and interests. The whole city poured out to accompany us to the station, and we were cheered and greeted all along the route. I had never yet seen a body of men in such high spirits as we were that February morning. Woe to the Germans that might have encountered us that day! Such was Russia going to war in those first months of the struggle. Hundreds of regiments like our own were streaming from east, north and south to the battlefields It was an inspiring, elevating, imperishable spectacle.

My mother felt none of the exaltations that moved me. She walked along the street, beside my line, weeping, appealing to the Holy Mother and all the saints of the Church to save her daughter. "Wake up! Marusia," she cried. "What are you doing?" But it was too late. The ardour of war held me securely in its embrace. Somewhere deep in my heart my beloved mother's wails found an echo, but my eyes were dimmed with tears of joy. And only when I bade my mother goodbye, hugging and kissing her for what she felt was the last time, and boarded the train, leaving her on the platform in a heap frantic with grief, did my heart quiver in my breast and a tremor shake me from head to foot. My resoluteness was on the point of melting as the train pulled out of the station.

I was going to war.

CHAPTER 7

Introduced to No Man's Land

Our train was composed of a number of box-cars and one passenger-car. A box-car, having two bunks on each side, in which the soldiers sleep, is called *teplushka*. There are no windows in a *teplushka*, as it is really only a converted freight-car. The passenger-car was occupied by the four officers of our regiment, including our new company commander, Grishaninov. He was a short, jolly fellow and soon won his men's love and loyalty.

There was much empty space in the passenger-car, and the officers bethought themselves to invite me to share it with them. When the invitation came the soldiers all shook their heads in disapproval. They suspected the motives of the officers and thought that Yashka could fare as well among them as among their superiors.

"Botchkareva," said Commander Grishaninov, when I entered his car, "would you prefer to be stationed in this carriage? There is plenty of room."

"No, your Excellency," I replied, saluting. "I am a plain soldier, and it is my duty to travel as a soldier."

"Very well," declared the commander, chagrined. And I returned to my *teplushka*.

"Yashka is back! Good fellow, Yashka!" the boys welcomed me enthusiastically, flinging some strong epithets at the officers. They were immensely pleased at the idea that Yashka preferred their company in a *teplushka* to that of the officers in a spacious passenger coach, and

65

made a comfortable place for me in a corner.

We were assigned to the Second Army, then commanded by General Gurko, with headquarters at Polotsk. It took us two weeks to get there from Tomsk. General Gurko reviewed us at Army Headquarters and complimented the officers upon the regiment's fitness. We were then assigned to the Fifth Corps. Before we started the word went out that there was a woman in our regiment. There was no lack of curiosity-seekers. Knots of soldiers gathered about my *teplushka*, peeped through the door and cracks in the sides to verify with their own eyes the incredible news. Then they would swear, emphasising by spitting the inexplicable phenomenon of a *baba* going to the trenches.

The attention of some officers was attracted by the crowd, and they came up to find out what the excitement was about. They reported me to the *commandant* of the station, who immediately sent for Colonel Grishaninov, demanding an explanation. But the colonel could not satisfy the *commandant's* doubts and was instructed not to send me along with the men to the fighting line.

"You can't go to the trenches, Botchkareva," my commander addressed me upon his return from the *commandant*. "The general won't allow it. He was much wrought up over you and could not understand how a woman could be a soldier."

For a moment I was shocked. Then the happy thought occurred to me that no general had the authority to overrule an order of the *Tsar*.

"Your Excellency!" I exclaimed to Colonel Grishaninov, "I was enlisted by the grace of the *Tsar* as a regular soldier. You can look up His Majesty's telegram in my record."

This settled the matter, and the *commandant* withdrew his objections. There were about twenty *versts* to Corps Headquarters to be walked. The road was in a frightful condition, sticky and full of mudholes. We were so tired at the end of ten *versts'* walking that a rest was ordered. The soldiers, although fatigued, made a dry seat for me with their overcoats. We then resumed our journey, arriving for supper at headquarters, and were billeted for the night in a stable. We slept like dead, on straw spread over the floor.

General Valuyev was then commander of the Fifth Corps. He reviewed us in the morning and was extremely satisfied, assigning us to the Seventh Division which was situated several *versts* distant. The commander of the division, by the name of Walter, was of German blood and a rascal of first rank. We were placed, during the night, in the woods back of the fighting line.

In command of the reserves was a colonel named Stubendorf, also of German blood, but a decent and popular officer. When informed that a woman was in the ranks of the newly arrived regiment, he was amazed.

"A woman!" he cried out, "she can't be permitted to remain. This regiment is going into battle soon, and women were not made for war."

There was a heated discussion between him and Commander Grishaninov, which ended in an order for my appearance before them. I received a thorough test and passed it well. Asked if I wanted to take part in the fight, I replied affirmatively. Muttering his wonderment, Colonel Stubendorf allowed me to remain till he looked into the matter further.

A big battle was raging at the time on that section of the front. We were told to be ready for an order to move at any moment to the front line. Meanwhile, we were sheltered in dugouts. My company occupied ten of these, all bomb-proof, though not in first-class condition. They were cold and had no windows. As soon as day broke we busied ourselves with cutting windows, building fireplaces, repairing the caved-in ceilings of timber and sand, and general house-cleaning. The dugouts were constructed in rows, the companies of odd numbers being assigned to the row on the right, while those of even numbers went to the left. Signs were posted on the streets and each company had a sentinel on duty.

Our position was eight *versts* behind the first line of trenches. The booming of the guns could be heard in the distance. Streams of wounded, some on vehicles and others trekking along on foot, flowed along the road. We drilled most of the time, the second day watched by Colonel Stubendorf. He must have kept a close eye on me, for at the end of the drilling he called me, praised my efficiency, and granted me permission to stay in the ranks.

On the third day came the order to move to the trench lines. Through mud and under shells we marched forward. It was still light when we arrived at the firing-line. We had two killed and five wounded. As the German positions were on a hill, they were enabled to observe all our movements. We were therefore instructed by field telephone not to occupy the trenches till after dark.

"So, this is war," I thought. My pulse quickened, and I caught the spirit of excitement that pervaded the regiment. We were all expectant, as if in the presence of a solemn revelation. We were eager to get into the fray to show the Germans what we, the boys of the Fifth Regiment, could do. Were we nervous? Undoubtedly. But it was not the nervousness of cowardice, rather was it the restlessness of young blood. Our hands were steady, our bayonets fixed. We exulted in our adventure.

Night came. The Germans were releasing a gas wave at us. Perhaps they noticed an unusual movement behind the lines, and wished to annihilate us before we entered the battle. But they failed. Over the wire came the order to put on our masks. Thus, were we baptised in this most inhuman of all German war inventions. Our masks were not perfect. The deadly gas penetrated some and made our eyes smart and water. But we were soldiers of Mother-Russia, whose sons are not unaccustomed to half-suffocating air, and so we withstood the irritating fumes.

The midnight hour passed. The commander went through our ranks to inform us that the hour had come to move into the trenches and that before dawn we would take the offensive. He addressed us with words of encouragement and was heartily cheered. The artillery had been thundering all night, the fire growing more and more intense every hour. In single file we moved along a communication trench to the front line. Some of us were wounded, but we remained dauntless. All our fatigue seemed to have vanished.

The front trench was a plain ditch, and as we lined up along it our shoulders touched. The positions of the enemy were less than one *verst* away, and the space between was filled with groans and swept by bullets. It was a scene full of horrors. Sometimes an enemy shell would land in the midst of our men, killing several and wounding many. Then we would be sprinkled with the blood of our comrades and spattered by the mud.

At two in the morning the commander appeared in our midst. He was seemingly nervous. The other officers came with him and took their positions at the head of the men. With drawn sabres they prepared to lead the charge. The commander had a rifle.

"*Viliezai!*" (Climb out!) his voice rang out. I crossed myself. My heart was filled with pain for the bleeding men around me and stirred by an impulse of savage revenge toward the Germans. My mind was a kaleidoscope of many thoughts and pictures. My mother, death, mutilation, various petty incidents of my life filled it. But there was no time for thinking.

I climbed out with the rest of the boys, to be met by a hail of machine gun bullets. For a moment there was confusion. So many dropped around us, like ripe wheat cut down by a gigantic scythe wielded by the invisible arm of Satan himself. Fresh blood was dripping on the cold corpses that had lain there for hours or days. And the moans, they were so heart-rending, so piercing!

Amid the confusion the voice of our company commander was raised:

"Forward!"

And forward we went. The enemy had perceived us go over the top, and he let loose Hell. As we ran ahead, we fired. Then the order came to lie down. The bombardment grew even more concentrated. Alternately running for some distance and then lying down for a while, we reached the enemy's barbed wire entanglements. We had expected to find them demolished by our artillery, but, alas! they were untouched. There were only about seventy of our company of two hundred and fifty left.

Whose fault was it? This was an offensive on a twenty-*verst* line, carried out by three army corps. And the barbed wire was uncut! Perhaps our artillery was defective! Perhaps it was the fault of someone higher up! Anyhow, there we were, seventy out of two hundred and fifty. And every fraction of a second was precious. Were we doomed to die here in a heap without even coming to grips with the enemy? Were our bodies to dangle on this wire tomorrow, and the day after, to provide food for the crows and strike terror into the hearts of the fresh soldiers who would take our places in a few hours?

As these thoughts flashed through our minds an order came to retreat. The enemy let a barrage down in front of us. The retreat was even worse than the advance. By the time we got back to our trenches there were only forty-eight of our company left alive. About a third of the two hundred and fifty were dead. The larger part of the wounded were in No Man's Land, and their cries of pain and prayers for help or death gave us no peace.

The remnant of our company crouched in the trench, exhausted, dazed, incredulous of their escape from injury. We were hungry and thirsty and would have welcomed a dry and safe place to recover our poise. But there we were, smarting under the defeat by the enemy's barbed wire barrier, with the heart-tearing appeals for succour coming from our comrades. Deeper and deeper they cut into my soul. They were so plaintive, like the voices of hurt children.

In the dark it seemed to me that I saw their faces, the familiar faces of Ivan and Peter and Sergei and Mitia, the good fellows who had taken such tender care of me, making a comfortable place for me in that crowded *teplushka*, or taking off their overcoats in cold weather and spreading them on the muddy road to provide a dry seat for Yashka. They called me. I could see their hands outstretched in my direction, their wide-open eyes straining in the night in expectation of rescue, the deathly pallor of their countenances. Could I remain indifferent to their pleas? Wasn't it my bounden duty as a soldier, as important as that of fighting the enemy, to render aid to stricken comrades?

I climbed out of the trench and crawled under our wire entanglements. There was a comparative calm, interrupted only by occasional rifle shots, when I would lie down and remain motionless, imitating a corpse. Within a few feet of our line there were wounded. I carried them one by one to the edge of our trench where they were picked up and carried to the rear. The saving of one man stimulated me to continue my labours, till I reached into the far side of the field. Here I had several narrow escapes. A sound, made involuntarily, was sufficient to attract several bullets, and only my anticipating that, by flattening myself against the ground, saved me. When dawn broke in the east, putting an end to my expeditions through No Man's Land, I had accounted for about fifty lives.

I had no idea at the time of what I had accomplished. But when the soldiers whom I had picked up were brought to the relief-station and asked who rescued them, about fifty replied, "Yashka." This was communicated to the commander, who recommended me for an Order of the 4th degree, "for distinguished valour shown in the saving of many lives under fire."

Our kitchen had been destroyed the previous night by the enemy's fire, and we hungered. Our ranks were refilled by fresh drafts, and our artillery again boomed all day, playing havoc with the enemy's wire fences. We knew that it meant another order to advance the following night, and our expectations proved correct. At about the same hour as the previous morning we climbed out and started on the run for the enemy's position. Again, a rain of shells and bullets, again scores of wounded and killed, again smoke and gas and blood and mud.

But we reached the wire parapet and it was down and torn to pieces this time. We halted for an instant, emitting an inhuman "Hurrah! Hurrah!" that struck terror into those Germans that were still alive in their half-demolished trenches, and with fixed bayonets rushed forward and jumped into them.

As I was about to descend into the ditch I suddenly observed a huge German aiming at me. Hardly did I have time to fire when something struck my right leg, and I had a sensation of a warm liquid trickling down my flesh. I fell. The boys had put the enemy to flight and were pursuing him. There were many wounded, and cries of "Save me, Holy Jesus!" came from every direction.

I suffered little pain and made several efforts to get up and reach our trenches. But every time I failed. I was too weak. There I lay in the dark of the night, within fifty feet of what was, twenty-four hours before, the enemy's position, waiting for dawn and relief. To be sure, I was not alone. Hundreds, thousands of gallant comrades were scattered on the field for *versts*.

It was four hours after I was wounded before day arrived and with it our stretcher-bearers. I was picked up and carried to a first-aid station in the immediate rear. My wound was bandaged, and I was sent on to the Division Hospital. There I was placed on a hospital train and taken to Kiev.

It was about Easter of 1915 when I arrived in Kiev. The station there was so crowded with wounded from the front that hundreds of stretchers could not be accommodated inside and were lined up in rows on the platform outside. I was picked up by an ambulance and taken to the Eugene Lazaret, where I was kept in the same ward with the men. Of course, it was a military hospital, and there was no women's ward. I spent the spring of 1915 there. The nurses and physicians took good care of all the patients in the hospital. My swollen leg was restored to its normal condition, and it was a restful two months that I passed in Kiev.

At the end of that period I was taken before a military medical commission, examined, pronounced in good health, provided with a ticket, money and a certificate and sent to the front again. My route now lay through Molodechno, an important railway terminal. When I arrived there in the early part of July I was sent to the Corps Headquarters by wagon, and thence I proceeded on foot to my regiment.

My heart throbbed with joy as I drew nearer to the front. I had been anxious to get back to the boys. They had endeared themselves to me so much that my company was as beloved to me as my own mother. I thought of the comrades whose lives I had saved and wondered how many of them had returned to the fighting line. I thought of the soldiers whom I had left alive and wondered if they were still among the living. Many familiar scenes came up in my imagination as

I marched along under the brilliant rays of the sun.

As I approached the Regimental Headquarters a soldier saw me in the distance and, turning to his comrade, he pointed toward me.

"Who could that be?" he asked, reminiscently.

The partner scratched his neck and said:

"Why, he looks familiar."

"That's Yashka!" exclaimed the first, as I moved nearer. "Yashka! Yashka!" they shouted at the top of their voices, running toward me as fast as they could.

"Yashka is back! Yashka is back!" went out the word to men and officers alike. There was such spontaneous joy that I was overwhelmed. Our regiment was then in the reserves, and soon I was surrounded by hundreds of old friends. There was intermittent kissing, embracing, handshaking. The boys pranced about like kids, shouting, "Look who's here! Yashka!" They had been under the impression that I was disabled and would never return. They congratulated me upon my recovery. Even the officers came out to shake hands with me, some even kissing me, and all expressing their gratification at my recovery.

I shall never forget the ovation I received from my comrades.

They carried me on their shoulders, shouting, "Hurrah for Yashka! Three cheers for Yashka!" Many of them wanted me to visit their dugouts and share with them the food parcels they had received from home. The dugouts were really in a splendid state, clean, furnished, well protected. I was reassigned to my old company, the Thirteenth, and was now considered a veteran.

Our company was detailed soon to act as the protecting force to a battery of artillery. Such an assignment was regarded by the men as a vacation, for it made possible a genuine rest in healthful surroundings. We spent between two and three weeks with the battery and were removed to Sloboda, a town in the vicinity of Lake Narotch, about forty *versts* from Molodechno. Our positions were in a swampy region, full of mud-holes and marshes. It was impossible to construct and maintain regular trenches there. We, therefore, built a barrier of sand-bags, behind which we crouched, knee-deep in water. One could not endure long in such circumstances. One was compelled to snatch bits of sleep standing, and even the strongest constitutions broke down quickly. We were relieved at the end of six days and sent to the rear for recuperation. Then we had to relieve the men who had taken our places.

Thus, we continued to hold the line. As the summer neared its end and the rains increased, the water would rise and at times reach our waists. It was important to maintain our front intact, although for several miles the bogs were practically impassable. The Germans, however, made an attempt in August to outflank the marshes, but failed.

Later we were shifted to another position, some distance away. There was comparative quiet at our front. Our main work consisted of sending out raiding parties and keeping a keen watch over the enemy's movements from our advanced listening-posts. We slept in the morning and stayed wide-awake all night.

I participated in numerous observation parties. Usually four of us would be detailed to a listening-post, located sometimes in a bush, another time in a hole in the ground, behind the stump of a tree, or some similar obstacle. We crawled to our post so noiselessly that not only the enemy but even our own men would not know our hiding places, which were on an average of fifty feet apart. Once at the post, our safety and duty demanded absolute immobility and caution. We were to make every effort to catch any unusual sound, and communicate it from post to post. Besides, there was always a chance of an enemy patrol or post being in close proximity without our knowing it. Every two hours the holders of the posts were relieved.

One foggy night, while on guard at a listening-post, I caught a dull noise. It sounded like a raiding party, and I took it at first for our own, but there was no answer to my sharp query for the password. It was impossible to see in the mist. We opened fire, and the Germans flattened themselves against the ground and waited.

There they lay for almost two hours, until we had forgotten the incident. Then they crawled toward our post and suddenly appeared in front of us. There were eight of them. One threw a grenade, but missed our hole, and it exploded behind us. We fired, killing two and wounding four. The remainder escaped.

When the company commander received an order to send out a scouting party, he would call for volunteers. Armed with hand-grenades, about thirty of the best soldiers would go out into No Man's Land to test the enemy's strength by drawing his fire, or to alarm him by intensive bombing and shooting. Not infrequently scouting parties from both sides would meet. Then there would be a regular battle. It has happened that one party would let an opposite party pass by, and then attack it from the rear and capture it.

The fifteenth of August, 1915, was a memorable day in our lives. The enemy opened a violent fire at us at three a. m. of that date, demolishing our barbed-wire defences, destroying some of our trenches and burying many soldiers alive. Many others were killed by his shells. Altogether we lost fifteen killed and forty wounded out of two hundred and fifty. It was clear that the Germans contemplated an offensive. Our artillery replied vigorously, and the earth shook from the thunders of the cannon. We sought every protection available, our nerves strained in momentary anticipation of an attack. We crossed ourselves, prayed to God, made ready our rifles, and awaited orders.

At six the Germans were observed climbing over the top and running in our direction. Closer and closer they came, and still we were kept inactive, while our artillery rained shells on them. When they approached within a hundred feet of our line the order was issued to us to open fire. It was such a concentrated hail of bullets that we let loose at the foe, decimating his ranks, that confusion resulted in his midst. We took advantage of the situation and rushed at the Germans, turning them back and pursuing them along the eighteen-*verst* front on which they started to advance. The enemy lost ten thousand that morning.

During the day we received reinforcements, also new equipment, including gas masks. Then word came that we would take the offensive the following night. Our guns began a terrific bombardment of the German positions at six in the evening. We were all in a state of suppressed excitement. Men and officers mixed, joking about death. Many expected not to return and wrote letters to their dear ones. Others prayed. Before an offensive the men's camaraderie reached a climax. There would be affectionate partings, sincere professions by some of their premonitions of death and the intrusting of messages to friends. Universal joy was displayed whenever a shell of ours tore a gap in the enemy's barrier of wire or fell into the midst of his trenches.

At three in the morning the order "Advance!" rang out. Buoyant in spirit, we started for the enemy's positions. Our casualties on the way were enormous. Several times we were ordered to lie down. Our first line was almost completely wiped out, but its ranks were filled up by men from the second row. On we went till we reached the Germans and overwhelmed them. Our own Polotsk Regiment alone captured two thousand prisoners and our jubilation was boundless. We held the enemy's positions and No Man's Land, strewn with wounded and dead, was now ours. There were few stretcher-bearers available, and a call went out for volunteers to gather in the wounded. I was among those who answered the call.

YASHKA IN UNIFORM WITH HER MEDALS

There is great satisfaction in aiding an agonised human being. There is great reward in the gratitude of some pain-convulsed boy that one wins. It gave me immense joy to sustain life in benumbed human bodies. As I was kneeling over one such wounded, who had suffered a great loss of blood, and was about to lift him, a sniper's bullet hit me between the thumb and forefinger and passed on and through the flesh of my left forearm. Fortunately, I realised quickly the nature of the wounds, bandaged them, and, in spite of his objections, carried the bleeding man out of danger.

I continued my work all night, and was recommended "for bravery in defensive and offensive fighting and for rendering, while wounded, first aid on the field of battle," to receive the Cross of St. George of the 4th degree. But I never received it. Instead, I was awarded a medal of the 4th degree and was informed that a woman could not obtain the Cross of St. George.

I was disappointed and chagrined. Hadn't I heard of the Cross being given to some Red Cross nurses? I protested to the commander. He fully sympathised with me and expressed his belief that I certainly deserved the Cross.

"But," he added, disdainfully, shrugging his shoulders, "it is *natchalstvo*." (Officialdom.)

My arm pained, and I could not remain in the front line. The medical assistant of our regimental hospital had been severely wounded, and I was sent to act in his place, under the supervision of the physician. I stayed there two weeks, till my arm improved, and attained such proficiency under the doctor's instructions that he issued a certificate to me, stating that I could temporarily perform the duties of a medical assistant.

The autumn of 1915 passed, for us, uneventfully. Our life became one of routine. At night we kept watch, warming ourselves with hot tea, boiled on little stoves in the front trenches. With dawn we would go to sleep, and at nine in the morning the day would begin for some of us, as that was the hour for the distribution of bread and sugar. Every soldier received a ration of two and a half pounds of bread daily. It was often burned on the outside and not done on the inside. At eleven o'clock, when dinner arrived, everybody was awake, cleaning rifles and repairing things generally. The kitchen was always about a *verst* in the rear, and we sent messengers to bring the dinner pails to the trenches.

The average dinner consisted of a hot cabbage soup, with some meat in it. The meat, frequently, was spoiled. The second dish was always *kasha*, Russia's popular gruel. Our daily ration of sugar was supposed to be three-sixteenths of a pound. By the time our dinner got to us it was cold, so that tea was resorted to again. After noon we received our assignments, and at six in the evening supper, the last meal, consisting only of one course, arrived. It was either cabbage soup or *kasha* or half a herring, with bread. Many ate all their bread before the supper hour, or if they were very hungry, with the first meal, and thus were forced to beg for morsels from their comrades, or go hungry in the evening.

Every twelve days we were relieved and sent to the rear for a six days' recuperation. There the baths of the Union of Zemstvos, which had already extended its activities in 1915 throughout the front, awaited us. Every Divisional bath was in charge of a physician and a hundred volunteer workers. Every bath-house was also a laundry, and the men, upon entering it, left their dirty underwear there, receiving in exchange clean linen. When a company was about to leave the trenches for the rear, word was sent to the bath-house of its coming. There was nothing that the soldiers welcomed so much as the bath-house, so vermin-ridden were the trenches, and so great was their suffering on this account.

More than anybody else did I suffer from the vermin. I could not think at first of going to the bath-house with the men. My skin was eaten through and through, and scabs began to form all over my body. I went to the commander to inquire how I could get a bath, telling him of my condition. The commander sympathised.

"But what can I do, Yashka?" he remarked, "I can't keep the whole Company out to let you alone make use of the bath-house. Go with the men. They respect you so much that I am sure they won't molest you."

I could not quite make up my mind for a while. But the vermin gave me no rest, and I was nearing the point of desperation. When we were relieved next and the boys were getting ready to march to the bath-house I plucked up courage and went up to my sergeant, declaring:

"I'll go to the bath-house, too. I can't endure it any longer."

He approved of my decision, and I followed the company, arousing general merriment. "Oh, Yashka is going with us to the bath-house!" the boys joked, good-naturedly. Once inside, I hastened to occupy a corner for myself and demanded that the men stay away from there.

They did, although they kept laughing and teasing. I was awfully embarrassed the first time, and as soon as I got through I hurried into my new underwear, dressed quickly and ran out of the building. But the bath did me so much good that I made it a habit to attend it with the company every two weeks. In time, the soldiers got so accustomed to it that they paid no attention to me, and were even quick to silence the fun-making of any new member of the company.

Chapter 8

Wounded and Paralyzed

Towards winter we were moved to a place called Zelenoye Polie. There I was placed in charge of twelve stretcher-bearers and served in the capacity of medical assistant for six weeks, exercising the authority of sending ill soldiers to the hospital and of granting a few days' rest from duty to the indisposed.

Our positions ran through an abandoned country estate. The manor lay between the lines. We were on the top of the hill, while the Germans occupied the low ground. We could, therefore, observe their movements and they, in turn, watch us. If anyone on either side raised his head he became the mark of some sniper.

It was in this place that our men fell victims to a high officer's treason. There had been rumours aplenty in the trenches of pro-German officials in the army and the court. We had our suspicions, too, and now they were confirmed in a shocking manner.

General Walter paid a visit to the front line. He was known to be of German blood, and his harsh treatment of the soldiers won for him the cordial hatred of the rank and file. The general, accompanied by a considerable suite of officers and men, exposed himself on his tour of inspection of our trenches completely without attracting a single enemy bullet! It was unthinkable to us who had to crawl on our bellies to obtain some water. And here was this party in open view of the enemy who kept such a strange silence.

The general acted queerly. He would stop at points where the barbed wire was torn open or where the fortifications were weak and wipe his face with his kerchief. There was a general murmur among the men. The word "treason!" was uttered by many lips in suppressed tones. The officers were indignant and called the general's attention to the unnecessary danger to which he exposed himself. But the general ignored their warnings, remarking, "*nitchevo!*" (It's nothing.)

The discipline was so rigorous that no one dared to argue the matter with the general. The officers cursed when he left. The men muttered:

"He is selling us out to the enemy!"

Half an hour after his departure the Germans opened a tremendous fire. It was particularly directed against those points at which the general had stopped, reducing their incomplete defences to dust. We thought at first that the enemy intended to launch an offensive, but our expectations did not materialise. He merely continued his violent bombardment, wounding and burying alive hundreds. The cries of the men were such that rescue work could not be postponed. While the shelling was still going on I took charge and dressed some hundred and fifty wounds. If General Walter had appeared in our midst at that moment the men would never have let him get away alive, so intense was their feeling.

For two weeks we worked at the reconstruction of our demolished trenches and altogether extracted about five hundred corpses. I was recommended for and received a gold medal of the 2nd degree for "saving wounded from the trenches under violent fire." Usually a medical assistant received a medal of the 4th degree, but I was given one of the 2nd degree because of the special conditions attending my work.

We were then relieved for the month and sent fifteen *versts* to the rear, to the village of Senky, on a stream called Uzlianka. An artillery base was located there, and once we got to the place our life was eased. But getting there was no easy task; the road was frightful. We were fatigued and exhausted, and most of us fell asleep without even eating the supper that had been prepared for us.

There was no work for a medical assistant in the rear, and besides my arm had fully recovered, so I applied to the commander for permission to return to the ranks. He granted it, promoting me to the grade of corporal, which placed me in charge of eleven men.

Here I received two letters, one from Yasha, in reply to mine, written from Yakutsk, in which I spoke of returning to him at the conclusion of the war. I had an answer sent to him reiterating my promise, on condition that he change his behaviour toward me and treat me with consideration and love. The other letter was from home. Mother wanted me to come back, telling of her hardships and sufferings.

It was October. This month, spent at the artillery base, was one of jollification. We were billeted in the village cabins, and engaged almost daily in sports and games. It was here that I was first taught how to sign my name and to copy the alphabet. I had learned to read previously, Yasha having been my first instructor. The literature that was allowed to circulate at the front was largely made up of lurid detective stories, and the name of "Nick Carter" was not unfamiliar even to me.

There were other pastimes, also. I remember one day during a downpour I sought shelter in a barn, where I found about forty officers and men, who had also sought protection there from the rain. The owner of the barn, a *baba* of middle-age, was there with her cow. I was in a mischievous mood and began to flirt with her, to the general merriment of the men. I paid her some flattering compliments and declared that she had captivated me. The woman did not recognise my sex and professed to be insulted. Encouraged by the uproar of the men, I persisted in my advances, and finally made an attempt to kiss her. The *baba*, maddened by the laughter of the soldiers, seized a big stick of stove-wood, and with curses threatened me and the men.

"Get out of here, you tormentors of a poor *baba!*" she cried.

I did not seek to provoke a fight and exclaimed to her: "Why, you foolish woman, I am a peasant girl myself."

This only further inflamed our hostess. She took it for more ridicule and became more menacing. The officers and soldiers interfered, trying to persuade her of the truth of my words, as none of us wanted to be put out into the rain. However, it required more than words to convince her, so I was compelled to unbutton my coat.

"Holy Jesus!" the woman crossed herself. "A *baba*, indeed." And immediately her heart softened, and her tone changed into one of tenderness. She broke out into tears. Her husband and son were in the army, she told me, and she hadn't heard from them for a long time. She gathered me into her arms, gave me food and treated me to some milk, inquiring about my mother and mourning over her lot. We parted affectionately, her blessings following me.

It was snowing when we returned to the front line. Our position was now at Ferdinandovi Nos, between Lake Narotch and Baranovitchi. The first night the commander of the company issued a call for thirty volunteers to go scouting and investigate the strength and position of the enemy. I was among the thirty.

We started out in single file, moving forward stealthily and as noiselessly as possible. We passed by some woods, in which an enemy patrol, upon hearing the crackling of the snow beneath some of our soldiers' boots, had hidden. We crawled on to the enemy trenches and lay in front of his barbed wide. Our chests were flattened against the snowdrifts. We were rather uneasy, as our presence seemed strangely unnoticed. Our officer, Lieutenant Bobrov, a former schoolteacher, but a fighting man of the first order, suddenly caught a noise in our rear.

"There is something on," he whispered to us.

We pricked up our ears, but scarcely had we time to look around when we found ourselves surrounded by an enemy force larger than our own. It was too late to shoot. We resorted to our bayonets, and it was a brief but savage scrap.

I found myself confronted by a German, who towered far above me. There was not an instant to lose. Life and death hung in the balance.

I rushed at the German before he had time to move and ran him in the stomach with the bayonet. It stuck. The man fell. A stream of blood gushed forth. I made an effort to pull the bayonet out, but failed. It was the first man that I had bayoneted. It was all so lightning-quick.

I fled, pursued by a German, toward our trenches, falling several times, rising always to go on. Our wire entanglements were zig-zagged, and I was unable to find quickly our positions. My situation was getting critical, when I discovered that I had some hand-grenades with me. I threw them at my pursuer, falling to the ground to avoid the shock of the explosion, and afterwards reached our trenches.

Only ten returned of our party of thirty. The commander personally thanked me, expressing his wonderment at my ability to bayonet a German. Deep in my soul I also wondered.

The year of 1915 was nearing its end. The winter was severe, and life in the trenches unbearable. Death was a welcome visitor. Even more welcome was a wound that enabled one to be sent to the hospital. There were many cases of men snowed under and frozen to death. There were many more cases of frozen feet that required amputation. Our equipment was running low. Our supply organisation was already breaking down. It was difficult to replace a worn pair of boots. Not infrequently something went wrong in the kitchen, and we were forced to hunger as well as suffer cold. But we were patient, like true children of Mother-Russia. It was dreadfully monotonous, this inactivity, the mere holding of those icy ditches. We longed for battles, for one mighty battle, to win the victory and end the war.

One bitter night I was detailed to a listening-post with three men. My boots were worn out. One can't move while on such duty. A motion may mean death. So, there we lay on the white ground, exposed to the attacks of King Frost. He went about his work without delay, and thoroughly. My right foot was undergoing strange sensations. It began to freeze. I felt like sitting up and rubbing it. But sitting up was not to be thought of. Didn't I hear a noise? I couldn't bother with my foot; I had to strain all my nerves to catch that peculiar sound. Or was it a mere freak of the wind? My foot grew numb. It was going to sleep.

"Holy Mother, what's to be done? My right foot is gone. The feet of the other three men are freezing, too. They just whispered that to me. If only the commander would relieve us now! But the two hours are not yet up," I thought.

Suddenly we perceived two figures in white crawling toward us, Germans provided with appropriate costumes for a deathly mission. We fired, and they replied. A bullet pierced my coat, just scratching the skin. Then everything quieted down again; and we were soon relieved. I barely had strength to reach my trench. There, I fell, exhausted, crying, "My foot! my foot!"

I was taken to the hospital, and there the horrible condition of my foot was revealed. It was as white as snow, covered with frost. The pains were agonising, but nothing terrified me as much as the physician's talk of the probable necessity of amputating it. But I put up a stubborn fight, and I saved my right limb. The doctors soon had it under control, and by persistent application succeeded in restoring it to its normal state.

The year of Our Lord, 1916, was ushered in while I lay in the hospital. Almost immediately upon my release our company was sent to the rear for a month's rest in Beloye, a village some distance back of the fighting line. We were billeted with the peasants in their homes. There we enjoyed the use of a bath-house and slept on the peasants' ovens, in true home fashion. We even had the opportunity to see motion pictures, the apparatus being carried from base to base in an automobile of the Union of Zemstvos. We also established our own theatre and staged a play, written by one of our artillery officers.

There were two women characters in the drama, and I was chosen for the leading role. The other feminine role was played by a young officer. It was with great reluctance that I consented to take the part, only after the urgent appeals of the commander. I did not believe myself capable of performing, and even the thunderous applause I won on that occasion has not changed my belief.

At Beloye many of the soldiers and officers were visited by their wives. I made many acquaintances there and some fast friendships. One of the latter was the wife of a stretcher-bearer with whom I had worked. She was a young, pretty and very lovable woman, and her husband adored her. When the month of our rest was about to expire and the order came for the women to leave, the *sanitar* (stretcher-bearer) borrowed the commander's horses to drive his wife to the station. On his way back, he suffered a stroke of apoplexy and died immediately. He received a military funeral, and I made and placed a wreath on his bier.

As we lowered his coffin into the grave the thought inevitably suggested itself to me whether I would be buried like this or my body lost and blown to the winds in No Man's Land. The same thought must have run through many a mind.

Another friend, made at the same time, was the wife of Lieutenant Bobrov, the former school teacher. Both of them helped me to learn to write and improve my reading. The peasant women of the locality were so poor and ignorant that I devoted part of my time to aiding them. Many of them were suffering from minor ills that were neglected. One evening I was even called to attend a woman in childbirth, my first experience in midwifery. Another time I was asked to visit a very bad case of fever.

Then came the trenches again. Again, intense cold, again eternal watchfulness and irritating inactivity. But there were great expectations in the air. As the winter drew to its close rumours of a gigantic spring offensive grew thicker and thicker. Surely the war can't end without a general battle, the men argued. And so, when, towards the end of February, we were again taken for a two weeks' rest, it was clear that we were to be prepared for an offensive. We received new outfits and equipment. On March the 5th the Commander of the Regiment addressed us. He spoke of the coming battle and appealed to us to be brave and win a great victory. He told us that the enemy's defences were enormous and that it would require a powerful effort to surmount them.

Then we started for the front. The slush and mud were unimaginable. We walked deep in water, mixed with ice. On the road we met many wounded being carried to the hospital. We also passed by a fraternal cemetery where the soldiers fallen in our lines were being buried in one huge grave. We were kept in the rear for the night, as reserves, and were told to await orders tomorrow to proceed to the trenches.

On March the 6th we began an unprecedented bombardment. The Germans replied intensively, and the earth fairly shook. The cannonade lasted several hours. Then an order came for us to form ranks and march into the trenches. We knew that it meant participation in the offensive.

Lieutenant Bobrov came up to me unexpectedly with these words:

"Yashka, take this and deliver it to my wife after the attack. I have had a premonition for three days that I would not survive this battle." He handed me a letter and a ring.

"But, Lieutenant," I tried to argue, well knowing that protestations are of no avail at such a moment, "it is not so. It will not be so. Premonitions are deceiving."

He grimly shook his head and pressed my hand.

"Not this one, Yashka," he said.

We were in the rear trenches already, under a veritable shower of shells. There were dead and dying in our midst. Waist-deep in water we crouched, praying to God. Suddenly a gas wave came in our direction. It caught some without masks on, and there was no escape for them. I, myself, narrowly missed this horrible death. My lips contracted and my eyes watered and burned for three weeks afterward.

The signal to advance was given, and we started, knee-deep in mud, for the enemy. In places the pools reached above our waists. Shells and bullets played havoc with us. Of those that fell wounded, many sank in the mud and drowned. The German fire was withering. Our lines grew thinner and thinner, and progress became so slow that our doom was certain in the event of a further advance.

The order to retreat rang out. How can one convey this march back through the inferno that No Man's Land presented that night of March 7th, 1916? There were bleeding human beings, all but their heads submerged, calling plaintively for help. "Save, for the sake of Christ!" came from every side. The trenches were filled with them, too, reverberating with their penetrating appeals. So long as we were alive we could not remain deaf to the pleadings of our comrades.

Fifty of us went out to do rescue work. Never before had I worked in such harrowing, hair-raising circumstances. One fellow was wounded in the neck or face, and I had to grip him under the arms and drag his body through the mud. Another had his side torn by a shell, requiring many difficult manoeuvres before I could extricate him. Several sank so deep that my own strength was not sufficient to drag them out.

I finally broke down, just as I reached my trench with a burden. I was so exhausted that all my bones ached. The soldiers got some drinking water, a very hard thing to get there, and made some tea for me. Somehow, they obtained for me a dry overcoat and put me to sleep in a protected corner. I slept about four hours, and resumed the fishing for wounded comrades.

All day the artillery boomed again, as violently as the previous day. At night, our ranks refilled with fresh drafts, we climbed out again and rushed for the enemy. Again, we suffered heavily, but our operation this time was more successful. When the Germans saw us push determinedly on in their direction they came out for a counter-attack. With bayonets fixed and a tremendous "Hurrah," we bounced at them.

The Germans never did like the Russian bayonets. As a matter of fact, they dreaded them more than any other arm of warfare, and so they gave way and took to their heels. We pursued them into their trenches, and there followed a hot scramble. Many of the Germans raised their hands in sign of surrender. They well understood that we were in a fierce, exasperated mood. Others fought to the end, and all this time German machine guns swept their own trenches, where Teuton and Slav were mixed in combat. We rushed the machine gun nests.

Our regiment captured in that attack two and a half thousand Germans and thirty machine guns. I escaped only with a slight bruise in the right leg and did not leave the ranks. Elated by our victory over the strong defences of the first line, we swept on toward the enemy's second line. His fire slackened considerably. A great triumph was in prospect, as behind the weak second and third lines there was an open stretch of undefended territory for many *versts*.

Our advance line was within seventy feet of the enemy's trenches when an order came from General Walter to halt and return to our positions. Men and officers alike were terribly shocked. Our colonel talked to the general on the field telephone, explaining to him the situation. The general was obdurate. All of us were so incensed at this treacherous order that, had any one of us taken charge at the moment, we would undoubtedly have snatched a great victory, as the breach in the German defences was complete.

The conversation between the colonel and general ended in a quarrel. The general had not, apparently, expected us to break through the first German line. So many waves of Russian soldiers had beaten in vain against it, and with such terrific losses. As our men saw it then, it was the general's traitorous program to have as many of us slaughtered as possible.

But discipline was rigid, and orders were orders. We had to go back. We were so exhausted that our bodies welcomed a rest. In those two days, the 7th and 8th of August, our ranks were refilled four times with fresh drafts. Our casualties were numberless. Like mushrooms after a rain the corpses lay thick everywhere, and there was no count to the wounded. One could not make a step in No Man's Land without striking a Russian or German dead body. Bloody feet, hands, sometimes heads, lay scattered in the mud.

That was the most terrible offensive in which I participated. It went down into history as the Battle of Postovy. We spent the first night in the German trenches we had captured. It was a night of unforgettable horrors. Darkness was impenetrable. The stench was suffocating. The ground was full of mud-holes. Some of us sat on corpses. Others rested their feet on dead men. One could not stretch a hand without touching a lifeless body. We were hungry. We were cold. Our flesh crawled in the dreadful surroundings. I wanted to get up. My hand sought support. It fell on the face of a corpse, stuck against the wall. I screamed, slipped and fell. My fingers buried themselves in the torn abdomen of a body.

I was seized with horror such as I had never experienced, and shrieked hysterically. My cries were heard in the officers' dugout, and a man was sent for me with an electric hand light to rescue Yashka, whom they had taken for wounded. It was warm and comfortable in the dugout, as it had previously been used by the enemy's regimental staff. I was given some tea, and little by little regained my poise.

The entrance of the dugout was, naturally, facing the enemy now. He knew its exact position and concentrated a fire on it. Although a bombproof, it soon began to give way under a rain of shells. Some of these blocked the entrance almost completely with debris. Finally, a shell penetrated the roof, putting out the light, killing five and wounding several. I lay in a corner, buried under wreckage, soldiers and officers, some of whom were wounded and others dead. The groans were indescribable. As the screech of a new shell would come overhead I thought death imminent. There was no question of making an immediate effort to extricate myself and escape while the bombs came crashing into the hole. When the bombardment finally ceased with dawn, and I was saved, I could hardly believe my own senses that I was unhurt.

The following day I discovered the body of Lieutenant Bobrov. His premonition was right, after all. A schoolteacher, he was an intrepid fighter, and a man of noble impulses. I fulfilled his wish, and had his ring and letter sent through the physician to his wife. Our own regiment had two thousand wounded. And when the dead were gathered from the field and carried out of the trenches, there were long, long rows of them stretched out in the sun awaiting eternal rest in the immense fraternal grave that was being dug for them in the rear.

With bowed heads and bleeding hearts we paid last homage to our comrades. They had laid down their lives like true heroes, without suspecting that they were being sacrificed in vain by a monster-traitor.

On March 10th, still suffering from the effects of the dreadful contact with corpses, I was sent to the Divisional Hospital for a three days' rest. I was back in the trenches on the 14th, when another advance was ordered. The German positions were not strongly fortified yet, and we captured their first line without serious losses. Then there was another few days' respite, during which our ranks were reformed.

Early in the morning of March 18th, after an ineffective bombardment of the enemy's positions by our artillery, the signal to go over the top was given. We advanced in the face of a stubborn German fire, dashing through No Man's Land only to find the foe's wire defences intact. There was nothing to do but retreat. It was while running back that a bullet struck me in the right leg, shattering the bone. I fell. Within a hundred feet of me ran the enemy's first line. Over my head bullets whizzed, pursuing my fleeing comrades.

I was not alone. Not far from me others groaned. Some prayed for death. . . . I grew thirsty. I had lost much blood. But I knew it was useless to move. The sun rose in the east, only to be swallowed by grey clouds.

"Will I be rescued?" I wondered. "Perhaps the enemy's stretcher-bearers will pick me up soon. But no, he just fired at that fellow yonder who raised himself in an effort to move."

I pressed myself closer to the ground. It seemed that I heard voices coming near. I held my breath in suspense.

"I am a German prisoner!" I thought. Then the voices died out, and again my thirst tortured me.

"Holy Mother, when will help come? Or am I doomed to lie here indefinitely till I lapse into unconsciousness and expire? . . . There, the sun is already in mid-sky. The boys are eating their soup and warm tea. What would I not give for a glass of hot tea! The Germans are eating, too. I can hear the clatter of their pans. Why, I can even smell faintly the steam from their soup.

"It is calm now. Only seldom a sniper's bullet crosses the field. . . . Night, night, night. . . . How I wish for night! Certainly, our men are not going to let all of us perish here. Besides, they must have missed me by now. They surely won't let Yashka, dead or alive, lie in the field. So, there is hope."

The thought of the boys' discovery of my absence gave me new strength. The seconds seemed hours and the minutes days, but the shadows arrived at last, creeping toward the side where the sun had disappeared. Then came darkness and rescue was not long postponed. Our brave *sanitars*, aided by comrades, were out on their holy mission. Cautiously they moved nearer and nearer to the German line, and finally picked me up. Yes, it was Yashka whom they carried into our trenches.

The boys were jubilant. "Yashka, alive! God speed you to recovery, Yashka!" I could only reply in a whisper. They took me to the first-aid station, cleansed my wound and dressed it. I suffered much. Then I was sent on to Moscow, where I lay in the Ekaterina Hospital, ward Number 20.

I was lonely in the hospital, where I spent nearly three months. The other patients would have their visitors or receive parcels from home, but nobody visited me, nobody sent anything to me. March, April, May came and went in the monotony of ward Number 20. Finally, one day in the beginning of June, I was declared fit again to return to the fighting line. My regiment was just then being transferred to the Lutzk front. On June the 20th I caught up with it. The reception accorded me even surpassed that of the previous year. I was showered with fruit and sweets. The soldiers were in a happy mood. The Germans had just been driven back at this sector by General Brusilov for scores of *versts*. The country was criss-crossed by their evacuated positions. Here and there enemy corpses were still unburied. Our men, though overjoyed, were worn out by forced marches and the long pursuit.

It was mid-summer, and the heat was prostrating. We marched on June 21st a distance of fifteen *versts* and stopped for rest. There were many prostrations among us and we felt too fatigued to go on, but the commander prayed us to keep going, promising a rest in the trenches. It was twenty *versts* to the front line, and we made it on the same day.

As we marched along we observed on both sides of the road that crops that had not been destroyed by the swaying armies were ripening. The fighting line ran near a village called Dubova Kortchma. We found in its neighbourhood a manor hastily left by the Germans. The estate was full of cattle, fowl, potatoes and other food. That night we had a feast royal.

We occupied abandoned German trenches. It was not the time for rest. The artillery opened up early in the evening and boomed ceaselessly throughout the night. It could mean nothing but an immediate attack. We were not deceived. At four in the morning we received word that the Germans had left their positions and started for our side. At this moment our beloved commander, Grishaninov, was struck to the ground. He was wounded. We attended to him quickly and had him despatched to the rear. There was no time to waste. We met the advancing Germans by repeated volleys, and when they approached our positions we climbed out and charged them with fixed bayonets.

Suddenly a terrific explosion deafened me, and I fell to the ground. A German shell had come my way, a shell I shall never forget, as part of it I still carry in my body.

I felt terrific pains in my back. I had been hit by a fragment at the end of the spinal column. My agony lasted long enough to attract a couple of soldiers. Then I lapsed into unconsciousness. They carried me to a dressing station. The wound was so serious that the physician in charge did not believe that I could survive. I was placed in an ambulance and taken to Lutzk. I required electrical treatments, but the Lutzk hospitals were not supplied with the necessary apparatus. It was decided to send me to Kiev. My condition, however, was so grave that for three days the doctors considered it dangerous to move me.

In Kiev the flow of wounded was so great that I was compelled to lie in the street on a stretcher for a couple of hours before I was taken to a hospital. I was informed, after an X-ray examination, that a fragment of shell was imbedded in my body and asked if I wished an operation to have it removed. I could not imagine living with a piece of shell in my flesh, and so requested its removal. Whether because of my condition or for some other reason, the surgeons finally decided not to operate, and told me that I would have to be sent either to Petrograd or to Moscow for treatment. As I was given the choice, I decided on Moscow, because I had spent the spring months of the year in the Ekaterina Hospital there.

The wound in the spine paralyzed me to such an extent that I could not move even a finger. I lay in the Moscow Hospital hovering between life and death for some weeks, resembling a log more than a human body. Only my mind was active and my heart full of pain.

Every day I was massaged, carried on a stretcher and bathed. Then the physician would attend me, probing my wound with iodine, and treating it with electricity, after which I was bathed again and my wound dressed. This daily procedure was a torture that could not be paralleled, in spite of the morphine injected into me. There was little peace in the ward in which I was kept. All the beds were occupied by serious cases, and the groans and moans must have reached to Heaven.

Four months I lay paralyzed, never expecting to recover. My food consisted of milk and *kasha*, fed to me by an attendant. Death would have been a welcome visitor on many a grey day. It seemed so futile, so hopeless to continue alive in such a state, but the doctor, who was a Jew, and a man of sterling heart, would not give up hope. He persisted in his daily grind, praising my stoicism and encouraging me with kind words. His faith was finally rewarded.

At the end of four months I began to feel life circulating in my inanimate body. My fingers could move! What a joy that was! In a few days I could turn my head a bit and stretch my arm. It was so marvellous, this gradual resurrection of my lifeless organs. To be able to close my fingers after four months of numbness! It was thrilling. To be in a position to bend a knee that had been torpid so long! It was a miracle. And I offered thanks to God with all the fervour that I could command.

One day a woman by the name of Daria Maximovna Vasilieva came to see me. I searched my mind in vain for an acquaintance of that name as I had her shown to my bed. But as I was perhaps the only patient in the ward that had no visitors and received no parcels one can imagine how joyous I was over the call. She introduced herself as the mother of Stepan, of my company. Of course, I knew Stepan well. He was a student before the war and volunteered as an under-officer.

"Stepan has just written me about you," Madame Vasilieva said, "urging me to look you up. 'Go to the Ekaterina Hospital and visit our Yashka,' he writes. 'She is lonely there, and I want you to do for her as much as you would do for me, for she saved my life once, and has been like a Godmother to the boys here. She is a decent, patriotic young woman and my interest in her is but that of a comrade, for she is a soldier, and a brave and gallant soldier.' He praised you so much, darling, that my heart just went out to you. May God bless you."

She brought me some dainties, and we became friends immediately. I told her all about her son and our life in the trenches. She wept and wondered how I had borne it. Her attachment to me grew so strong that she made it a habit to visit me several times a week, although she lived on the outskirts of the city. Her husband was assistant superintendent at a factory and they occupied a small but comfortable dwelling in keeping with their means. Daria Maximovna herself was a woman of middle-age, modestly dressed and of gentle appearance. She had a married daughter, Tonetchka, and another son a youth of about seventeen, who was a high school student.

My friend buoyed up my spirits and my recovery progressed. As I gradually regained full control of my muscles and nerves, I teased the doctor sometimes:

"Well, doctor," I would say to him, "I am going to war again."

"No, no," he would answer, "there will be no more war for you, *golubushka*."

I wondered whether I really would be able to return to the front. There was that fragment of shell yet in my body. The doctor would not extract it. He advised me to await complete recovery and have it removed at some future date through an abdominal operation, as the fragment is lodged in the omentum. I have not yet found the opportunity to undergo such an operation, and still carry with me that piece of shell. The slightest indigestion causes me to suffer from it even now.

I had to learn to walk as if I had never mastered that art before. I was not successful at the first attempt. Having asked the doctor for a pair of crutches, I tried to stand up, but fell back weakened and helpless into the bed. The attendants, however, placed me in a wheelchair and took me out into the garden. This movement gave me deep satisfaction. Once, in the absence of my attendant, I tried to stand up alone and make a step. It was very painful, but I maintained my balance, and tears of joy came streaming down my cheeks. I was jubilant.

It was only a week later, however, that I was permitted by the doctor to walk a little, supported by the attendants. But I made only ten steps, beaming with triumph and making every effort to overcome my pain, when I collapsed and fainted. The nurses were alarmed and called the doctor, who instructed them to be more cautious in the future.

My improvement was, nevertheless, steady, and a couple of weeks later I was able to walk. Naturally I did not feel sure of my legs at first; they trembled and seemed so weak. Gradually they regained their former strength and at the end of six months spent in the hospital I was again in possession of all my faculties.

CHAPTER 9

Eight Hours in German Hands

The morning on which I was taken before the military medical commission I was in a very jolly, devilish mood. It was a late December day, but the sun glowed warmly in my heart as I was led into the large room in which about two hundred other patients awaited examination and word whether they would be sent home or considered fit to be returned to the front.

The chairman of the commission was a general. As my turn came and he reached the name of Maria Botchkareva he thought it a mistake and corrected it to Marin Botchkarev. By that name I was called out of the crowd.

"*Razdievaysia!*" (Undress) the general bawled the order that was given to every soldier awaiting discharge.

I walked up determinedly and threw off my clothes. "A woman!" went up from a couple of hundred throats, followed by an outburst of laughter that shook the building. The members of the commission were too amazed for words.

"What the devil!" cried the general. "Why did you undress?"

"I am a soldier, Excellency, and I obey orders without question," I replied.

"Well, well. Hurry up and dress," came the order.

"How about the examination, Excellency?" I queried, as I put my things on.

"That's all right. You are passed."

In view of the seriousness of the wound I had sustained the commission offered me a couple of months' leave, but I declined the opportunity and requested to be sent to the front in a few days. Supplied with fifteen *rubles* and a railroad ticket, I left the grounds of the hospital and went to Daria Maximovna, who had invited me previously to stay with her for a while. It was a stay of short duration, lasting only three days, but of genuine delight. It was so pleasant to be in a home again, eat home food and be under the care of a woman who became to me a second mother. With packages for myself and Stepan and the blessings of the whole family following me, I left Moscow from the Nikolaiev Station. The train was crowded and there was only standing room.

On the platform my attention was attracted to a poor woman with a nursing baby in her arms, another tot on the floor and a girl of about five hanging on to her skirt. All the woman's property was packed in a single bag. The children were crying for bread, the woman tried to calm them, evidently in dread of something. It touched my heart to watch this little group, and I offered some bread to the children.

Then the woman confided in me the cause for her fear. She had no money and no ticket and expected to be put off at the next station. She was the wife of a soldier from a village in German hands and was now bound for a town three thousand *versts* away, where she had some relatives. Something simply had to be done for this woman. I made an appeal to the soldiers that filled the car, but they did not respond immediately.

"She is the wife of a soldier, of one like you," I said. "Suppose she were the wife of one of you! For all you know, the wives of some of you here may be floating about the country in a similar state. Come, let us get off at the next station, go to the station-master and request for her permission to go to her destination."

The soldiers softened and helped me to take the woman and her belongings off the train at the next stop. We went to the station-master, who was very kind, but explained that he could do nothing in the matter. "I have no right to give permission to travel without a ticket, and I can't distribute tickets free," he said, sending us to the military *commandant*. I went along with the woman, deserted by the soldiers, who had heard the train whistle and did not wish to miss it. I remained for another train.

The *commandant* repeated the words of the stationmaster. He had no right to provide her with a military pass, he said.

"No right!" I exclaimed, beside myself. "She is the wife of a soldier and her husband is probably now, at this very moment, going into battle to defend the country, while you, safe and well-fed in the rear here, won't even take care of his wife and children. It is an outrage. Look at the woman. She needs medical attention, and her children are starved."

"And who are you?" sharply asked the *commandant*. "I will show you who I am," I answered, taking off my medals and cross and showing him my certificate. "I have shed enough blood to be entitled to demand justice for the helpless wife of a soldier."

The *commandant* turned away and went out. There was nothing to be done but make a collection. I made my way into the First-Class waiting room, which was filled with officers and well-to-do passengers, took my cap in my hand and went the rounds, begging for a poor soldier's wife. When I got through there were eighty *rubles* in the cap. With this money I went to the *commandant* again, turned it over to him with a request that he provide accommodations for the woman and her children, who did not know how to express her gratitude to me.

The next train pulled in. I never before saw one so packed. There could be no thought of getting inside a car. The only space available was on the top of a coach. There were plenty of passengers even there. With the aid of some soldiers I climbed to the top, where I spent two days and two nights. It was impossible to get off at every station to take a walk. Even for the tea we had to send emissaries, and our food consisted of that and bread.

Accidents were not uncommon. On the very roof on which I travelled a man fell asleep and rolled off, being killed instantly. I almost suffered a similar fate, escaping by a hair's breadth. I began to doze and drifted to the edge, and had not a soldier caught me at the very last moment I would undoubtedly have gone over. We finally arrived at Kiev.

That journey on the train was the symbol of the country's condition in the winter of 1916. The government machinery was breaking down. The soldiers had lost faith in their superiors, and the view that they were being led to slaughter by the thousands prevailed in many minds. Rumours flew thick and fast. The old soldiers were killed off and the fresh drafts were impatient for the end of the war. The spirit of 1914 was no more.

In Kiev I had to obtain information as to the location of my regiment. It was now near the town of Berestechko. In my absence the boys had advanced fifteen *versts*. The train from Kiev was also badly crowded and offered nothing but standing room. At stations we sent out a few soldiers to fill our kettles with hot water. The men could seldom get in and out through the entrances, so they used the windows. The train passed through Zhitomir and Zhmerinka on the way to Lutzk. There I changed to a branch road, going to the station Verba, within thirty *versts* of our position.

It was muddy on the road to the front. Overhead flew whole flocks of aeroplanes, raining bombs. I got used to them. In the afternoon there was a downpour, and I was thoroughly soaked. Dead tired, with water streaming from my clothes, I arrived in the evening within five *versts* of the first line. There was a regimental supply train camping on both sides of the road. I approached a sentry with the question:

"What regiment is billeted here?"

"The Twenty-Eighth Polotsk Regiment."

My heart leaped with joy. The soldier did not recognise me. He was a new man. But the boys must have told him of me.

"I am Yashka," I said.

That was a pass. They all knew the name and had heard from the veterans of the regiment many stories about me. I was taken to the colonel in command of the supply train, a funny old chap who kissed me on both cheeks and jumped about, clapping his hands and shouting, "Yashka! Yashka!"

He was kind-hearted and immediately became solicitous for me. He promptly ordered an orderly to bring a new outfit and had the bath, used by the officers, prepared for me. Clean and in the new uniform, I accepted the invitation to sup with the colonel. There were several other officers at the table and all were glad to see me. The word went out that Yashka had arrived, and some soldiers could not restrain their desire to shake hands with me. Every now and then there would be a meek knock at the door and in answer to the colonel's question, "Who's there?" a plaintive voice would say:

"Excellency, may I be allowed to see Yashka?"

In time quite a number of comrades were admitted into the house. One part of it was occupied by the owner, a widow with a young daughter. I spent the night with the latter and in the morning started out to the front. Some of our companies were in reserve and my progress became a triumphal journey. I was feasted on the way and given several ovations.

I presented myself to the commander of the regiment, who invited me to dine that afternoon with the regimental staff, unquestionably the first case of an underofficer receiving such an invitation in the history of the regiment. At dinner the commander toasted me, telling the history of my service with the regiment and wishing me many more years of such service.

At the conclusion he pinned a cross of the 3rd degree on my breast, marked with a pencil three stripes on my shoulder, thus promoting me to the grade of senior under-officer. The staff crowded around me, pressing my hands, praising me and expressing their best wishes. I was profoundly shaken with this demonstration of sincere appreciation and affection on the part of the officers. This was my reward for all the suffering I had undergone.

And it was a reward very much worthwhile. What did I care for a wound in the spine and a four months' paralysis if this was the return that I received for my sacrifice? Trenches filled with bloody corpses held no horror for me then. No Man's Land seemed quite an attractive place in which to spend a day with a bleeding leg. The screech of shells and the whistle of bullets presented themselves like music to my imagination. Ah, life was not so bleak and futile, after all. It had its moments of bliss that compensated for years of torment and misery.

The commander had, in his order of the day, stated the fact of my return and promotion. He furnished me an orderly to show me the way to the trenches. Again, I was hailed by everybody as I emerged from the dugout of the commander of the company, who had placed me in charge of a platoon of seventy men. In this capacity I was to keep an inventory of the supplies and equipment of my men, for which purpose I had a soldier perform the duties of a clerk.

Our positions were on the bank of the Styr, which is very narrow and shallow in that section. On the opposite bank were the German trenches. Several hundred feet from us was a bridge across the stream that had been left intact by both sides. At our end of it we maintained a post while the enemy kept a similar watch at the opposite end. Our line, because of the irregularity of the river's course, was extremely zigzagged. The Germans were very active at mine-throwing. However, the mines travelled so slowly that we could take to cover before they fell on our side. My Company occupied a position close to the enemy's first line.

I had not spent a month in the trenches when a local battle occurred which resulted in my capture by the Germans. They had conducted their mine-throwing operations for a period of about twelve days so regularly that we grew accustomed to them, expecting no attack. Besides, it was after the fighting season, and the cold was intense.

One morning about six o'clock, when we had turned in for our daily sleep, we were suddenly awakened by a tremendous "Hurrah!" We nervously seized our rifles and peeped through the loop-holes. Great Heavens! There, within a hundred feet of us, in front and in the rear, the Germans were wading the Styr! Before we had time to organise resistance they were upon us, capturing five hundred of our men. I was in the batch taken.

We were brought before the German Staff for examination. Every one of us was grilled with questions, intended to draw out valuable military information. Threats were made to those who refused to disclose anything. Some cowards among us, especially those of non-

Russian stock, gave away important facts. As the test was proceeding our artillery on the other side opened up a violent bombardment of the German defences. It was evident that the German commander did not have many reserves, as he made frantic appeals by wire for support. It required quite a force to keep us under guard and even a larger force to take us to the rear. As the enemy momentarily expected a Russian attack, he decided not to send us away before help arrived.

"So, I am a German prisoner," I thought. "How unexpected! There is still hope that the boys on the other side will come to our rescue. Only, every minute is precious. They must hurry or we are lost. Here, my turn is coming. What will I tell them? I must deny being a soldier and invent some kind of a story."

"I am a woman and not a soldier," I announced as soon as I was called.

"Are you of noble blood?" I was asked.

"Yes," I answered, simultaneously deciding to claim that I was a Red Cross nurse, dressed in man's uniform, in order to pay a visit to my husband, an officer in the front line trenches.

"Have you many women fighting in the ranks?" was the next question.

"I don't know. I told you that I was not a soldier."

"What were you doing in the trenches, then?"

"I came to see my husband, who is an officer of the regiment."

"Why did you shoot, then? The soldiers tell that you shot at them."

"I did it to defend myself. I was afraid to be captured. I serve as a Red Cross nurse in the rear hospital, and came over to the fighting line for a visit."

The Russian fire was growing hotter every minute. Some of our shells wounded not only enemy soldiers but several of the captives. Noon had arrived, but the Germans were too nervous to eat their lunch. The expected reserves were not forthcoming, and there was every sign of a fierce counter-attack by our troops.

At two o'clock our soldiers went over the top and started for the German positions. The enemy commander decided to retreat with his batch of prisoners to the second line rather than defend the front trenches. It was a critical moment. As we were lined up the "Hurrah" of our comrades reached us. It stimulated us to a spontaneous decision.

We threw ourselves, five hundred strong, at our captors, wrested many of their rifles and bayonets and engaged in a ferocious hand-to-hand combat, just as our men rushed through the torn wire entanglements into the trenches. The confusion was indescribable; the killing merciless. I grasped five hand-grenades that lay near me and threw them at a group of about ten Germans. They must have all been killed. Our entire line across the river was advancing at the same time. The first German line was occupied by our troops and both banks of the Styr were then in our hands.

Thus, ended my captivity. I was in German hands for a period of only eight hours and amply avenged even this brief stay. There was great activity among us for a couple of days. We fortified the newly-won positions and prepared for another attack at the foe. Two days later we received the signal to advance. But again, our artillery had failed to cut the German wire defences. After pushing on against the withering fire and incurring heavy losses, we were compelled to retreat, leaving many of our comrades wounded and dying on the field of battle.

Our commander improvised a relief party by calling for twenty volunteers. I responded among the first. Provided with twenty red crosses which we prominently displayed, and leaving our rifles in the trenches, we went out in the open daylight to rescue the wounded. I was allowed to proceed by the Germans almost to their barbed wire. Then, as I leaned over a wounded man whose leg was split, I heard the click of a trigger and immediately flattened myself against the ground. Five bullets whistled over me, one after another, most of which landed in the wounded soldier, killing him outright. I continued to lie motionless, and the German sniper was evidently satisfied that he had killed me as well. I remained in this position till night, when I crawled back to our trenches.

Of the twenty Red Cross volunteers only five returned alive.

The following day an order of thanks was issued by the commander to all those soldiers who had been captured three days previous and took the initiative to save themselves by fighting their captors. My name appeared first on the list. Those of us who had refused to give any information to the enemy were praised in the order. One soldier, who had revealed to the Germans many vital things, was executed. I was recommended for a cross of the 2nd degree, but, being a woman, I received only a medal of the 3rd degree.

We met the year 1917 while resting three *versts* in the rear. There was much fun-making and merriment in the reserve billets. Although the discipline was as strict as ever, the relations between the officers and men had undergone, in the three and a half years of the war, a complete transformation.

The older officers, trained in pre-war conditions, were now gone, having died in battle or been disabled. The new junior officers, all young men taken from civil life, many of them former students and school teachers, were liberal in their views and very human in their treatment. They mixed freely with the men in the ranks and allowed us more liberty than we had ever enjoyed. At the New Year festival, we all danced together. These new relations were not entirely due to the new attitude from above. In a sense, they were generated from below by a dumb and yet potent undercurrent of restlessness.

We were reviewed before returning to the front line by General Valuyev, the commander of the Fifth Corps. I was presented to him by our commander. The general shook my hand warmly, remarking that he had heard many praiseworthy things of me.

Our positions were now on a hill, in the vicinity of Zelenaya Kolonia, while the enemy was at our feet in the valley. The trenches we occupied had been in German hands some time before.

It was late in January when I made an expedition into No Man's Land at the head of a patrol of fifteen men. We crawled along a ditch that was formerly a German communication trench. It ran along a very exposed part of the field and the utmost caution was exercised by us. As we came nearer to the enemy's trench line I thought I heard German conversation. Leaving ten men behind, with instructions to rush to our aid in case of a fight, five of us crept forward at a snail's pace and with perfect noiselessness. The German voices grew clearer and clearer.

Finally, we beheld a German listening-post. There were four of them, all seated with their backs toward us. Their rifles were scattered on the ground while they warmed their hands over a fire. Two of my men stretched their hands out, reached the rifles and removed them. It was a painstaking operation, as slow as eternity. The Germans chattered on unconcernedly. As I was cautiously going after the third rifle two of the Germans, having apparently heard a noise, were about to turn.

In an instant my men were upon them. The two were bayoneted before I had an opportunity to realise what was on. It was my intention to bring in the four alive. The other two Germans were safe in our hands.

In all my experience in patrol duty, and I must have participated in at least a hundred expeditions into No Man's Land, it was the first case of a German listening-post being caught in such a manner. We returned triumphantly with our prizes.

One of the prisoners was a tall, red-headed fellow, the other was evidently an educated person, with *pince-nez*. We took them to Regimental Headquarters, accompanied on the way by numerous ovations and congratulations. The commander inquired as to the details of the capture and had them recorded *verbatim*. He congratulated me, pressing my hand, and so did all the other officers, telling me that my name would live forever in the annals of the Polotsk Regiment. I was recommended for a gold cross of the 1st degree and given two days' leave for recuperation in the village.

At the end of the two days my company joined me in the reserve. Strange things were occurring in our midst. In subdued voices the men repeated dark rumours about Rasputin's death. Wild stories about his connections with the court and Germany were communicated from mouth to mouth. The spirit of insubordination was growing in the soldiers' midst. It was still suppressed at that time. The men were weary, terribly weary of the war. "How long shall we continue this fighting?" and "What are we fighting for?" were on the lips of everybody. It was the fourth winter and still there was no end in sight.

Our boys were genuinely anxious to solve the great puzzle that the war had become to them. Hadn't it been proven again and again that the officers at headquarters were selling them to the enemy? Hadn't a multitude of reports reached them that the court was pro-German? Hadn't they heard of the War Minister placed under arrest and charged with being a traitor? Wasn't it clear, therefore, that the government, the official class, was with the enemy? Then why continue indefinitely this carnage? If the government was in alliance with Germany, what prevented it from concluding peace? Was it the desire to have millions more of them slaughtered?

This was the riddle that forced itself upon the peasant mind. It was complicated by a hundred other suggestions that were injected into his brain from various channels. Depressed in spirit, discouraged and sullen in appearance was the Russian soldier in February, 1917.

We returned to our positions and took up the heavy burden. It was not long before an attack was organised against the German line. Our artillery again displayed little effectiveness and again we climbed out of the trenches and swept across No Man's Land while the enemy's wire defences were intact. It was not the first wave of Russian breasts that had beaten itself in vain against that parapet of death, to be hurled back with grave losses without even coming to grips with the foe. But each of those waves had left its quantity of bitterness in the hearts of the survivors. And it was a particularly leavening dose of bitterness that this last futile attack had left in the souls of the soldiers of our sector.

Nevertheless, in February, 1917, the front was unprepared for the eruption that was to shake the world soon. The front maintained its fierce hatred for the Germans and could conceive of no righteous peace otherwise than through the efficient organisation of a gigantic offensive against the enemy. In the way of such an offensive was the treasonable government. Against this government were directed the indignation and suppressed dissatisfaction of the rank and file. But so old, so stable, so deep-rooted was the institution of *Tsarism* that, with all their secret contempt for the court, with all the hidden hatred for the officials of the government, the armies at the front were not ripe yet for a conscious and deliberate rising.

PART THREE REVOLUTION

CHAPTER 10

The Revolution at the Front

The first swallow to warn us of the approaching storm was a soldier from our company who had returned from a leave of absence at Petrograd.

"Oh, my! If you but knew, boys, what is going on in the rear! Revolution! Everywhere they talk of overthrowing the *Tsar*. The capital is aflame with revolution."

These words spread like wildfire among the men. They gathered in knots and discussed the possibilities of the report. Would it mean peace? Would they get land and freedom? Or would it mean another huge offensive before the end of the war? The arguments, of course, took place in whispers, behind the backs of the officers. The consensus of opinion seemed to be that revolution meant preparation for a general attack against the Germans to win a victory before the conclusion of peace.

For several days the air was charged with electricity. Everybody felt that earth-quaking events were taking place and our hearts echoed the distant rumblings of the raging tempest. There was something reticent about the looks and manners of the officers, as if they kept important news to themselves.

Finally, the joyous news arrived. The *commandant* gathered the entire regiment to read to us the glorious words of the first manifesto, together with the famous Order No. 1. The miracle had happened! *Tsarism*, which enslaved us and thrived on the blood and marrow of the toiler, had fallen. Freedom, Equality and Brotherhood! How sweet were these words to our ears! We were transported. There were tears of joy, embraces, dancing. It all seemed a dream, a wonderful dream. Whoever believed that the hated *régime* would be destroyed so easily and in our own time?

The *commandant* read to us the manifesto, which concluded with a fervent appeal to us to hold the line with greater vigilance than ever, now that we were free citizens, to defend our newly won liberty from the attacks of the *Kaiser* and his slaves. Would we defend our freedom? A multitude of throats shouted in a chorus, that passed over No Man's Land and reverberated in the German trenches, "Yes, we will!"

Would we swear allegiance to the Provisional Government, which wanted us to prepare to drive the Germans out of Free Russia before we returned home to divide the land?

"We swear!" thundered thousands of men, raising their right hands, and thoroughly alarming the enemy.

Then came Order No. 1, signed by the Petrograd Soviet of Workmen and Soldiers. Soldiers and officers were now equal, it declared. All the citizens of the Free Russia were equal henceforth. There would be no more discipline. The hated officers were enemies of the people and should no longer be obeyed and kept at their posts. The common soldier would now rule the army. Let the rank and file elect their best men and institute committees; let there be Company, Regimental, Corps and Army Committees.

We were dazzled by this shower of brilliant phrases. The men went about as if intoxicated. For four days the festival continued unabated, so wild with the spirit of jubilation were the boys. The Germans could not at first understand the cause of our celebration. When they learned it they ceased firing.

There were meetings, meetings and meetings. Day and night the regiment seemed to be in continuous session, listening to speeches that dwelt almost exclusively on the words of peace and freedom. The men were hungry for beautiful phrases and gloated over them.

All duty was abandoned in the first few days. While the great upheaval had affected me profoundly, and the first day or two I shared completely the ecstasy of the men, I awoke early to a sense of responsibility. I gathered from the manifestoes and speeches that what was demanded of us was to hold the line with much more energy than before. Wasn't this the concrete significance for us of the Revolution? To my questions the soldiers replied affirmatively, but had no power of will to tear themselves away from the magic circle of speechmaking and visions. Still dazed, they appeared to me like lunatics at large. The front became a veritable insane asylum.

One day, in the first week of the revolution, I ordered a soldier to take up duty at the listening-post. He refused.

"I will take no orders from a *baba*," he snorted, "I can do as I please. We have freedom now."

I was painfully stunned. Why, this very same soldier would have gone through fire for me a week before. And now he was sneering at me. It seemed so incredible. It was overwhelming.

"Ha, ha," he railed. "You can go yourself."

Flushed with chagrin, I seized a rifle and answered:

"Can I? I will show you how a free citizen ought to guard his freedom!"

And I climbed over the top and made my way to the listening-post where I remained on duty for the full two hours.

I talked to the soldiers, appealing to their sense of honour and arguing that the revolution imposed greater responsibilities upon the man in the ranks. They agreed that the defence of the country was the most important task confronting us. But didn't the revolution bring them also freedom, with the injunction to create their own control of the army, and the abolition of discipline? The men were in a high state of enthusiasm, but obedience was contrary to their ideas of liberty. Seeing that I could not get my men to perform their duties, I went to the commander of the company and asked to be released from the army and sent home.

"I see no good in sticking here and doing nothing," I said. "If this is war, then I want to be out of it. I can't get my men to do anything."

"Have you gone insane, Yashka?" the commander asked. "Why, if you, who are a peasant yourself, one of them, beloved by all the rank and file, can't remain, then what should we officers do? It is the obligation of the service that we stay to the last, till the men awake. I am having my own troubles, Yashka," he confided, in a low voice. "I can't have my way, either. So, you see, we are all in the same boat. We have got to stick it out."

It was abhorrent to my feelings, but I remained. Little by little things improved. The soldiers' committees began to function, but did not interfere with the purely military phases of our life. Those of the officers who had been disliked by the men, or who had had records typical of *Tsaristic* officials, disappeared with the revolution. Even Colonel Stubendorf, the commander of the regiment, was gone, retiring perhaps because of his German name. Our new commander was Kudriavtzev, a popular officer.

Discipline was gradually re-established. It was not the old discipline. Its basis was no longer dread of punishment. It was a discipline founded on the high sense of responsibility that was soon instilled into the grey mass of soldiery. True, there was no fighting between us and the enemy. There were even the beginnings of the fraternisation plague that later destroyed the mighty Russian Army. But the soldiers responded to the appeals from the Provisional Government and the Soviet in the early weeks of the spring of 1917. They were ready to carry out unflinchingly any order from Petrograd.

Those were still the days of immense possibilities. The men worshipped the distant figures in the rear who had brought them the boon of liberty and equality. We knew almost nothing of the various parties and factions. Peace was the sole thought of the men. They were told that peace could not come without defeating or overthrowing the *Kaiser*. We, therefore, all expected the word for a general advance. Had that word been given at that time nothing in the world could have withstood our pressure. Nothing. The revolution had given birth to elemental forces in our hearts that defied and ever will defy description.

Then there began a pilgrimage of speakers. There were delegates from the army, there were members of the *Duma*, there were emissaries of the Petrograd Soviet. Almost every day there was a meeting, and almost every other day there were elections. We sent delegates to Corps Headquarters and delegates to Army Headquarters, delegates to a congress in Petrogad and delegates to consult with the government. The speakers were almost all eloquent. They painted beautiful pictures of Russia's future, of universal brotherhood, of happiness and prosperity. The soldiers' eyes would light up with the glow of hope. More than once even I was caught by those enticing traps of eloquence. The rank and file were carried away to an enchanted land by the orators and rewarded them with tremendous ovations.

There were speakers of a different kind, too. These solemnly appealed for a realisation of the immediate duty which the revolution imposed upon the shoulders of the army. Patriotism was their keynote. They called us to defend our country, to be ready at any moment for an attack to drive the Germans out and win the much-desired victory and peace. The soldiers responded to these calls to duty with equal enthusiasm. They were ready, they would swear. Was there any doubt that they were? No. The Russian soldier loved his Mother Country before. He loved her a hundred-fold now.

The first signs of spring arrived. The rivers had broken, the ice fields had thawed. It was muddy, but the earth was fragrant. The winds were laden with intoxicating odours. They were carrying across the vast fields and valleys of Mother-Russia tidings of a new era. There was spring in our souls. It seemed that our longsuffering people and country were being born for a new life, and one wanted to live, live, live.

But there, a few hundred feet away, were the Germans. They were not free. Their souls did not commune with God. Their hearts knew not the immense joy of this unusual spring. They were still slaves, and they would not let us alone in our freedom. They stretched themselves over the fair lands of our country and would not retire. They had to be removed before we could embark upon a life of peace. We were ready to remove them. We were awaiting the order to leap at their throats and show them what Free Russia could do. But why was the order postponed? Why wait? Why not strike while the iron was hot?

Yet the iron was allowed to cool. There was an ocean of talk in the rear; there was absolute inactivity at the front. And as hours grew into days and days into weeks there sprang forth out of this inactivity the first sprouts of fraternisation.

"Come over here for a drink of tea!" a voice from our trenches would address itself across No Man's Land to the Germans. And voices from there would respond:

"Come over here for a drink of vodka!"

For several days they did not go beyond such mutual summons. Then one morning a soldier from our midst came out openly into No Man's Land, announcing that he wanted to talk things over. He stopped in the centre of the field, where he was met by a German and engaged in an argument. From both sides soldiers flocked to the debaters.

"Why do you continue the war?" asked our men. "We have thrown over the *Tsar* and we want peace, but your *Kaiser* insists on war. Throw over your *Kaiser* and then both sides will go home."

"You don't know the truth," answered the German. "You are deceived. Why, our *Kaiser* offered peace to all the Allies last winter. But your *Tsar* refused to make peace. And now your Allies are forcing Russia to continue in the war. We are always ready for peace."

I was with the soldiers in No Man's Land and saw how the German argument impressed them. Some of the Germans had brought vodka along and gave it to our boys. While they were returning to the positions, engaged in heated arguments over the story of the *Kaiser's* peace offer, Commander Kudriavtzev came out to admonish them.

"What are you doing, boys? Don't you know that the Germans are our enemies? They want to entrap you."

"Kill him!" a voice shouted in the crowd. "Enough have we been deceived! Kill him!"

The commander got out of the way quickly before the crowd had caught up the shout of the ruffian. This incident, when the revolution was still in its cradle, was an early symptom of the malady to which the Russian army succumbed in months to come. It was still an easily curable malady. But where was the seer-physician to diagnose the disease at its inception and uproot it then?

We were relieved and sent to the reserve billets. There a mass meeting was organised in honour of a delegate from the Army Committee who came to address us. He was welcomed by Krylov, one of our enlightened soldiers, who spoke well and to the point.

"So long as the Germans keep their *Kaiser* and obey him we will not have peace," he declared. The *Kaiser* wants to rob Russia of many provinces and subject their populations. The German soldiers do his will just as you did the will of the *Tsar*. Isn't that the truth?"

"The truth! The truth, indeed! Right!" the multitude roared.

"Now," resumed Krylov, "the *Kaiser* liked the *Tsar* and was related to him. But the *Kaiser* does not and cannot love Free Russia. He is afraid that the German people will learn from us and start a revolution in their country. He is, therefore, seeking to destroy our freedom because he wants to keep his throne. Is this plain?"

"Yes! Yes! Good! It's the truth!" shouted thousands of throats, cheering wildly for Krylov.

"Therefore," continued the speaker, "it is our duty to defend the country and the precious liberty from the *Kaiser*. If we don't destroy him, he will destroy us. If we defeat him, there will be a revolution in his land and the German people will throw him over. Then our freedom will be secure. Then we will go home and take possession of all the available land. But we can't return home with an enemy at our back. Can we?"

"No! No! No! Sure not!" thundered the swaying mass of soldiery.

"And we can't make peace with a ruler who hates us at heart and who was the secret associate of the *Tsar*. Isn't this correct?"

"Correct! Correct! The truth! Hurrah for Krylov!" bawled the vast gathering, applauding strenuously.

Then the delegate from the Army Committee mounted the speaker's stool. The soldiers were in high spirits, thirsting for every word of enlightenment.

"Comrades!" the delegate opened up. "For three years we have bled, suffered from hunger and cold, wallowed in the muddy and vermin-eaten trenches. Myriads of our brethren have been slaughtered, maimed for life, taken into captivity. Whose war was it? The *Tsar's*. He made us fight and perish while he and his clique bathed in gold and luxury. Now the *Tsar* is no more. Why, then, comrades, should we continue his war? Do you want to lay down your lives again by the thousand?"

"No! No! No! We have had enough of war!" thousands of voices rang out.

"Well," continued the delegate, "I agree with you. We have had enough of war, indeed. You are told that our enemy is in front of us. But what about our enemies in the rear? What about the officers who are now leaving the front and scurrying to cover? What about the land-owners who are holding fast to the large estates donated to them by former *Tsars?* What about the *bourgeoisie* who have sucked our blood for generations and grown rich through our sweat and toil? Where are they all now? What do they want with us? They want you to fight the enemy here so that they, the enemies of the people, can pillage and loot in the rear! So that when you come home, if you live to come home, you will find all the land and the wealth of the country in their hands!"

"It is the truth! The truth! He's right!" interrupted the vast crowd.

"Now you have two enemies," resumed the speaker. "One is foreign and the other domestic. You can't fight both at once. If we continue the war the enemy at your back will rob you of the freedom, the land and the rights that the revolution won for you. Therefore, we must have peace with the Germans in order to be able to combat the *bourgeois* bloodsuckers. Isn't that so?"

"Yes! Yes! It's the truth! It's correct! We want peace! We are tired of the war!" came in a chorus from every side.

The passions of the soldiers were inflamed. The delegate was right, they said. If they continued to sit in the trenches they would be robbed of the land and the fruits of the new freedom, they argued among themselves heatedly. It ached my heart to see the effect of the orator's words. All the impression of Krylov's speech had been eradicated. The very same boys who so enthusiastically acclaimed his call to duty now applauded just as fervidly, if not more so, the appeal of the delegate for a fratricidal war. It maddened me. I could not control myself.

"You stupid asses!" I burst out. "You can be turned one minute one way, the other minute in an opposite direction. Didn't you cheer Krylov's truthful words when he said that the *Kaiser* was our enemy and that we must drive him out of Russia first before we can have peace? And now you have been incited to start a civil war so that the *Kaiser* can walk over Russia and take it all into his grip. This is war! War, you understand, war! And in war there can be no compromise with the enemy. Give him an inch and he will take a mile! Come, let's get down to work. Let's fulfil our duty."

There was a commotion among the soldiers. Some expressed their dissatisfaction loudly.

"Why stand here and listen to this silly *baba?*" sounded one.

"Give her a shove!" shouted another.

"Kick her!" cried a third.

In a moment I was being handled roughly. Blows showered on me from every side.

"What are you doing, boys? Why, that is Yashka! Have you gone crazy?" I heard a friendly voice appeal to the men. Other comrades hurried to my aid and I was rescued without suffering much injury. But I decided to ask for leave to go home and get away from this war without warfare. I would not be thwarted by the commander. No, not this time.

The following day Michael Rodzianko, the President of the *Duma*, arrived at our sector. We were formed for review, and although the men were somewhat lax in discipline they made up for it in enthusiasm. Rodzianko was given a stormy ovation as he appeared before the crowd.

"The responsibility for Russia," he said, "which rested before on the shoulders of the *Tsar* and his government now rests on the people, on you. This is what freedom means. It means that we must, of our own volition, defend the country against the foe. It means that we must all get together, forget our differences and quarrels and present a solid front to the Germans. They are subtle and hypocritical. They talk to you sweetly but their hearts are full of hatred. They claim to be your brothers, but they are your enemies. They seek to divide us so that it will be easier for them to destroy our liberty and country."

"True! True! Right! Right! It is so! It is so!" the throng voiced its approval.

"Free Russia will never be secure until the *Kaiser's* soldiers are driven out of Russia," the speaker continued. "We must, therefore, prepare for a general offensive to win a great victory. We must work together with our Allies who are helping us to defeat the Germans. We must respect and obey our officers, as there can be no army without chiefs, just as there can be no flock without a shepherd."

"Correct! Correct! Well said! It's the truth! It's the truth!" the soldiers shouted from every corner.

"Now, boys, tell me what you think of launching an attack against the foe?" asked the President of the *Duma*. "Are you ready to advance and die, if necessary, to secure our precious freedom?"

"Yes, we are! We will go!" thundered the thousands present.

Then Orlov, the chairman of the Regimental Committee, an educated fellow, rose to answer for the rank and file. He expressed what all of us at the front had in our minds:

"Yes, we are ready to strike. But we want those millions of soldiers in the rear, who spread all over the country, overflowing the cities, overcrowding all the railroads and doing nothing, returned to the front. Let's advance all together. The time for speeches has passed. We want action, or we will leave here."

Comrade Orlov was boisterously acclaimed. Indeed, he said what we all so keenly felt. It wasn't just to the boys in the trenches to allow hundreds of thousands of their comrades to holiday in the rear without interruption. Rodzianko agreed with us. He would do his best to alter this inequality, he promised. But, privately, in reply to the insistent questions of the officers why the golden opportunity for an offensive was being wasted, he confessed that the Provisional Government and the *Duma* were powerless.

"It is the Soviet, Kerensky and its other leading spirits, that have the say in such matters," he said. "They are shaping the policy of the country. I have urged on them not to delay, but to order a general attack immediately."

Chairman Orlov then presented me to Rodzianko with a little

speech in which he recounted my record since the beginning of the war. The President of the Duma was greatly surprised and moved.

"I want to bow before this woman," he said, shaking my hand warmly. He then inquired as to my feeling about conditions at the front. I poured my bitter heart out.

"I can't stand this new order of things. The soldiers don't fight the Germans any more. My object in joining the army was to defend the country. Now, it is impossible to do so. There is nothing left for me, therefore, but to leave."

"But where are you going from here?" he asked.

"I don't know. I suppose I will go home. My father is old, and my mother is sick, and they almost have to go begging for bread."

Rodzianko patted me on the shoulder. "Won't you come to me in Petrograd, *heroitchik?* (little heroine) I will see what I can do for you."

I joyously accepted the invitation, and told the boys of my leaving soon. I was provided with a new outfit and one hundred *rubles* by the commander. The word went out that Yashka was to depart and about a thousand soldiers, many of whose lives I had saved in battle, presented me with a testimonial.

A thousand signatures! They were all the names of dear fellows who were attached to me by ties of fire and blood. There was a record, on that long scroll, of every battle which we had fought and of every episode of lifesaving and self-sacrifice in which I had participated. It made my heart thump with joy and my eyes fill with tears, while deep in my soul something ached and yearned.

It was May, but there was autumn in my breast. There was autumn also in the heart of Mother-Russia. The sun glowed dazzlingly. The fields and the forests rioted in all the glories of spring. There was peace in the trenches, calm in No Man's Land. My country was still exhilarating in the festival of the newly born Freedom. It was scarcely two months old, this child of generations of pain and suffering. It came into being with the first warm wind, and how deep were the forces that it aroused in us, how infinite the promises it carried! My people still entertained the marvellous illusions of those first days. It was spring, the beginning of eternal spring to them.

But my heart pined. All joy was dead in it. I heard the autumn winds howling. I felt instinctively an immense tragedy developing, and my soul went out to Mother-Russia.

The entire regiment was formed in line so that I could bid them farewell. I addressed myself to them as follows:

"You know how I love you, how I cared for you. Who picked you up on the field of battle? Yashka. Who dressed your wounds under fire? Yashka. Who braved with you all dangers and shared with you all privations? A *baba*, Yashka. I bore with your insults and rejoiced in your caresses. I knew how to receive them both, because I knew your souls. I could stand anything with you, but I can't stand this any longer. I can't bear fraternisation with the enemy. I can't tolerate these ceaseless meetings. I can't endure this endless chain of orators and their empty phrases. It is time to act. The time for talk is gone. Otherwise, it will be too late. Our country and freedom are perishing.

"Nevertheless, I love you and want to part from you as a friend."

Here I stopped. I could not continue. The boys gave me a hearty goodbye. They were sorry, very sorry, to lose me, they said, but of course I was entitled to my opinion of the situation. They assured me that they respected me as ever and that, while on leave home, they had always told their mothers to pray for me. And they swore that they would always be ready to lay down their lives for me.

The commander placed his victoria at my disposal to go to the railway station. A delegate from the regiment was leaving the same day for Petrograd, and we went together. As the horses started, tearing me away from the men, who clasped my hands and wished me luck and Godspeed, something tore a big hole in my heart, and the world seemed desolate. . . .

CHAPTER 11

I Organise the Battalion of Death

The journey to Petrograd was uneventful. The train was crowded to capacity with returning soldiers who engaged in arguments day and night. I was drawn into one such debate. Peace was the subject of all discussions, immediate peace.

"But how can you have peace with the Germans occupying parts of Russia?" I broke in. "We must win a victory first or our country will be lost."

"Ah, she is for the old *régime*. She wants the *Tsar* back," murmured threateningly some soldiers.

The delegate accompanying me here advised me to keep my mouth shut if I wanted to arrive safely in Petrograd. I heeded his advice. He left me at the station when we got to the capital. It was in the afternoon, and I had never been in Petrograd before. With the address of Rodzianko on my lips I went about making inquiries how to go there. I was finally directed to board a certain tram-car.

About five in the afternoon I found myself in front of a big house. For a moment I lost courage. "What if he has forgotten me? He may not be at home and nobody will know anything about me." I wanted to retreat, but where could I go? I knew no one in the city. Making bold, I rang the bell and awaited the opening of the door with a trembling heart. A servant came out and I gave my name, with the information that I had just arrived from the front to see Rodzianko. I was taken up in an elevator, a novelty to me, and was met by the secretary to the *Duma* President. He greeted me warmly, saying that he had expected me and invited me to make myself at home.

President Rodzianko then came out, exclaiming cheerfully: "*Heroitchik* mine! I am glad you came," and he kissed me on the cheek. He then presented me to his wife as his *heroitchik*, pointing to my military decorations. She was very cordial and generous in her praise. "You have come just in time for dinner," she said, showing me into her bathroom to remove the dust of the journey. This warm reception heartened me greatly.

At the table the conversation turned to the state of affairs at the front. Asked to tell of the latest developments, I said, as nearly as I can remember:

"The agitation to leave the trenches and go home is growing. If there will be no immediate offensive, all is lost. The soldiers will leave. It is also urgent to return the troops now scattered in the rear to the fighting line."

Rodzianko answered approximately:

"Orders have been given to many units in the rear to go to the front. However, not all obeyed. There were demonstrations and protests on the part of several bodies, due to Bolshevist propaganda."

That was the first time I ever heard of the Bolsheviki. It was May, 1917.

"Who are they?" I asked. "They are a group, led by one Lenine, who just returned from abroad by way of Germany, and Trotzki, Kollontai and other political emigrants. They attend the meetings of the Soviet at the Taurida Palace, in which the *Duma* meets, incite to strife among classes, and call for immediate peace."

I was further asked how Kerensky then stood with the soldiery, being informed that he had just left for a tour of the front.

"Kerensky is very popular. In fact, the most popular man with the front. The men will do anything for him," I replied.

112

Rodzianko then related an incident which made us all laugh. There was an old door-man in the Government Offices who had served many ministers of the *Tsar*. Kerensky, it appeared, made it a habit to shake hands with everybody. So that whenever he entered his office he shook hands with the old door-man, quickly becoming the laughing-stock of the servants.

"Now, what kind of a minister is it," the old footman was overheard complaining to a fellow-servant, "who shakes hands with me?"

After dinner Rodzianko took me to the Taurida Palace, where he introduced me to a gathering of soldiers' delegates, then in session. I was given an ovation and a prominent seat. The speakers told of conditions at various sections of the front that tallied exactly with my own observations. Discipline was gone, fraternisation was on the increase, the agitation to leave the trenches was gaining strength. Something had to be done quickly, they argued. How can the men be kept fit till the moment when an offensive is ordered? That was the problem.

Rodzianko arose and suggested that I be asked to offer a solution. He told them that I was a peasant who had volunteered early in the war and fought and suffered with the men. Therefore, he thought, I ought to know what was the right thing to do. Naturally, I was thrown into confusion. I was totally unprepared to make any suggestions and, therefore, begged to be excused for a while till I thought the matter over.

The session continued, while I sank deep into thought. For half an hour I raked my brain in vain. Then suddenly an idea dawned upon me. It was the idea of a Women's Battalion of Death.

"You heard of what I have gone through and what I have done as a soldier," I turned to the audience upon getting the floor. "Now, how would it do to organise three hundred women like me to serve as an example to the army and lead the men into battle?"

Rodzianko approved of my idea. "Provided," he added, "we could find hundreds more like Maria Botchkareva, which I greatly doubt."

To this objection I replied that numbers were immaterial, that what was important was to shame the men and that a few women at one place could serve as an example to the entire front. "It would be necessary that the women's organisation should have no committees and be run on the regular army basis in order to enable it to serve as a restorative of discipline," I further explained.

Rodzianko thought my suggestion splendid and pictured the enthusiasm that would be bound to be provoked among the men in case of women occupying some trenches and taking the lead in an offensive.

There were objections, however, from the floor. One delegate got up and said:

"None of us will take exception to a soldier like Botchkareva. The men of the front know her and have heard of her deeds. But who will guarantee that the other women will be as decent as she and will not dishonour the army?"

Another delegate remarked:

"Who will guarantee that the presence of women soldiers at the front will not yield there little soldiers?"

There was a general uproar at this criticism. I replied:

"If I take up the organisation of a women's battalion, I will hold myself responsible for every member of it. I would introduce rigid discipline and would allow no speech-making and no loitering in the streets. When Mother-Russia is drowning it is not a time to run an army by committees. I am a common peasant myself, and I know that only discipline can save the Russian Army. In the proposed battalion I would exercise absolute authority and get obedience. Otherwise, there would be no use in organising it."

There were no objections to the conditions which I outlined as preliminary to the establishment of such a unit. Still, I never expected that the government would consider the matter seriously and permit me to carry out the idea, although I was informed that it would be submitted to Kerensky upon his return from the front.

President Rodzianko took a deep interest in the project. He introduced me to Captain Dementiev, *commandant* of the Home for Invalids, asking him to place a room or two at my disposal and generally take care of me. I went home with the captain, who presented me to his wife, a dear and patriotic woman who soon became very much attached to me.

The following morning Rodzianko telephoned, suggesting that before the matter was broached to the War Minister, Kerensky, it would be wise to take it up with the commander in chief, General Brusilov, who could pass upon it from the point of view of the army. If he approved of it, it would be easier to obtain Kerensky's permission.

General Headquarters were then at Moghilev and there we went, Captain Dementiev and I, to obtain an audience with the commander in chief. We were received by his adjutant on the 14th of May. He announced our arrival and purpose to General Brusilov, who had us shown in.

Hardly a week had elapsed since I left the front, and here I was again, this time not in the trenches, however, but in the presence of the commander in chief. It was such a sudden metamorphosis and I could not help wondering, deep in my soul, over the strange ways of fortune. Brusilov met us with a cordial hand-shaking. He was interested in the idea, he said. Wouldn't we sit down? We did. Wouldn't I tell him about myself and how I conceived the scheme?

I told him about my soldiering and my leaving the front because I could not reconcile myself to the prevailing conditions. I explained that the purpose of the plan would be to shame the men in the trenches by having the women go over the top first. The commander in chief then discussed the matter from various angles with Captain Dementiev and approved of my idea. He bade us *adieu*, expressing his hope for the success of my enterprise, and, in a happy frame of mind, I left for Petrograd.

Kerensky had returned from the front. We called up Rodzianko and told him of the result of our mission. He informed us that he had already asked for an audience with Kerensky and that the latter wanted to see him at seven o'clock the following morning, when he would broach the subject to him. After his call on Kerensky Rodzianko telephoned to tell us that he had arranged for an audience for me with Kerensky at the Winter Palace at noon the next day.

Captain Dementiev drove me to the Winter Palace and a few minutes before twelve I was in the ante-chamber of the War Minister. I was surprised to find General Brusilov there and he asked me if I came to see Kerensky about the same matter. I replied in the affirmative. He offered to support my idea with the War Minister, and introduced me right there to General Polovtzev, Commander of the Petrograd Military District, who was with him.

Suddenly the door swung open and a young face, with eyes inflamed from sleeplessness, beckoned to me to come in. It was Kerensky, at the moment the idol of the masses. One of his arms was in a sling. With the other he shook my hand. He walked about nervously and talked briefly and dryly. He told me that he had heard about me and was interested in my idea. I then outlined to him the purpose of the project, saying that there would be no committees, but regular discipline in the battalion of women.

Kerensky listened impatiently. He had evidently made up his mind on the subject. There was only one point of which he was not sure.

Would I be able to maintain a high standard of morality in the organisation? He would allow me to recruit it immediately if I made myself answerable for the conduct and reputation of the girls. I pledged myself to do so. And it was all done. I was granted the authority there and then to form a unit under the name of the First Russian Women's Battalion of Death.

It seemed unbelievable. A few days ago, it had dawned upon me as a mere fancy. Now the dream was adopted as a practical policy by the highest in authority. I was transported. As Kerensky showed me out his eyes fell on General Polovtzev. He asked him to extend to me all necessary help. I was overwhelmed with happiness.

A brief consultation took place immediately between Captain Dementiev and General Polovtzev, who made the following suggestion:

"Why not start at the meeting to be held tomorrow night in the Mariynski Theatre for the benefit of the Home for Invalids? Kerensky, Rodzianko, Tchkheidze, and others will speak there. Let us put Botchkareva between Rodzianko and Kerensky on the program."

I was seized with fright and objected strenuously that I could never appear publicly and that I would not know what to talk about.

"You will tell the same things that you told Rodzianko, Brusilov and Kerensky. Just tell how you feel about the front and the country," they said, brushing away my objections.

Before I had time to realise it I was already in a photographer's studio, and there had my picture taken. The following day this picture topped big posters pasted all over the city, announcing my appearance at the Mariynski Theatre for the purpose of organising a Women's Battalion of Death.

I did not close an eye during the entire night preceding the evening set for the meeting. It all seemed a weird dream. Where did I come in between two such great men as Rodzianko and Kerensky? How could I ever face an assembly of educated people, I, an illiterate peasant woman? And what could I say? My tongue had never been trained to smooth speech. My eyes had never beheld a place like the Mariynski Theatre, formerly frequented by the *Tsar* and the Imperial Family. I tossed in bed in a state of fever.

"Holy Father," I prayed, my eyes streaming with tears, "show Thy humble servant the path to truth. I am afraid; instil courage into my heart. I can feel my knees give way; steady them with Thy strength. My mind is groping in the dark; illumine it with Thy light. My speech is but the common talk of an ignorant *baba*; make it flow with Thy wisdom and penetrate the hearts of my hearers. Do all this, not for the sake of Thy humble Maria, but for the sake of Russia, my unhappy country."

My eyes were red with inflammation when I arose in the morning. I continued nervous all day. Captain Dementiev suggested that I commit my speech to memory. I rejected his suggestion with the comment:

"I have placed my trust in God and rely on Him to put the right words into my mouth." It was the evening of May the 21st, 1917. I was driven to the Mariynski Theatre and escorted by Captain Dementiev and his wife into the former Imperial box. The house was packed, the receipts of the ticket office amounting to twenty thousand *rubles*. Everybody seemed to point at me, and it was with great difficulty that I controlled my nerves.

Kerensky appeared and was given a tremendous ovation. He spoke only about ten minutes. Next on the program was Mrs. Kerensky, and I was to follow her. Mrs. Kerensky, however, broke down as soon as she came out in the limelight. That did not add to my courage. I was led out as if in a trance.

"Men and women-citizens!" I heard my voice say. "Our mother is perishing. Our mother is Russia. I want to help save her. I want women whose hearts are crystal, whose souls are pure, whose impulses are lofty. With such women setting an example of self-sacrifice, you men will realise your duty in this grave hour!"

Then I stopped and could not proceed. Sobs choked the words in me, tremors shook me, my legs grew weak. I was caught under the arm and led away under a thunderous outburst of applause.

Registration of volunteers for the battalion from among those present took place the same evening, there and then. So great was the enthusiasm that fifteen hundred women applied for enlistment. It was necessary to put quarters at my immediate disposal and it was decided to let me have the building and grounds of the Kolomensk Women's Institute, and I directed the women to come there on the morrow, when they would be examined and officially enlisted.

The newspapers carried accounts of the meeting and other publicity helped to swell the number of women who volunteered to join the Battalion of Death to two thousand. They were gathered in the garden of the Institute, all in a state of jubilation. I arrived with Staff Captain Kuzmin, assistant to General Polovtzev, Captain Dementiev and General Anosov, who was introduced to me as a man very interested in my idea. He looked about fifty and was of impressive appearance. He wanted to help me, he explained. In addition, there was about a score of newspaper men. I mounted a table in the centre of the garden and addressed the women in the following manner:

"Women, do you know what I have called you here for? Do you realise clearly the task lying ahead of you? Do you know what war is? War! Look into your hearts, examine into your souls and see if you can stand the great test.

"At a time when our country is perishing it is the duty of all of us to rise to its succour. The morale of our men has fallen low, and it is up to us women to serve as an inspiration to them. But only those women who have entirely sacrificed their own personal interests and affairs could do it.

"Woman is naturally light-hearted. But if she can purge herself for sacrifice, then through a caressing word, a loving heart and an example of heroism she can save the motherland. We are physically weak, but if we be strong morally and spiritually we will accomplish more than a large force.

"I will have no committees in the battalion. There will be strict discipline and guilt will be severely punished. There will be punishment for even slight disobediences. No flirtations will be allowed and any attempts at them will be punished by expulsion and sending home under arrest. It is the purpose of this battalion to restore discipline in the army. It must, therefore, be irreproachable in character. Now, are you willing to enlist under such conditions?"

"Yes! We are! All right! All right!" the women responded in a chorus.

"I will now ask those of you who accept my terms to sign a pledge, binding you to obey any order of Botchkareva. I warn you that I am stern by nature, that I will personally punish any misdemeanour, that I will demand absolute obedience. Those of you who hesitate, better not sign the pledge. There will now be a medical examination."

There were nearly two thousand signed pledges. They included names of some of the most illustrious families in the country, as well as those of common peasant girls and domestic servants. The physical examination, given by ten physicians, some of whom were women, was not of the same standard as that required of the men. There were, naturally, very few perfect specimens of health among the women. But we rejected only those suffering from serious ailments. Altogether there were a few score rejections. Those accepted were allowed to go home with instructions to return on the day following when they would be quartered permanently in the Institute and begin training.

It was necessary to obtain outfits, and I applied to General Polovtzev, Commander of the Military District of Petrograd, for them. The same evening two thousand complete outfits were delivered at my headquarters. I also asked General Polovtzev for twenty-five men instructors, who were well disciplined, could maintain good order and knew all the tricks of the military game, so as to be able to complete the course of instruction in two weeks. He sent me twenty-five petty officers of all grades from the Volynski Regiment.

Then there was the question of supplies. Were we to have our own kitchen? It was found more expedient not to establish one of our own but to make use of the kitchen of a guard regiment, stationed not far from our quarters. The ration was that of regular troops, consisting of two pounds of bread, cabbage soup, *kasha*, sugar and tea. I would send a company at a time, equipped with pails, for their meals.

On the morning of May 26th all the recruits gathered at the grounds of the Institute. I had them placed in rows, so as to distribute them according to their height, and divided the whole body into two battalions of approximately one thousand each. Each battalion was divided into four companies, and each company sub-divided into four platoons. There was a man instructor in command of every platoon, and, in addition, there was a petty officer in command of every company, so that altogether I had to increase the number of men instructors to forty.

I addressed the girls again, informing them that from the moment they entered upon their duties they were no longer women, but soldiers. I told them that they would not be allowed to leave the grounds and that only between six and eight in the evening they would be permitted to receive relatives and friends. From among the more intelligent recruits—and there were many university graduates in the ranks—I selected a number for promotion to platoon and company officers, their function being limited at first to the internal management of the organisation, since the men officers were purely instructors, returning to their barracks at the end of the day's training.

Next, I marched the recruits to four barber shops, where from five in the morning to twelve at noon a number of barbers, using clippers, closely cropped one girl's head after another. Crowds outside the shops watched this unprecedented procedure, greeting with derision every hairless girl that emerged, perhaps with an aching heart, from

Battalion of Death

the barber's parlours.

The same afternoon my soldiers received their first lessons in the large garden. A recruit was detailed to stand guard at the gate and not to admit anybody without the permission of the officer in charge. The watch was changed every two hours. A high fence surrounded the grounds, and the drilling went on without interference. Giggling was strictly forbidden, and I kept a sharp surveillance over the girls. I had about thirty of them unceremoniously dismissed the first day. Some were cast out for too much laughing, others for frivolities. Several of them threw themselves at my feet, begging mercy.

However, I made up my mind that without severity I might just as well give it up at the beginning. If my word was to carry weight, it must be final and unalterable, I decided. How could one otherwise expect to manage two thousand women? As soon as one of them disobeyed an order I quickly removed her uniform and let her go. In this work it was quality and not quantity that counted, and I determined not to stop at the dismissal of even several hundred of the recruits.

We received five hundred rifles for training purposes, sufficient only for a quarter of the force. This necessitated the elaboration of a method whereby the supply of rifles could be made use of by the entire body. It was thought wiser to have the members of the Battalion of Death distinguished by special insignia. We, therefore, devised new epaulets, white, with a red and black stripe. A red and black arrowhead was to be attached to the right arm. I had two thousand of such insignia ordered.

When evening came and the hour for going to bed struck, the girls ignored the order to turn in for the night at ten o'clock and continued to fuss about and make merry. I called the officer in charge to account, threatening to place her at attention for six hours in the event of the soldiers keeping awake after ten. Fifty of the girls I had right there punished by ordering them at attention for two hours. To the rest I exclaimed:

"Every one of you to bed this instant! I want you to be so quiet that I could hear a fly buzz. Tomorrow you will be up at five o'clock."

I spent a sleepless night. There were many things to think about and many worries to overcome.

At five only the officer in charge was up. Not a soul stirred in the barracks. The officer reported to me that she had called a couple of times on the girls to arise, but none of them moved. I came out and in a thundering voice ordered:

Firing Exercise

"*Vstavai!*" (Get up.)

Frightened and sleepy, my recruits left their beds. As soon as they got through dressing and washing there was a call to prayer. I made praying a daily duty. Breakfast followed, consisting of tea and bread.

At eight I had issued an order that the companies should all, in fifteen minutes, be formed into ranks, ready for review. I came out, passed each company, greeting it. The company would answer in a chorus:

"*Zdravia zhelaiem, gospodin Natchalnik!*" (Good health, sir, chief!)

Training was resumed, and I continued the combing out process.

As soon as I observed a girl *coquetting* with an instructor, carrying herself lightly, playing tricks and generally taking it easy, I quickly ordered her out of the uniform and back home. In this manner I weeded out about fifty on the second day. I could not emphasise too much the burden of responsibility I carried. I constantly appealed for the most serious attitude possible on the part of the soldiers toward our task. The battalion had to be a success or I would become the laughing-stock of the country, disgracing at the same time the sponsors of my idea, who grew in numbers daily. I took no new applicants, because haste in completing the course of training to rush the battalion to the front was of the greatest importance.

For several days the drilling went on, the girls acquiring the rudiments of soldiering. On several occasions I resorted to slapping as punishment for misbehaviour.

One day the sentry reported to the officer in charge that two women, one a famous Englishwoman, came to see me. I ordered the battalion at attention while I received the two callers, who were Emmeline Pankhurst and Princess Kikuatova, the latter of whom I knew.

Mrs. Pankhurst was introduced to me and I had the battalion salute "the eminent visitor who had done much for women and her country." Mrs. Pankhurst became a frequenter of the battalion, watching it with absorbing interest as it grew into a well-disciplined military unit. We became very much attached to each other. Mrs. Pankhurst invited me to a dinner at the Astoria, Petrograd's leading hotel, at which Kerensky was to be present and the various Allied representatives in the capital.

Meanwhile, the battalion was making rapid progress. At first, we were little annoyed. The Bolshevik agitators did not think much of the idea, expecting it to collapse quickly. I received only about thirty threatening letters in the beginning. It gradually, however, became

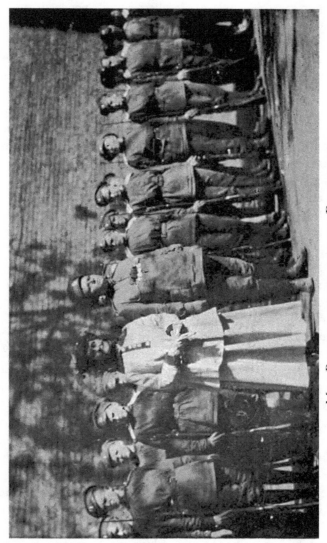

Mrs. Pankhurst watching the Battallion

known that I maintained the strictest discipline, commanding without a committee, and the propagandists recognised a menace in me, and sought a means for the destruction of my scheme.

On the evening appointed for the dinner I went to the Astoria. There Kerensky was very cordial to me. He told me that the Bolsheviki were preparing a demonstration against the Provisional Government and that at first the Petrograd garrison had consented to organise a demonstration in favour of the government. However, later the garrison wavered in its decision. The War Minister then asked me if I would march with the battalion for the Provisional Government.

I gladly accepted the invitation. Kerensky told me that the Women's Battalion had already exerted beneficial influence, that several bodies of troops had expressed a willingness to leave for the front, that many invalids of the war had organised for the purpose of going to the fighting line, declaring that if women could fight then they—the cripples—would do so, too. Finally, he expressed his belief that the announcement of the marching of the Battalion of Death would stimulate the garrison to follow suit.

It was a pleasant evening that I spent at the Astoria. Upon leaving, an acquaintance who went in the same direction offered to drive me to the Institute. I accepted the invitation, getting off, however, within a block of headquarters, as I did not wish him to drive out of his way. It was about eleven o'clock when I approached our temporary barrack. There was a small crowd at the gate, about thirty-five men, of all descriptions, soldiers, hooligans, vagrants, and even some decent-looking fellows.

"Who are you? What are you doing here?" I questioned sharply.

"*Natchalnik*," cried out the sentry, "they are waiting for you. They have been here more than an hour, breaking the gate and scouring the grounds and building for you. When they became convinced that you were away they decided to wait here for your return."

"Now, what do you want?" I demanded of the group as they surrounded me.

"What do we want, eh? We want you to disband the battalion. We have had enough of this discipline. Enough blood has been shed. We don't want any more armies and militarism. You are only creating new troubles for the common people. Disband your battalion and we will leave you alone."

"I will not disband!" was my answer.

Several of them pulled out revolvers and threatened to kill me. The sentry raised an alarm and all the girls appeared at the windows, many of them with their rifles ready.

"Listen," a couple of them argued again, "you are of the people and we only want the weal of the common man. We want peace, not war. And you are inciting to war again. We have had enough war, too much war. We only now understand the futility of war. Surely you don't like to see the poor people slaughtered for the sake of the few rich. Come, join our side, and let's all work for peace."

"Scoundrels!" I shouted with all my strength. "You are idiots! I am myself for peace, but we will never have peace without driving the Germans out of Russia. They will make slaves of us and ruin our country and our freedom. You are traitors!"

"Suddenly I was kicked violently in the back. Someone dealt me a second blow from the side.

"Fire!" I shouted to my girls at the windows as I was knocked down, knowing that I had instructed them always to shoot in the air first as a warning.

Several hundred rifles rang out in a volley. My assailants quickly dispersed, and I was safe. However, they returned during the night and stoned the windows, breaking every pane of glass fronting the street.

CHAPTER 12

My Fight against Committee Rule

It was after midnight when I entered the barracks. The officer in charge reported to me on the happenings of the evening. It appeared that at first one of the group, a Bolshevik agitator, had made his way inside by telling the sentry that he had been sent by me for something. As soon as he was admitted he got the women together and began a speech, appealing to them to form a committee and govern them-selves, in accordance with the new spirit. He ridiculed their toleration of the system of discipline I had inaugurated, calling it *Tsaristic*, and expressing his compassion for those poor girls that I had punished. Agitating against the war, inciting to peace at any price, he urged my recruits to act as free citizens, depose their reactionary *Natchalnik* and democratically elect a new one.

The result of the oration was a split in the ranks of my battalion. More than half of them approved of the speaker, crying, "We are free. This is not the old *régime*. We want to be independent. We want to exercise our own rights." And they seceded from the body, finding themselves in the majority after a vote, and elected a committee.

I was deeply aroused, and in spite of the late hour ordered the girls to form into ranks. As soon as this was accomplished I addressed the following command to the body:

"Those who want a committee move over to the right. Those who are against it go to the left."

The larger part was on the right. Only about three hundred stood at the left.

"Now, those of you who are willing to be treated by me as heretofore, to receive punishment when necessary, to maintain the severest possible discipline in the battalion and to be ruled without a committee, say yes," I exclaimed.

The group of three hundred on the left shouted in a chorus, "Yes! We consent! We are willing, *Gospodin Natchalnik!*"

Turning to the silent crowd on the right, I said:

"Why did you join? I told you beforehand that it would be hard. Didn't you sign pledges to obey? I want action, not phrases. Committees paralyze action in a flood of words."

"We are not slaves; we are free women!" many of the mutineers shouted. "This is not the old *régime*. We want more courteous treatment, more liberty. We want to govern our own affairs as the rest of the army."

"Ah, you foolish women!" I answered with a pained heart. "I did not organise this battalion to be like the rest of the army. We were to serve as an example, and not merely to add a few *babas* to the ineffective millions of soldiers now swarming over Russia. We were to blaze a path and not follow the demoralised army. Had I known what stuff you were made of, I would not have come within a thousand miles of you. Consider, we were to lead in a general attack. Now, suppose we had a committee and the hour for the offensive was here. Then the committee suddenly decides not to advance and our whole idea is destroyed."

"That's it," the recalcitrants shouted. "We would want to decide for ourselves whether to attack or not."

"Well," I turned on them, disgusted, "you are not worth the uniforms you are wearing. This uniform stands for noble sacrifice, for unselfish patriotism, for purity and honour and loyalty. Every one of you is a disgrace to the uniform. Take them off and get out!"

My order was met by an outburst of derision and insubordination.

"We are in the majority. We refuse to obey your orders. We no longer recognise your authority. We will elect a new *Natchalnik!*"

Some of the Female Soldiers

I was deeply hurt but controlled myself not to act rashly. I resolved to make another appeal to them and said:

"You will elect no new *Natchalnik*. But if you want to go, go quietly. Make no scandal, for the sake of womanhood. If all this becomes public it will mar and humiliate all of us. Men will say that women are unfit for serious work, that they don't know how to run things and that they simply must quarrel. We will become the talk of the world and your act will be an eternal blot on our sex."

"But, why are you so cruel to us, so rigid?" the secessionists began to argue again. "Why do you keep us as if in a prison, allowing us no leave, giving us no opportunity to go promenading, always shouting and ordering us about? You want to enslave us."

"I told you at the beginning that I would be strict, that I would shout and punish. As to not letting you out of the grounds, you know that I do it because I can't be sure of your conduct outside. I wanted this house to be a holy place. I prayed to God to hallow us all with His chastity. I wished you to go to the front as saintly women, hoping that the enemy's bullets would not touch you."

All night an argument raged between the few hundred loyal girls and the mutineers. I retired, leaving instructions with the officers to let the recalcitrants do as they pleased, even to leave in the uniforms. My frame of mind was one of despair as I reflected on the outcome of my enterprise. My soul ached for all women as I thought of the disgraceful act of the girls who had pledged their honour to an idea and then deserted the banner they had themselves raised.

In the morning I was informed that the secessionists had elected a delegation to go to General Polovtzev, Commander of the Military District, to make complaint against me, and that they all departed in the uniforms. The same day I was called to report to General Polovtzev on the whole matter. The general advised me to meet some of the demands of the rebels and make peace.

"The whole army is now being run by committees of soldiers. You can't remain alone with the old system. Let your girls form a committee so that a scandal will be averted and your big work thereby saved," General Polovtzev tried to persuade me. But I would not be persuaded.

He then went on to tell me that the soldiers of the First and Tenth Armies, having heard of my work, had bought for me two icons, one of the Holy Mother and the other of Saint George, both of silver, framed in gold. They telegraphed instructions to embroider two

A Female Soldier

standards with appropriate inscriptions. Kerensky, the general told me, had thought of making the presentation a solemn occasion and had my record in the army fully investigated, after which he decided to buy a gold cross to present to me at the same time.

"Now what will become of this celebration if you do not conciliate your girls?" the general asked.

I was, naturally, flattered by the story of Polovtzev but I considered that duty was first and that I would not give in because of the honours promised to me, in spite of the assurances he gave me that the women would ask my pardon in accordance with instructions from him if I consented to form a committee.

"I would not keep the rebels in the battalion for anything. Once insulted by them, I will always consider them harmful in the organisation. They would sap my strength here and would disgrace me at the front. The purpose of the battalion was to set an example to the demoralised men. Give them a committee, and all is lost. I will have the same situation as in the army. The disintegration there is a sufficient reason for my determination not to introduce the new system," I argued.

"Yes, I agree with you that the committees are a curse," confided the general. "But what is to be done?"

"I know this much, that I, for one, will have nothing to do with committees," I declared emphatically.

The general jumped to his feet, struck the table with his fist and thundered:

"And I order you to form a committee!"

I jumped up as well, also struck the table and reiterated loudly:

"I won't! I started this work on condition that I be allowed to run the battalion as I see fit and without any committees."

"Then there is nothing left but to disband your battalion!" proclaimed General Polovtzev.

"Even this minute if you wish!" I offered.

I drove to the Institute. Knowing that the girls were instructed to return I placed ten sentries with rifles in hand at the gates with instructions not to allow anyone to enter, and to shoot in case of trouble. Many of the rebels came but in face of the muzzles they retired. Again, they went to Polovtzev, who, for the moment, at least, could do nothing for them. He reported the matter to Kerensky with a recommendation for some action that would curb me.

I proceeded to reorganise my battalion. There was only a remnant

A Female Soldier

of three hundred left of it, but it was a loyal remnant and I was not upset by the diminution in numbers. Most of the remaining women were peasants like myself, illiterate but very devoted to Mother-Russia. All of them but one were under thirty-five. The exception was one Orlova, who was forty but of an unusually powerful constitution. We resumed the drilling with greater zeal than ever.

A day or two later Kerensky's adjutant called up. He wanted me to come to the Winter Palace to see the War Minister. The ante-chamber was again crowded with many people and I was greeted by several acquaintances. At the appointed minute I was shown into Kerensky's study.

Kerensky was pacing the room vigorously as I entered. There was a cloud on his brow.

"Good morning, Gospodin Minister," I greeted him.

"Good morning," he answered coldly, without extending his hand.

"Are you a soldier?" he asked abruptly.

"Yes," I replied.

"Then why don't you obey your superiors?"

"Because I am in the right in this case. The orders are against the interests of my country and in violation of my charter."

"You must obey!" Kerensky raised his voice to a high pitch, his face suffused with anger. "I demand that you form a committee to-morrow! that you treat the girls courteously! that you cease punishing them! Otherwise I will reduce you to dust!" The War Minister banged his fist on the table for emphasis.

But I felt that I was right, so this fit of temper did not frighten me but, on the contrary, fortified my determination.

"No!" I shouted, letting down my fist, too, "no, I am not going to form any committees. I started out with the understanding that there would be the strictest discipline in the battalion. You can disband it now. A soldier I was and a soldier I shall remain. I will go home, retire to a village and settle there in peace." And I ran out, slamming the door angrily in the face of the astonished minister.

Agitated, I returned to the Institute and had the girls gathered before me. I addressed them as follows:

"I am going home tomorrow. The battalion will be disbanded, because I would not consent to form a committee. You all know that I had warned all the applicants previously that I would be a severe disciplinarian. I sought to make this battalion an example that would shine forever in the history of our country. I hoped to show that where men failed women could succeed. I dared dream that women would inspire men to great deeds and save our unhappy land. But my hopes are now shattered. Cowardly, weak girls proved to be the majority of those who responded to my appeal and they wrecked my scheme for the salvation of suffering Russia. I have just come back from Kerensky. He told me that I should form a committee, but I refused. Have you any idea what a committee would mean?"

"No, no, *Natchalnik*," the women answered.

"A committee," I explained, "means nothing but talk and talk. The committees have destroyed the army and the country. This is war and in war there should be no talk, but action. I can't submit to the order to introduce in this battalion the very system that has disrupted our glorious army. So I am going home. . . . Yes, tomorrow I leave. . . ."

The girls threw themselves at my feet in tears. They wept and begged me to remain with them. "We love you. We will stand by you to the last," they cried. "You can punish us, beat us if you will. We know and appreciate your motives. You want to help Russia and we want you to make use of us. You can treat us as you please, you can kill us, but don't leave us. We will go anywhere for you. We will go to General Polovtzev and tear him to pieces!"

They embraced my feet, hugged me, kissed me, professed their affection and loyalty. I was profoundly stirred. My heart was filled with gratitude and love for these brave friends. They seemed like children to me, like my children, and I felt like a tender mother. If I had alienated fifteen hundred bad ones, I had won the deep devotion of these three hundred noble souls. They had tasted the rigors of soldiering but did not flinch. The others were cowards, masquerading their worthlessness under the cover of "democracy." These sought no excuses. The prospect of actual sacrifice did not daunt them. The thought of three hundred Russian girls, courageous of heart, pure of soul, ready for self-sacrifice, was one to comfort my aching heart.

"I wish I could, but it is impossible for me to remain," I replied to the pleadings of my girls. "The orders from the superiors are to form a committee or disband the battalion. Since I unqualifiedly refused to do the former there remains nothing for me but to go home. Goodbye for the time being; I will go to the Duchess of Lichtenberg for the afternoon."

The duchess was one of the circle of society women who had taken a deep interest in my work. She was a very simple and lovable soul, and I needed someone to whom I could pour out my heart. I was always sure that the duchess would understand and be helpful.

"What ails you, Maria?" were the words with which she greeted me as soon as I appeared on the threshold of her house.

I could not restrain my sobs and told her haltingly of the mutiny and the consequent collapse of the battalion. It weighed heavily on me and I seemed crushed by the disaster. She was struck by the news and cried with me. The beautiful dream we had nurtured was shattered. In truth, it was an evening of mourning. I remained there for dinner.

About eight o'clock one of my girls sought admission and was shown in. She had been sent from the barracks as a messenger to report to me the results of a visit they had paid to General Polovtzev. It appeared that my three hundred loyalists armed themselves with the rifles and went to the Commander of the Military District, demanding that he come out to see them. They were not in a light mood and meant business. The general came out.

"What have you done to our *Natchalnik?*" they demanded sternly.

"I haven't done anything to her," Polovtzev answered, amazed at this threatening demonstration.

"We want back our *Natchalnik!*" my girls shouted. "We want her back immediately. She is a holy woman; her heart is bleeding for unhappy Russia. We will have nothing to do with those bad, unruly girls, and we will not disband the battalion. We are the battalion. We want our *Natchalnik.* We want strict discipline in accordance with our pledges to her, and we will not form any committees."

It was reported to me that General Polovtzev was actually frightened, surrounded by the throng of raging and menacing women. He sent them back to the Institute, promising that he would not disband them and that he would come to the barracks at nine o'clock the following morning. I went with the messenger to the quarters and found everything in splendid order. The girls seemed anxious to comfort their *Natchalnik* and so maintained calm and moved on tiptoe.

In the morning everything went as usual, the rising hour, prayers, breakfast and drilling. At nine I was informed that General Polovtzev, the adjutant of Kerensky, Captain Dementiev and several of the women who took an interest in the Battalion were at the gate. I quickly formed the Battalion. The general greeted us and we saluted. He then shook hands with me and gave orders to let the girls out into the garden, for he wanted to talk things over with me.

I asked myself, as I led the group of distinguished visitors into the house, what it all meant. "If it means that they came to persuade me to form a committee," I thought, "then it will make it mighty hard for me, but I shall refuse all pleas."

My anticipation proved correct. The general had brought all these patronesses of mine to help him break my obstinacy. He immediately launched into an exposition of the necessity to comply with general regulations and introduce, the committee system in the army. He argued along the already familiar lines, but I would not budge. He gradually became angry.

"Are you a soldier?" he repeated the question put to me by Kerensky.

"Yes, Gospodin General!"

"Then why don't you obey orders?"

"Because they are against the interests of the country. The committees are a plague. They have destroyed our army," I answered.

"But it is the law of the country," he declared.

"Yes, and it is a ruinous law, designed to disrupt the front in time of war."

"Now I ask you to do it as a matter of form," he argued in a different tone altogether, perhaps himself realising the truth of my words. "All the army committees are beginning to wonder about you. 'Who is this Botchkareva?' they ask, 'and why is she allowed to command without a committee?' Do it only for the sake of form. Your girls are so devoted to you that a committee elected by them would never seriously bother you. At the same time, it would save us trouble."

Then the women surrounded me and begged me and coaxed me to give way. Some of them wept, others embraced me, all got on my nerves. Nothing could enrage me so much as this wheedling. I grew exasperated and completely lost control of myself, gripped by hysteria.

"You are rascals, all of you! You want to destroy the country! Get out of here!" I shrieked madly.

"Shut up! How dare you shout like that? I am a general. I will kill you!" Polovtzev thundered at me, trembling with ire.

"All right, you can kill me! kill me!" I cried out, tearing my coat open and pointing to my chest. "Kill me!"

The general then threw up his hands, muttering angrily under his breath, "What the devil! This is a demon, not a woman! You can do nothing with her," and he, with his mixed suite, withdrew.

The following morning a telegram came from General Polovtzev, notifying me that I would be allowed to continue my work without a committee!

Thus, ended the row caused by the mutiny in the battalion, and which nearly wrecked the entire undertaking. It was a hard fight that I had made but, convinced of my right, there was no retreating for me.

Events have completely justified my feeling. The Russian Army, once the most colossal military machine in the world, was wrecked in a few months by the committee system. Coming from the trenches, where I learned at first hand what a curse the committees proved, I realised early their portentous significance. To me it has always been clear that a committee meant ceaseless speech-making. That was the outstanding factor about it and I considered no other aspect of it. I knew that the Germans worked all day while our boys talked, and in war I always understood it was action that counted and conquered.

CHAPTER 13

The Battalion at the Front

The same morning on which the telegram came from General Polovtzev there also arrived a banner, with an inscription that read something like this:

Long Live the Provisional Government!
Let Those Who Can, Advance!
Forward, Brave Women!
To the Defense of the Bleeding Motherland!

We were to march with this banner in the demonstration, organised in opposition to the Bolshevik demonstration, set for that day. The Invalids were to march in the same parade. I talked matters over with their chief when we met at Morskaya.

The air was charged with alarming rumours. The captain of the Invalids placed fifty revolvers at my disposal. I distributed them among the instructors and my other officers, leaving a pair for myself.

The band of the Volynski Regiment headed the Battalion of Death, as half the soldiers of that regiment had refused to march against the Bolsheviki, having already been contaminated with Bolshevist ideas, although it was only June.

Mars Field, our destination, was about five *versts* from our barracks. The whole route was lined with enormous crowds which cheered us and the Invalids, of whom there were only about five hundred. Many women on the sidewalks wept, mourning the girls that I was leading into what seemed a conflict with the Bolsheviki. Everybody said,

"Something is going to happen today."

As we approached the Mars Field where the opposing demonstration was held I ordered my soldiers to sit down and rest for fifteen minutes.

"*Stroysia!*" (Form ranks) I ordered at the end of that time. We were all more or less nervous, as if on the eve of an offensive. I addressed a few words to the Battalion, instructing them to stick by me to the end, not to insult anybody, not to run at the slightest provocation, in order to avoid a panic. They all pledged themselves to fulfil my instructions.

Before resuming the march, the captain of the Invalids, several of his subordinate officers and all my instructors came forward and asked to march in the front row with me. I objected, but they insisted, and I finally had to give way, in spite of my desire to show the Bolsheviki that I was not afraid.

The crowds on the Mars Field were indeed enormous. A stream of marchers, with Bolshevist banners, flowed into the great square. We stopped within fifty feet of a Bolshevist crowd and were met promptly by a hail of jokes and curses. The opponents derided the Provisional Government and shouted: "Long live the revolutionary democracy! Down with the war!"

Some of the girls could not suppress their indignation and began to reply, provoking a hot argument.

"When you cry, 'Down with the war!' you are helping to destroy Free Russia," I exclaimed, stepping forward and addressing myself to the turbulent neighbours. "We must beat the Germans first and then there will be no war."

"Kill her! Kill her!" several voices threatened.

Greatly aroused, I rushed a few steps nearer to the crowd. My fingers gripped the two pistols but in all the excitement that followed, the idea was fixed in my mind that I must not shoot at my own people, common workers and peasants.

"Wake up, you deluded sons of Russia! Think what you are doing! You are destroying the Motherland! Scoundrels!" I concluded as their derision continued.

My instructors tried to hold me back as the throng swarmed around me, but I tore myself out of their arms and plunged into the thick of it. I worked myself up to such a state of frenzy that I did not cease talking even when a volley of shots was sent into our midst. Then my officers ordered the battalion to fire. There followed an awful mix-up.

Two of my instructors were killed, one while defending me. Two others were wounded. Ten of my girls were also wounded. Many bullets grazed me, but I escaped till struck unconscious by a blow on the head with an iron bar from behind. Many onlookers became mixed up in the scrap and the result was a panic.

I recovered consciousness in the evening. I was in my own bed with a physician beside it. He told me that although I had lost considerable blood, my wound was not serious and that I would be able to resume my duties soon.

Late in the evening the officer in charge reported that Michael Rodzianko had come to see me. The physician went out to meet him and I heard the two conversing in the room next to mine. Rodzianko's first question was whether I had been killed. It appeared that rumours circulated about town that I was struck dead on the Mars Field. The doctor's statement of my condition apparently gladdened the heart of the President of the *Duma*.

He then came in and smilingly approached my bed and kissed me.

"*Heroitchik* mine, I am very glad that you escaped serious injury. There were many alarming reports about you. It was a brave act on your part to march straight into the midst of the Bolsheviki. Nevertheless, it was foolish of you and the Invalids to oppose such tremendous odds. I have heard of your victory in the fight against the introduction of the committee system in the battalion. Good for you! I wanted to call and congratulate you earlier but was very occupied."

I sat up in bed to show my visitor that I was quite well. He told me of the appointment of General Kornilov to the command of the southwestern front and of a luncheon on the morrow at the Winter Palace at which Kornilov would be present. Rodzianko inquired if I would be strong enough to attend it, and the physician thought that I probably would. Rodzianko then took leave, assuring me of his readiness to help me at all times and wishing me a speedy recovery.

The following morning, I spent at the window, with my head bandaged, watching my girls drill. I felt steady enough to go with Rodzianko to the luncheon. He called before noon and drove me to the Winter Palace. In the reception room there I was introduced by the President of the *Duma* to General Kornilov.

A thin, virile, dynamic body; a wiry face of middle-age; grey moustache; Mongol eyes; semi-Mongol cheekbones; this was Kornilov. He spoke little, but each word he uttered had a ring in it. One felt instinctively that here was a man of power, of dogged perseverance.

"Very glad to meet you," he said, shaking my hand. "Congratulations on your determined fight against the committees."

"Gospodin General," I replied, "I was determined because my heart told me that I was in the right."

"Always follow the advice of your heart," he said, "and you will do right."

At this moment Kerensky appeared. We arose to greet him. He shook hands with Kornilov, Rodzianko and me. The War Minister was in good humour and smiled benignly at me.

"Here is a little hard-head. I never saw one like her," Kerensky pointed at me. "She took it into her head not to form a committee, and nothing could break her will. One must do her justice. She is a sticker, holding out all alone against us all. She foolishly stuck to the argument that 'there ain't such law.'"

"Well," joked Rodzianko in my defence. "She isn't such a fool. She is perhaps wiser than you and I together."

We were then asked into the dining room. Kerensky was seated at the head of the table, I at its opposite end. Rodzianko was on Kerensky's right, Kornilov was on my right. There were also three Allied Generals present. One was on my left, and the other two were between Kerensky and Kornilov.

The conversation was carried on mostly in a foreign tongue and I understood nothing. Besides, I had my troubles with the dishes and table etiquette. I did not know how to handle the unfamiliar courses and blushed several times deeply, watching my neighbours from the corners of my eyes.

Now and then I engaged in bits of conversation with Kornilov. He liked my decided opinions about the necessity of discipline in the army, and expressed himself to the effect that if discipline were not restored, then Russia was lost. The burden of Kerensky's conversation at the table was, that in spite of the considerable disintegration that was eating away the army, it was not too late as yet. He planned a trip to the front, feeling certain that it would result in an offensive blow by our troops.

Finally, Kerensky got up, and the luncheon was over. He told me before leaving that there would be a solemn presentation to me of the two standards and icons sent by the soldiers from the front to the battalion. I replied that I did not deserve such honours, but hoped to be able to justify his trust in me.

Kornilov parted from me cordially, also inviting me to call on him at his headquarters when I arrived at the front. Rodzianko then took me home and asked me to come to see him before leaving for the front.

The time left until the date set by Kerensky for the dedication of the Battalion's battle flags was spent in intensive training and rifle practise. The women were getting ready to go to the front and awaited June 21st with impatience.

Finally, that day arrived. The girls were in high spirits. My heart beat with anticipation. The battalion arose early. Every soldier had a new uniform. The rifles were spick and span. The atmosphere was one of a holiday. We were all cheerful though nervous under the weight of the responsibility of the day.

At nine in the morning two bands arrived at our gates. They were followed by Captain Kuzmin, assistant commander of the Petrograd Military District, with instructions for the battalion to be at the St. Isaac Cathedral at ten o'clock in full military array. We started out almost immediately, led by the two army bands.

The movement of people in the direction of the cathedral was enormous. The entire neighbourhood was lined up with units of the garrison. There were troops of all kinds. Even a body of Cossacks, with flags on the tops of their spears, was there. A group of distinguished citizens and officers was on the stairs leading to the entrance of the church. There were Kerensky, Rodzianko, Miliukov, Kornilov, Polovtzev and others. The battalion saluted as we marched inside of the huge edifice.

The officiating persons were two archbishops and twelve priests. The church was filled to overflow. A hush fell on the vast gathering as I was asked to step forward and give my name. I was seized with fear, as if in the presence of God Himself. The standard that was to be consecrated was placed in my hand and two old battle flags were crossed over it, hiding me almost completely in their folds. The officiating archbishop then addressed me, telling of the unprecedented honour of dedicating an army standard to a woman.

It was not customary to inscribe the name of a commander on the flag of a military unit, he explained, but the name of Maria Botchkareva was emblazoned on this standard, which, in case of my death, would be returned to the cathedral and never used by another commander. As he spoke and said the prayers, in the course of which he sprinkled me three times with holy water, I prayed to the Lord with all my heart and might. The ceremony lasted about an hour, after which

An Award Ceremony for the Batallion of Death

two soldiers, delegates from the First and Third armies, presented to me two icons, given by fellow soldiers, with inscriptions on the cases, expressing their confidence in me as in the woman who would lead Russia to honour and renown.

I was humbled. I did not consider myself worthy of such honours. When asked to receive each of the two icons I fell on my knees before them and prayed for God's guidance. How could I, a dark woman, justify the hopes and trust of so many enlightened and brave sons of my country?

General Kornilov, representing the army, then placed on me a revolver and sabre with handles of gold.

"You have deserved these gallant arms, and you will not disgrace them," he said, and kissed me on the cheek.

I kissed the sabre and pledged myself never to disgrace the weapons and to use them in the defence of my country.

Kerensky then pinned the epaulets of a lieutenant on my shoulders, promoting me to the rank of an officer. He, also, kissed me and was followed by some of the distinguished guests, who congratulated me warmly.

The high officials departed and General Polovtzev took charge for the rest of the day. I was too overcome to regain my self-possession quickly. I was lifted in the hands of General Polovtzev and General Anosov first. Then some officers of junior ranks carried me. Next, I was raised above the crowd by some enthusiastic soldiers and picked out of their hands by even more jubilant sailors. All the time I was very uncomfortable, but the ovation continued and the cheers would not subside. Women in the throng forced their way to me, kissing my feet and blessing me. It was a patriotic mass of people, and love for Russia was the dominant note of the celebrating crowd.

Orators mounted improvised tribunes and talked of the coming offensive and the Battalion of Death, finishing with a "Long Live Botchkareva!" The spiritual state of the soldiers at the moment was such that they cried, "We will go with Botchkareva to the front." Speakers pointed to the women as heroes, calling upon every able-bodied man to rise to the defence of Russia.

It was a wonderful day; a dream, not a day. Had my fancy come true? Had this group of women already accomplished the object for which it was organised? It seemed so that day. I felt that Russia's manhood was ready to follow the battalion and strike the final blow for the salvation of the country.

It was an illusion and my disenchantment was not very long delayed. But it was such a beautiful illusion that one gained enough strength from it to labour patiently for its revival and realisation. What those thousands of Russian soldiers, assembled in the vicinity of the St. Isaac Cathedral, felt on June 21st, 1917, was the thrill that comes from self-sacrifice for the truth, from unselfish devotion to the motherland, from lofty idealism. It convinced me that the millions of Russian soldiers, scattered over their vast country, were amenable to the word of truth, and instilled into me the faith in the ultimate righting of itself of my country.

After the consecration of the battalion's standard, there remained less than three days before leaving for the front. These were spent in preparations. We had to organise a supply unit of our own, as we could not take along the kitchen of the guard regiment that we had used. Also, every member of the battalion received full war equipment.

On June 24th we left the grounds of the Institute and marched to the Kazan Cathedral, on the way to the railroad station. The archbishop addressed us, pointing to the significance of the moment and blessing us. Again, large crowds followed us into the cathedral and to the station. When we started out from the church a group of Bolsheviki blocked our way. The girls immediately began to load their rifles. I ordered them to stop this, put my sabre in the scabbard and marched forward to the Bolsheviki.

"Why do you block the way? You make fun of us women, claiming that we can't do anything. Then, why did you come here to interfere with our going? It is a sign that you are afraid of us," I said to the obstructionists. They dispersed, jeering.

Accompanied by the lusty cheers of the people who lined the streets, we marched to the station. Our train consisted of several *teplushkas* and one second-class passenger coach. We boarded the train under orders to proceed to Molodechno, the headquarters of the Tenth Army, to which the battalion was assigned.

The journey was a triumphal procession. At every station we were hailed by crowds of soldiers and civilians. There were ovations, demonstrations and speeches. My girls had straight orders not to leave the cars without permission. Our meals were provided for us at certain stations, through telegraphic orders, and we would get off the train in those places to eat. At one stop, while I was at rest, a demonstration took place in our honour, and I was suddenly taken out of bed and carried out in view of the crowd.

Thus, we moved to the front, finally arriving at Molodechno. I was met there by a group of about twenty officers and taken to dine with the staff. The battalion was quartered in two barracks upon our arrival at Army Headquarters.

There were about a score of barracks in Molodechno. Almost half of these were filled with deserters from the front, former police and *gendarmes* who had been impressed into the army at the outbreak of the Revolution and soon escaped from the ranks. There were also some criminals and a number of Bolshevist agitators. In a word, the lot consisted of the down-and-outs of that sector of the front.

They scented the arrival of the battalion quickly, and while I was being driven to dinner they descended upon my girls in flocks and began to deride and molest them. The officer in charge perceived with alarm the growing insolence of the rogues and hurried to the *commandant* of the station to beg protection.

"But what can I do?" answered the *commandant*, helplessly. "I am powerless. There are fifteen hundred of them, and there is nothing to be done but to bear patiently with their derision and win their favour by kindness."

The death penalty had already been abolished in the army.

The officer in charge returned with empty hands. She found a few of the outlaws in the barracks, behaving offensively towards the women. Having tried vainly to get rid of them by persuasion, she telephoned to me. I had barely seated myself at the dinner table as her call reached me. I hastened into an automobile and to the barracks.

"What are you doing here?" I yelled, sharply, as soon as I jumped off the car and ran inside. "What do you want? Get out! I will talk to you outside if you want anything."

"Ha, ha, ha!" the men jeered. "Who are you? What sort of a *baba* is this?"

"I am the *Natchalnik*."

"The *Natchalnik*, eh? Ha, ha, ha! Look at this *Natchalnik!*" they scoffed.

"Now," I spoke slowly and firmly, "you have no business here whatever. You have got to get out. I will be at your services outside. If you want anything you will tell it to me there. But you must get out of here!"

The men, there was only a score of them, took themselves to the door, still jeering and muttering curses. I followed them. Immediately outside a large crowd had collected, attracted by the noise. As I faced these depraved men in soldiers' uniforms my heart was pained by the sight of them. A more ragged, tattered, demoralised lot of soldiers I had never seen. Most of them had the faces of out-and-out murderers. Others were mere boys, corrupted by the Bolshevist propaganda.

In other times, in the old days of January, 1917, it would have been sufficient to execute a couple of them to transform the fifteen hundred into respectable and obedient human beings. Now, the mighty Russian military organisation, while engaged in a mortal combat with a stupendous enemy, was rendered unable to cope with such a small group of recalcitrants! This was my first contact with the front in two months. But what a great stride had been made by the disintegrating influences in this short period of time. It was four months after the Revolution, and the front was already seriously affected by the blight of disobedience.

"Why did you come here? What devil brought you here? You want to fight? We want peace! We have had enough fighting!" showered on me from every side.

"Yes, I want to fight. How, otherwise, could we have peace if not by fighting the Germans? I have had more war than you, and I want peace as much as anyone here. If you want me to talk more to you and answer any questions you might put to me, come tomorrow. It is getting late now. I shall be at your disposal tomorrow."

The gang drifted away in groups, some still scoffing, others arguing. I transferred the girls from the second barrack into the first for greater safety and posted sentinels at every entrance. This buoyed up the girls somewhat, but they were even more encouraged when they heard me refuse an invitation to spend the night at Staff Headquarters. How could I leave my girls alone with these fifteen hundred ruffians in the neighbourhood? So, I resolved to sleep with them, under the same roof.

Night came and my soldiers went to bed. Many of us must have wondered that evening whether the deserters would heed my words or return during the night and attack the barracks. It was not midnight yet when a party of them came knocking at the windows and the thin wooden walls. They cursed us all and particularly me. They tried to enter through one or the other doors but were met by fixed bayonets. Getting no further through their raillery, they stoned the barrack, breaking some window panes.

Still we remained docile. If the *commandant* confessed his powerlessness to control them, what could we do? Besides, we were going to the front to fight the Germans, not to engage in a battle with three times our number of desperadoes.

The more patience we exercised the greater grew the encroachments of the men. Some of them would thrust suddenly their hands through the shattered window-panes, grab some of the girls by their hair, causing them pain and resulting in sharp outcries. Nobody slept. All were excited and on edge. The crashing of the stones against the board walls would shake the structure every now and then. It required a lot of patience to endure it all, but my orders were not to bring about a fight.

However, as the night wore on and the noises and catcalls did not cease, my blood began to boil in me, and I finally lost control of myself. Hastily putting on my overcoat, I ran out of the barrack. The day was just breaking, an early July day. The band of thugs, about fifty in all, halted for an instant.

"Villains, rogues, you! What are you doing?" I shouted with all my strength. "Didn't you seek a rest on the way to the trenches? Can't you let us alone, or do you know not what shame is? Perhaps some of the girls here are your sisters. And some of you are old men, one can see. If you want anything, come to see me. I am always ready to talk and argue and answer questions. But leave the girls alone, you shameless rascals!"

My tirade was met by an outburst of laughter and drollery that incensed me even more.

"You will get away this instant or kill me here!" I shrieked, bouncing forward. "You hear? Kill me!" I was trembling with rage. The outcasts were struck by my tone and words. They left one by one, and we settled down for a couple of hours of sleep.

One morning General Valuyev, now commander of the Tenth Army, reviewed the battalion. He was greatly pleased and expressed his gratification to me over the perfect discipline and bearing of the unit. Our own two kitchens then prepared dinner, after they had received a supply of food and provender. There were twelve horses attached to the battalion, six drivers, eight cooks, two shoemakers. In addition to these sixteen men, there were two military instructors accompanying us. The men were always segregated from the girls.

After dinner the deserters began to assemble around our barracks. I had promised to debate with them on the preceding day, and they now took me at my word.

"Where are you taking your soldiers? To fight for the *bourgeoisie*?

What for? You claim to be a peasant woman, then why do you want to shed the people's blood for the rich exploiters?"

These and many similar questions were fired at me from many directions.

I stood up, folded my arms and eyed the crowd sternly. I must confess a tremor ran over me as my eyes passed from one hooligan to another. They were a desperate lot, appearing more like beasts than humans. The dregs of the army, truly.

"Look at yourselves," I opened up, "and think what has become of you! You, who have advanced before like heroes against a withering enemy fire and suffered like faithful sons of the motherland in the defence of Russia, lying for weeks in the muddy, vermin-ridden trenches, and crawling through No Man's Land. Consider for a moment what you are now and what you were a while ago. You were the pride of the country and the world only last winter. Now you are the execration of the army and the nation. Surely there are some among you who belonged to the Fifth Siberian Corps, aren't there?"

"Yes, yes."

"Then you ought to remember me—Yashka—or have heard of me."

"Yes, we do! We know you!" came from several corners.

"Well, if you know me, you ought also to know that I wallowed in the mud of the trenches together with you; that I slept on the same wet ground as you or your brother; that I faced the same dangers, suffered the same hunger, shared the same cabbage soup that you had. Why then do you attack me? Why do you jeer at me? How and when have I earned your contempt and derision?"

"When you were a common soldier," answered a couple of voices, "you were like one of us. But now, being an officer, you are under the influence of the *bourgeoisie.*"

"Who made me an officer if not you? Didn't your brethren, the common soldiers of the First and Tenth Armies, send special delegates to honour me and present icons and standards to me, thus raising me to the grade of officer? I am of the people, blood of your blood, a toiling peasant girl."

"But we are tired of war. We want peace," they complained, unable to find fault with me personally.

"I want peace, too. But how will you have peace? Show me how!" I pounded vigorously, observing that my talk was softening the crowd's temper considerably.

148

"Why, simply leave the front and go home. That's how we can have peace."

"Leave the front!" I bawled, with all the power I could command. "What will happen then? Tell me! Will you have peace? Never! The Germans will just walk over our impregnable defences and crush the people and the freedom. This is war. You are soldiers and you know what war is. You know that all is fair in war. To leave the trenches! Why not hand Russia over to the *Kaiser!* It's the same thing, and you know it as well as I. No, there is no other way to peace than through an offensive and the defeat of the enemy. Conquer the Germans and there will be peace! Shoot them, kill them, sabre them, but do not fraternise with the foes of our beloved Russia!"

"But they fraternise with us. They are tired of the war, too. They want peace as much as we," said a few men.

"They deceive. They fraternise here and send soldiers to fight our Allies."

"What Allies are they to us if they want no peace?" some argued. "They want no peace now because they know that the Germans are treacherous. You and I know it too. Haven't the Germans asphyxiated thousands of our brethren with their deadly gases? Haven't we all suffered from their dirty tricks? Aren't they now occupying a large part of our country? Let's drive them out and have peace!"

There was silence. Nobody had anything to say. Greatly encouraged, I resumed, just as a happy idea dawned upon me.

"Yes, let us drive them out of Russia. Suppose I were to take you along to the front, to feed you well, to equip you with new uniforms and boots, would you go with me to attack the treacherous enemy?"

"Yes, yes! We will go! You are our comrade. You are not a *bourgeois* blood-sucker! With you, we will go!" many voices rang from all sides.

"But if you go with me," I said, "I would keep you under the severest discipline. There can be no army without discipline. I am a peasant like you, and I would take your word of honour to stick it out. But should any one of you attempt to escape, I would have him shot promptly."

"We agree! We are willing to follow you! You are one of us! Hurrah for Yashka! Hurrah for Botchkareva!" the crowd roared almost unanimously.

It was a soul-stirring spectacle. But an hour ago these tattered men acted as if their hearts were congealed. Now they were beating warmly. A brief while ago they looked like the most depraved thugs; now their faces were lit with the spark of humanity. It seemed a miracle. But it was not. Such is the soul of the Russian; now it is hardened and brutal, now it is full of devotion and love.

I called up General Valuyev and begged permission to take the body of deserters to the front, asking for equipment for them. The general refused. He was afraid that they would disintegrate the rest of the men. I assumed responsibility for their conduct, but the general could not see it the way I did.

So, I had to return with empty hands, but I did not disclose the truth to the men. I told them that there was no equipment on hand and that as soon as it arrived they would be despatched to the battalion's sector. Meanwhile, I invited them to escort us out of Molodechno as comrades.

We started out, in full array, early the following week. Each of the girls carried her full equipment, a burden of about sixty-five pounds. There were thirty *versts* ahead of us to Corps Headquarters. The road was open, fields alternating with woods stretching on both sides of it.

I had telegraphed to headquarters for supper, expecting to arrive there early in the evening. But clouds gathered overhead and showers impeded our progress to such an extent that the girls could scarcely keep up. Whenever we passed a village the temptation was great to let them take a rest in it, but I knew that I would never be able to collect them again that day if I once allowed them to spread out. So, I was compelled to hold the battalion in the open and move ahead regardless of the condition of the road or the weather.

It was eleven at night when we arrived at Corps Headquarters and were met by General Kostiayev, chief of staff, who asked us to go to eat the meal prepared for us. The commanding general would review us tomorrow he said. The girls were too tired to sup. They fell like dead in the barn assigned to the battalion and slept all night in their clothes.

The Corps Headquarters were situated at Redki. We breakfasted in the barracks, after which we proceeded to prepare for review by the commanding general. I had been invited to lunch with the staff after review.

It was then found that several of my girls were suffering from the effects of the arduous march on the preceding day. Two of them, Skridlova, my adjutant, the daughter of an admiral who had commanded the Black Sea Fleet, and Dubrovskaya, the daughter of a general, were too ill to remain in the ranks and were sent to a hospital. I

FEMALE SOLDIERS OF THE BATALLION OF DEATH ON THE MARCH

appointed Princess Tatuyeva, of a famous Grusin family in Tiflis, the Caucasus, to be my adjutant. She was a brave and loyal girl, of high education and spoke fluently three foreign languages.

At twelve I formed the battalion for review. Knowing how much the girls had gone through the twenty-four hours before, I abandoned for a moment my severe attitude and joked and coaxed my soldiers into an effort to make a striking impression on the general. The girls tried their best to appear in good shape and were ready to show the general what the battalion was worth. The corps commander arrived soon. He reviewed my soldiers, gave them a thorough examination, resorting even to some catch tests.

"Magnificent!" he said enthusiastically at conclusion of the quiz, congratulating me and shaking my hand. "I would not have believed it possible for men, let alone women, to master the game in six weeks so well. Why, we get recruits here who had undergone three months' drilling, and they could not compare with your girls."

He then spoke a few words of praise to the rank and file, and my soldiers were immensely pleased. I proceeded with the general and his suite to headquarters, where luncheon was awaiting us. He nearly kissed me when he learned that there were no committees in my battalion, so genuine was his joy over it.

"Since the committees were instituted in the army, everything has changed," he said. "I love the soldiers and they always loved me. But now it is all gone. There is no end to trouble. Every day, almost every hour, there come some impossible demands from the ranks. The front has lost almost all of its former might. It is a comedy, not war."

We had not had time to begin the luncheon when a telegram arrived from Molodechno, notifying the staff of Kerensky's arrival there for luncheon and requesting the general's and my attendance. Losing no time, the general ordered his car and we drove to Molodechno at top speed.

There were about twenty persons present at the luncheon at Army Headquarters. Kerensky sat at the head of the table. The commander of my corps was on my right and another general on the left. During the meal the conversation was about the condition at the front and the state of preparedness for a general offensive. I took practically no part in the discussion. At the end of the meal, when all arose, Kerensky walked up to the commander of my corps and delivered himself unexpectedly of the following peremptory speech:

"You will see to it that a committee be formed immediately in

YASHKA WITH SENIOR OFFICERS INSPECTING THE BATALLION

the Death Battalion and that she," pointing at me, "cease punishing the girls!"

I was thunderstruck. All the officers in the room pricked up their ears. There was a tense instant. I felt my blood rush to my head, setting me ablaze. I was furious.

With two violent jerks I tore off my epaulets and threw them into the face of the War Minister.

"I don't want to serve under you!" I exclaimed. "Today you are this way, tomorrow, the opposite. You allowed me once to run the battalion without a committee. I shall not form any committees! I am going home."

I flung these words at the reddened Kerensky before anyone in the room had recovered from the shock, ran out of the house, threw myself into the corps commander's automobile and ordered his chauffeur to drive to Redki instantly.

There was a great commotion as soon as I left the room, a friend of the Chief of Staff, Kostiayev, told later. Kerensky raged at first.

"Shoot her!" he ordered in the flush of anger.

"Gospodin Minister," General Valuyev, the commander of the Tenth Army, said in my defence, "I have known Botchkareva for three years. She first tasted war as a member of my corps. She suffered more than any other soldier at the front, because she suffered both as a woman and as a soldier. She was always in the lead of any enterprise, serving as an example. She is a plain soldier and a word is a pledge to her. If she had been promised the command of the battalion without the aid of a committee, then she could never understand a reversal of the pledge."

The commander of my corps and other officers also spoke up for me. Finally, some remembered that Kerensky had abolished capital punishment.

"Capital punishment has been abolished, Gospodin Minister," they said. "If Botchkareva is to be shot, then why not let us shoot some of those fifteen hundred deserters who are raising the devil here?"

Kerensky then abandoned the thought of shooting me, but insisted before departing from Molodechno that I be tried and punished. The trial never came off.

The corps commander was wrought up when he discovered that I had disappeared with his car. He had to borrow one to get to Redki, and although glad at heart at my outburst, he decided to give me a scolding and remind me of discipline. I was too excited and nervous to do anything when I returned from Molodechno, and so laid down in my barrack, trying to figure out what would now become of the battalion. I knew I had committed a serious breach of discipline and reproached myself for it.

I was called before the commander late in the afternoon, and he reprimanded me for my unmilitary conduct. The general's rebuff was severe. I acknowledged every point of it without argument, recognising that my behaviour was unpardonable.

The hour for dinner came, and I went to headquarters. The scene at the table was one of suppressed merriment. Everybody knew of what had happened at Molodechno. The officers winked knowingly and interchanged smiles. I was the hero of the clandestine celebration. Nobody dared to laugh out loud, for the general at the head of the table had assumed a grave expression, as if struggling not to sanction inadvertently by a smile the illegitimate levity of the staff over my treatment of Kerensky. At the end the general could not maintain his poise and joined in the laughter. The ban was lifted.

"Bravo, Botchkareva!" one of the men exclaimed.

"That's the way to treat him," said another.

"As if there weren't enough committees in the army, he wants still more!" spoke a third.

"He had himself abolished capital punishment, and now wants her shot!" laughed a fourth.

The officers were plainly hostile toward Kerensky. Why? Because they saw that Kerensky did not understand the temper of the Russian soldier. His flying trips to the front perhaps made Kerensky and the world think that the army was a living, powerful, intelligent organism. The officers who were with the soldiers day and night knew that the identical crowd which gave an enthusiastic welcome to Kerensky would accord a similar reception to a Bolshevist or Anarchist agitator an hour later. Above all, it was Kerensky's development of the committee system in the army that undermined his standing with officers.

After dinner I applied to the general for seven officers and twelve men instructors to accompany the battalion to the trenches. One of the officers, a young lieutenant named Leonid Grigorievitch Filippov, was recommended to me for the post of adjutant in battle. Filippov was known as a brave fellow, as he had escaped from a German prison camp. I addressed to the group of instructors a warning to the effect that if any of them would be unable to consider my soldiers as men it would be better for them not to join the battalion, and thus avoid unpleasantness in the future.

The battalion was assigned to the 172nd Division, located within six *versts* of Redki, in the village of Beloye. We were met by the units in reserve, formed in ranks to greet us, with great enthusiasm.

It was a sunny day in midsummer. We spent little time at Division Headquarters. After lunching we resumed our march, having been further assigned to the 525th Kuriag-Daryinski Regiment, about a *verst* and a half from Beloye and two *versts* from the fighting line. We arrived at Senki, Regimental Headquarters, after sunset and were met by a "shock battalion," formed of volunteer soldiers for offensive warfare. There were many such battalions scattered throughout the army, comprising in their ranks the best elements of the Russian soldiery.

Two barns were placed at the disposal of the battalion and one dugout for the officers. Another dugout was occupied by the instructors and members of the supply detachment. However, as the men in the place began to manifest a certain amount of curiosity in my girls, I decided to sleep in one barn and let Tatuyeva take charge of the second. At night many soldiers surrounded the barns and would not let us sleep. They were inoffensive. They made no threats. But they were simply curious, intensely curious.

"We merely want to see. It is something new," they replied to the remonstrating sentinels; "*babas* in breeches!" they made merry, "and soldiers, to boot! Isn't it outlandish enough to attract attention?"

In the end I had to go out and talk with the soldiers. I sat down and argued it out. Didn't they think it right for the girls to want a rest after a day of marching? Yes, they did. Wouldn't they admit that recuperation was necessary before taking the offensive? Yes, they would. Then why not suppress their curiosity and give the fatigued women a chance to collect new strength? The men agreed and dispersed.

The girls were in high spirits the following day. The Russian artillery had opened up early and poured a stream of fire into the enemy positions. Of course, that meant an offensive. The commander of the regiment came out to review us and made a warm speech to the battalion, calling me their mother and expressing his hope that the girls would love me as such. The cannonade grew in violence as the 6th of July, 1917, was declining. The German artillery did not remain silent long. Shells began to fall here and there.

The night was passed in the same barns at Senki. How many of the girls slept, I do not know. Certainly, most of them must have been awed in the presence of war itself. The guns were booming incessantly, but my brave little soldiers, whatever their hearts felt, behaved with fortitude. Weren't they going to lead in a general attack against the foe that would set the entire Russian front ablaze? Weren't they sacrificing their lives for beloved Russia, who would surely remember with pride this gallant group of three hundred girls? Death was dreadful. But a hundred times more dreadful was the ruin of Mother-Russia. Besides, their *Natchalnik* would lead them over the top, and with her they would go anywhere.

And what was the *Natchalnik* thinking about? I had a vision. I saw millions of Russian soldiers rise in an invincible advance after I and my three hundred women had disappeared in No Man's Land on the way to the German trenches. Surely, the men would be shamed at the sight of their sisters going into battle. Surely, the front would awake and rush forward like one man, to be followed by the powerful armies of the rear. No force on earth could withstand the irresistible momentum of fourteen million Russian soldiers. Then there would be peace. . . .

CHAPTER 14

An Errand from Kerensky to Kornilov

In the dusk of July, the 7th we made our last preparations before going into the trenches. The Battalion was provided with a detachment of eight machine guns and a crew to man them. A wagon load of small ammunition was also put in my possession.

I addressed my girls, telling them that the whole regiment would participate in an offensive the coming night.

> Don't be cowards! Don't be traitors! Remember that you volunteered to set an example to the laggards of the army. I know that you are of the stuff to win glory. The country is watching you set the stride for the entire front. Place your trust in God, and He will help us save the motherland.

To the men who were standing by I spoke of the necessity of cooperation. As Kerensky had just completed a tour of this section, the soldiers were still under the influence of his passionate appeals to defend the country and freedom. The men responded to my call, promising to join us in the expected attack.

Darkness settled on earth, interrupted now and then by the flare of explosions. This was to be the night of nights. The artillery roared louder than ever as we stealthily entered a communication trench and filed singly into the front line. The rest of the regiment was pouring in the same direction through other communication trenches. There were casualties during the proceeding. Some soldiers were killed, and many were wounded, among the latter being several of my girls.

The order from General Valuyev, commander of the Tenth Army, was for our whole corps to go over the top at 3 a.m., July the 8th. The battalion occupied a section of the front trench, flanked on both sides by other companies. I was at the extreme right of the line held by the battalion. At the extreme left was Captain Petrov, one of the instructors. My adjutant, Lieutenant Filippov, was in the centre of the line. Between him and me two officers were stationed among the girls at equal distances. Between him and Captain Petrov another two officers occupied similar positions. We waited for the signal to advance.

The night was passed in great tension. As the hour set for the beginning of the attack approached strange reports reached me. The officers were uneasy. They scented a certain restlessness among the men and began to wonder if they would advance after all.

The hour struck three. The colonel gave the signal. But the men on my right and to the left of Captain Petrov would not move. They replied to the colonel's order with questions and expressions of doubt as to the wisdom of advancing. The cowards!

"What for should we die?" asked some.

"What's the use of advancing?" joined others.

"Perhaps it would be better not to attack," vacillated many more.

"True, let us see first if an offensive is necessary," debated the remaining companies.

The colonel, the company commanders and some of the braver soldiers tried to persuade the regiment to go over the top. Meanwhile, day was breaking. Time did not wait. The other regiments of the corps were also vacillating. The men, raised to a high pitch of courage by Kerensky's oratory, lost heart when the advance became imminent. My battalion was kept in the trench by the pusillanimous conduct of the men on both flanks. It was an intolerable situation, unthinkable, grotesque.

The sun crept out in the east, only to cast its rays on the extraordinary spectacle of an entire corps debating their commander's order to advance. It was four. The debate still raged. The sun rose higher. The morning mist had almost vanished. The artillery fire was slackening. The debate continued. It was five. The Germans were wondering what in the world those Russians were going to do with their offen-

FEMALE SOLDIERS ON PARADE

sive. All the spirit accumulated in the battalion during the night was waning, giving way to the physical strain under which we laboured. And the soldiers were still discussing the advisability of attacking!

Every second was precious. "If they would only decide in the affirmative, even now it might not be too late to strike," I thought. But minutes rolled into hours, and there was no sign of a decision. It struck six, and then seven. The day was surely lost. Perhaps all was lost. One's blood boiled with indignation at the absurdity, the futility of the procedure. The weak-kneed hypocrites! They feigned interest in the prudence of starting an offensive on general principles, as if they hadn't talked for weeks about it to their hearts' content. They were plain cowards, concealing their fear in bushels of idle talk.

Orders were given to the artillery to continue the bombardment. All day the cannon boomed while the men debated. The shame, the humiliation of it! These very men had given their words of honour to attack! Now the fear for the safety of their hides had overwhelmed their minds and souls. The hour of noon still found them in the midst of the debate! There were meetings and speeches in the immediate rear. Nothing more stupid, more empty of meaning could be imagined than the arguments of the men. They were repeating in halting tones those old, vague phrases that had been proven false again and again, to the complete satisfaction of their own minds. And yet they lingered, drawn by their faint souls towards doubt and vacillation.

The day declined. The men had arrived at no final resolution. Then, about seventy-five officers, led by Lieutenant-Colonel Ivanov, came to me to ask permission to enter the ranks of the battalion for a joint advance. They were followed by about three hundred of the most intelligent and gallant soldiers in the regiment. Altogether, the battalion's ranks had swollen to about a thousand. I offered the command to Lieutenant-Colonel Ivanov as to a superior, but he declined.

Every officer was provided with a rifle. The line was so arranged that men and women alternated, a girl being flanked by two men. The officers, now numbering about a hundred, were stationed at equal distances throughout the line.

We decided to advance in order to shame the men, having arrived at the conclusion that they would not let us perish in No Man's Land. We all felt the gravity of the decision. We had nothing to guide us in the belief that the boys would not abandon us to our fate, except a feeling that such a monstrosity could not happen. Besides, something had to be done. An offensive had to be launched soon. The front was rapidly deteriorating to a state of impotence.

Colonel Ivanov communicated to the commander by telephone the decision of the battalion. It was a desperate gamble, and every one of us realised the grimness of the moment. The men on our flanks were joking and deriding us.

"Ha, ha! Women and officers will fight!" they railed.

"They are faking. Who ever saw officers go over the top like soldiers, with rifles in hand?"

"Just watch those women run!" joked a fellow, to the merriment of a chorus of voices.

We gritted our teeth in fury but did not reply. Our hope was still in these men. We stuck to the belief that they would follow us and, therefore, avoided alienating them.

At last the signal was given. We crossed ourselves and, hugging our rifles, leaped out of the trenches, every one of our lives dedicated to "the country and freedom." We moved forward against a withering fire of machine guns and artillery, my brave girls, encouraged by the presence of men on their sides, marching steadily against the hail of bullets.

Every particle of time carried death with it. There was but one thought in every mind: "Will they follow?" Each fleeting instant seemed like an age that lurid morning. Already several of us were struck down, and yet no one came after us. We turned our heads every now and then, piercing the darkness in vain for support. Many heads were sticking out from the trenches in our rear. The laggards were wondering if we were in earnest. No, it was all a ruse to them. How could a bare thousand of women and officers attack after a two days' bombardment on a front of several *versts*? It seemed incredible, impossible.

But, dauntless of heart and firm of step, we moved forward. Our losses were increasing, but our line was unbroken. As we advanced more and more into No Man's Land, the shadows finally swallowing us completely, with only the fire of explosions revealing our figures at times to the eyes of our boys in the back, their hearts moved.

Through the din and crash of the bombardment we suddenly caught the sound of a great commotion in the rear. Was it a feeling of shame that stirred them from their lethargy? Or was it the sight of this handful of intrepid souls that aroused their spirit? Anyhow, they were awake at last. Bounding forward with shouts, numberless bodies climbed over the top, and in a few moments the front to the right and left of us became a swaying mass of soldiers. First our regiment poured out and then, on both sides, the contagion spread and unit after unit joined in the advance, so that almost the entire Corps was on the move.

We swept forward and overwhelmed the first German line, and then the second. Our regiment alone captured two thousand prisoners. But there was poison awaiting us in that second line of trenches. Vodka and beer were in abundance. Half of our force got drunk right there, throwing themselves ravenously on the alcohol. My girls did splendid work here, destroying the stores of liquor at my orders. If not for that, the whole regiment would have been drunk. I rushed about appealing to the men to stop drinking.

"Are you going insane?" I pleaded. "We must take the third line yet, and then the Ninth Corps will come to relieve us and keep up the drive."

I realised that the opportunity was too precious. "We must take the third line and rip their defences open," I thought, "so as to turn this blow into a general offensive."

But the men were succumbing one by one to the bitter scourge. And there were the wounded to be taken care of. Some of my girls were killed outright, many were wounded. The latter almost all behaved like Stoics. I can see, even now, the face of Klipatskaya, one of my soldiers, lying in a pool of blood. I ran up to her and sought to aid her, but it was too late. She had twelve wounds, from bullets and shrapnel. Smiling faintly her last smile, she said: "*Milaya, nitchevo!*" (My dear, it's nothing).

The Germans organised a counter-attack at this moment. It was a critical instant, but we met the shock of the attack with our bayonets. As usual in such cases, the enemy turned and fled. We pursued them and swept them out of their third line, driving them into the woods ahead of us.

We had hardly occupied the enemy's third line when orders came by field telephone from the commander to keep up the chase so as not to allow the Germans to entrench themselves, with a promise that the supporting corps would start out immediately. We cautiously sent some patrols into the woods to find out the strength of the foe. I led one such scouting party, and was able to detect that the German force was being slowly but steadily augmented. It was then decided that we immediately advance into the forest and hold positions there till reinforcements arrived enabling us to resume the movement.

It was the half-light hour of morning. The Germans, being in the thick of the woods, had the advantage of observing every movement we made, while we could not see them at all. We were met by such a violent and effective fire that our soldiers lost heart and took to their heels by the hundred, reducing our force to about eight hundred, two hundred and fifty of whom were those of my girls who had escaped death or injury.

Our situation rapidly grew perilous. The line running through the forest was long. Our numerical strength was wholly inadequate for it. Our flanks were in the air. Our ammunition was running low. Fortunately, we turned on the enemy several of his own abandoned machine guns. We stripped the dead of rifles and bullets. And we reported to the commander that we had been deserted under fire by the men and were in danger of imminent capture. The commander begged us to hold out till three o'clock when the Ninth Corps would come up to our succour.

Had the Germans any idea at first of the size of our force we would not have remained there more than a few minutes. We dreaded momentarily being outflanked and surrounded. Our line was stretched out so that each soldier held a considerable number of feet, our force altogether covering a distance of three *versts*. The Germans organised an attack on the left flank. Aid was despatched from the right flank, which was left almost without machine guns, and the attack was repulsed. In this scrap Lieutenant-Colonel Ivanov was wounded. There were many other officers and men lying about disabled. We could not spare the hands necessary to carry them to the first-aid dressing stations far away in our rear.

Three o'clock came, and the expected reinforcements were not yet in sight. The Germans made an attack on the right flank. My adjutant, Lieutenant Filippov, was now commanding there. As our line was curved, he ordered the machine guns on the left flank to direct a slanting fire at the advancing enemy. At the same time our artillery was instructed to let down a barrage in the same section, and the attack was repulsed.

At my request the commander sent out about a hundred stretcher-bearers to collect the dead and wounded scattered between our former line and the captured German third line. About fifty of my girls were dead or wounded.

Meanwhile the sun had risen and time was fast passing. Our condition grew desperate. We sent an urgent appeal for help to headquarters. This shocking answer came from the other end of the wire:

The Ninth Corps has been holding a meeting. It arrived from the reserve billets and went forward till it came to the trenches we had held before the attack. There it stopped, wavered, and began to deliberate whether to advance or not.

We were struck by the news as if by some colossal weight. It was crushing, unimaginable, unbelievable.

Here we were, several hundred women, officers, men—all on the brink of a precipice, in momentary danger of being surrounded and squeezed out of existence. And there, within a *verst* or two, were they, thousands of them, with the fate of our lives, the fate of this whole movement, nay, the fate, perhaps, of all Russia, in their hands. And they were deliberating!

Where was justice? Where was brotherhood? Where was manhood and decency?

"How can you leave your comrades and those brave women," the commander appealed to them, "to certain destruction? Where is honour and right and comradeship?"

The officers begged, implored their men to go forward as our calls for help grew more and more insistent. There was no response. The men said they would defend their positions in case of a German attack, but would not participate in any offensive operation.

It was in these desperate circumstances, as I was rushing about from position to position, exposing myself to bullets in the hope that I might be struck dead rather than see the collapse of the whole enterprise, when I came across a couple sneaking behind a trunk of a tree. One of the pair was a girl of the battalion, the other a soldier. They were making love!

This was even more overpowering than the deliberations of the Ninth Corps, which doomed us to annihilation. It was sufficient to drive one mad. My mind failed to comprehend such a thing at a moment when we were trapped like rats in the enemy's vise. My heart turned into a raging caldron. In an instant I bounced upon the couple.

I ran the bayonet through the girl. The man took to his heels before I could strike him, and escaped.

There being no immediate prospect for the conclusion of the debate in the Ninth Corps, the commander ordered us to save ourselves by retreat. The difficult task was that of extricating ourselves without being detected by the Germans. I had first one group go back some distance and stop, and then another and a third group do the same till we reached almost the fringe of the forest. It was a slow and perilous job, full of anxious moments during the shiftings of the line, but everything went along smoothly, and there was hope.

Our line was drawn in, and we were preparing for the final dash when terrifying shouts of "Hurrah!" suddenly rang out, almost in unison, on both flanks. We were half surrounded! Another quarter of an hour and the net would have been drawn tight around us. There was no time to lose. I ordered a free-for-all run.

The German artillery increased in violence, and the enemy's rifles played havoc with us from both sides. I ran for all I was worth several hundred feet, till knocked unconscious by the terrific concussion of a shell that landed near me. My adjutant, Lieutenant Filippov, saw me fall, picked my body up and dashed with it through the devastating fire, the German trench system, the open space that was No Man's Land before the offensive, and into the Russian trenches.

There the Ninth Corps was still deliberating. But it was already too late. As the breathless, mud-covered, blood-bespattered survivors of the battalion trekked one by one into our trenches, it became obvious that there was no use in any further deliberations. The offensive movement proved abortive. The Germans re-occupied, without opposition, all the ground and trenches we had won at such high cost. There were only two hundred women left in the ranks of my battalion.

I regained consciousness at a hospital in the rear. I was suffering from shell-shock. My hearing was affected and, while I could understand when spoken to, I was unable to talk. I was sent to Petrograd and was met at the station by a distinguished gathering, including many of my patronesses and some high army officers. Kerensky sent his adjutant. General Vasilkovsky, successor to Polovtzev as commander of the Petrograd Military District, was also present. I was showered with flowers and kisses. But to all congratulations I could not even reply with a sound, lying motionless on the stretcher.

I was taken to a hospital and given a large, beautiful room. Kerensky came to see me, kissed me on the forehead, and presented to me a handsome bouquet. He made a little speech, apologising for the trouble he had given me in the controversy about introducing the committee system in the battalion and praising me for my bravery, declaring that I had set a wonderful example to the men all over the front. He invited me to call on him as soon as I got well.

President Rodzianko visited me the following day. He was very depressed and pessimistic over the condition of the country.

"Russia is perishing," he said, "and there is no salvation in prospect for her. Kerensky relies too much on his own power, and is blind to what is going on around him. General Kornilov requested that Kerensky grant him the authority to restore discipline in the army, but the latter refused, claiming that he was able to accomplish it himself in his own manner."

While I was in the hospital a delegate from the front brought me a testimonial from my corps committee! It appeared that two days after I was wounded the committee, which usually comprised the more intelligent soldiers, met in session and discussed all night how they could best award my conduct. A resolution was passed in which praise and thanks were expressed to me for leading bravely in an attack which resulted in the capture of two thousand prisoners. The testimonial was a record of the resolution, signed by the members of the corps committee. Later, the men would have done anything to revoke their signatures, as they deeply regretted this tribute to me, an implacable enemy of the Germans, from the entire corps, which was permeated even then with the Bolshevist spirit.

I learned that Lieutenant Filippov took charge of the battalion, gathering the survivors from all the units with which they identified themselves during and after the retreat. However, he did not remain with the battalion, resigning to join some aviation detachment in the south, after his reorganisation of the remnant of my unit. It was also reported to me that the commander of the corps had recommended me for a cross.

Another week passed before I recovered my speech and poise, although the effects of the shock did not disappear completely for some weeks. A woman friend of mine told me that Kornilov was expected to arrive in Petrograd on the morrow, and that his relations with Kerensky were strained, on account of their difference as to the restoration of discipline at the front. I telephoned to the Winter Palace for an appointment, and the War Minister's adjutant reported my request to Kerensky, who said that he could receive me immediately, even sending his car for me.

Kerensky welcomed me heartily, expressing his gladness over my recovery. He asked me for the reason why the soldiers would not fight. In reply I told him in detail the story of my abortive offensive, how the men had called meetings to deliberate for hours and days whether to advance or not. I told only facts, as narrated above, and Kerensky was deeply impressed. In conclusion I said:

"You can see for yourself that the committees stand for talk, endless talk. An army that talks is not a fighting army. In order to save the front, it is necessary to abolish the committees and introduce strict discipline. General Kornilov seems to be the man for the job. I believe he can do it. Not all is lost yet. With an iron hand the Russian Army can be revived. Kornilov has such a hand. Why not give him the right to use it?"

Kerensky agreed with me generally. "But," he said, "Kornilov wants to restore the old regime. He may take power into his own hands and put the *Tsar* back on the throne."

This I could not believe, and I said so to Kerensky. He replied that he had grounds for believing that Kornilov wanted the monarchy re-established.

"If you are not convinced," Kerensky continued, "go over to General Headquarters, have a talk with Kornilov, find out all you can about his intentions, and come back to report to me."

I realised immediately that Kerensky was asking me to act for him in the role of a secret agent, but I was interested. The thought occurred to me again and again:

"What if Kerensky is right, and Kornilov really wants the *Tsar* back?"

My country was in bad shape, but I dreaded to think of a return of *Tsarism*. If Kornilov was for the old *régime*, then he was an enemy of the people, and Kerensky was right in his hesitancy to clothe the general with supreme authority. I therefore accepted his proposal.

I was, however, troubled by the thought of the errand I had undertaken and resolved to go to Rodzianko, whom I consider my best friend, and make a clean breast of it. When I told him of my conversation with Kerensky he said:

"This is Kerensky's old game—suspecting everybody of being for the old *régime*. I don't believe it of Kornilov. He is an honest, straightforward man. Still, if you seem to be in doubt about it yourself, come, let's go over together to headquarters. Do no spying, but tell Kornilov the truth to his face."

We took a train for General Headquarters and were admitted to Kornilov soon after our arrival. I told him frankly of what had transpired between Kerensky and me a couple of days before. Kornilov grew red. He jumped up and began to pace the room in a rage.

"The scoundrel! The upstart! I swear by the honour of an old soldier that I do not want *Tsarism* restored. I love the Russian *moujik* as much as any man in the country. We fought together and understand one another. If I were only given authority, I would restore discipline quickly by punishing, if necessary, a few regiments. I could organise an offensive in several weeks, beat the Germans and have peace this year yet. He is driving the country to perdition, the rascal!"

Kornilov's words sank like daggers. There was no question that the man spoke from the depth of his soul. His agitation was real beyond a doubt. He continued to walk the room fiercely, talking of the certain collapse of the front if measures were not taken without delay.

"The idiot! He can't see that his days are numbered. Bolshevism is spreading rapidly in the army, and it will not be long before the tide swamps him. Today he allows Lenine to carry on his propaganda in the army without hindrance. Tomorrow Lenine will have his head, and everything will be wrecked."

We left Kornilov, and I had to decide whether to report to Kerensky or not. I must confess to a feeling of shame when I thought of how I carried out the errand. I therefore asked Rodzianko to tell Kerensky of Kornilov's attitude toward Tsarism and boarded a train for Moscow, where I had been invited to review the local Women's Battalion, organised after the fashion of mine. There were many such battalions formed all over Russia.

When I arrived at the barracks and was taken before the fifteen hundred girls who had enlisted in the Moscow unit, I nearly fainted at the sight of them. They were nearly all rouged, wearing slippers and fancy stockings, loosely dressed and of very nonchalant bearing. There were plenty of soldiers around, and their relations with the girls were revolting.

"What's this, a house of shame?" I cried out in anguish. "You are a disgrace to the army! I would have you disbanded at once, and will do my best to see to it that you are not sent to the front!"

A storm of protest broke loose.

"Aha, what is it, the old *régime* or what?" shouted some indignant voices.

"What's that? Discipline? How dare she talk like this?" cried others.

In a moment I was surrounded by a mob of indignant men who drew nearer and nearer, threatening to kill me. The officer who accompanied me apparently knew the temper of the crowd and realised the peril I had provoked. He sent a hurry call to General Verkhovsky, commander of the Moscow Military District, and a very popular man with all troops.

Meanwhile my escort was doing his best to calm the raging throng which soon grew to about one thousand. Closer and closer the circle got to me, and I was ready to say my last prayers. One fellow tripped me by the foot, and I fell. Another let the heel of his boot down on my back. One more minute and I would have been lynched. But God was with me. Verkhovsky arrived not an instant too soon and dashed into the crowd, which split to make way for him. He addressed a few words to the men. They had a magic effect. I was saved.

From Moscow I went to the front, and when my girls saw me arrive there was general jubilation. "The *Natchalnik* has come back!" they sang and danced about. It was hard life for them in my absence, but unfortunately, I did not remain long. In the evening of the day of my arrival a telegram came from General Kornilov, requesting my immediate presence. I left without delay for Army Headquarters, and there met the commander in chief and Rodzianko. The three of us went to Petrograd to see Kerensky. It was on the eve of the great Moscow Assembly, which met on the 28th of July.

During this journey Kornilov talked of his childhood. He was born in Mongolia, the son of a Russian father and Mongol mother. Conditions of life some fifty years ago in the Far East were such as to inure one to any hardships. This is where Kornilov imbibed his contempt for danger and spirit of adventure. He was given a good education by his father, who, I believe, was a frontier trader of peasant stock, but rose to his high position by sheer ability and doggedness. He learned to speak a dozen languages and dialects, more from mixing with all kinds of people than from books. In brief, Kornilov was not of an aristocratic family or brought up in exclusive surroundings. His knowledge of men and affairs was gained at first hand. His contact with the Russian *moujik* and labourer was close. Himself of reckless valour, he came to love the Russian peasant-soldier for his disdain of death.

Upon our arrival at Petrograd we all went together to the Winter Palace. Kornilov entered Kerensky's study first, leaving us to wait in the ante-chamber. It was a long wait for Rodzianko and me. Kornilov remained locked up with Kerensky for two whole hours, and our ears bore witness to the storminess of the session inside. When the commander in chief finally emerged from the office his face was flushed.

Rodzianko and I were admitted next. Kerensky was visibly agitated. He said that he had not expected me to carry out his errand in such a manner. I did not do the right thing, he declared.

"Perhaps I am guilty towards you, Gospodin Minister," I replied. "But I acted according to my conscience, and did what I felt was my duty to the country."

Rodzianko then addressed Kerensky in some such manner:

"Botchkareva reports from the front that both men and officers are turning fast against you; the officers because of the destruction of discipline, the men because of their desire to go home. Now, see what's becoming of the army. It is going to pieces. If the soldiers could have allowed a group of women and officers to perish, then the situation is critical. Something must be done immediately. Give untrammelled authority in the army to Kornilov, and he will save the front. And you remain at the head of the government, to save us from Bolshevism."

I joined Rodzianko in his plea. "We are rapidly nearing an abyss," I urged, "and it will soon be too late. Kornilov is an honourable man, I convinced myself. Let him save the army now, so that people shall not say afterwards that Kerensky destroyed the country!"

"This will not happen!" he cried out, banging his fist on the table. "I know what I am doing!"

"You are destroying Russia!" exclaimed Rodzianko, angered by Kerensky's arrogance. "The blood of the country will be on your head."

Kerensky turned red, then white as a corpse. His appearance frightened me. I thought he would topple over dead.

"Get out!" he shrieked, beside himself, pointing toward the door. "Get out of here!"

Rodzianko and I moved to the exit. At the door Rodzianko stopped for a moment, turned his head and flung a few caustic words at the minister.

Kornilov was waiting for us in the ante-room. We drove to Rodzianko's home for luncheon. There, Kornilov related to us the substance of his conference with Kerensky. He had told him that the soldiers were deserting the front in droves and that those who remained were useless, as they visited the German trenches every night and came back drunk in the morning. The fraternisation had extended to the entire front. A whole Austrian regiment, well provided with liquor, came over to our trenches at one point and a debauch followed. Kornilov repeated the experience of my battalion from official reports that reached him and declared that numerous inquiries from officers were coming to him daily, seeking instructions. But what instructions could he give? He had to seek instructions himself from Kerensky.

At this point the minister asked him what was to be done, and he replied that capital punishment must be re-established, that the committees must be abolished, that the commander in chief must be given the full authority to disband units and execute agitators and rebels, if the front was to be saved from collapse and the country from immense disaster.

Kerensky replied that Kornilov's suggestions were impossible, that all that could be done was for the officers to submit the various complications arising at the front to the Regimental, Corps and Army Committees for solution. But Kornilov retorted that the committees had already, again and again, been confronted with such problems, had them investigated and confirmed, passed condemnatory resolutions and obtained pledges from the men that they would not repeat the offenses, but like weak children the soldiers would immediately resume drinking and fraternising. Only rigid discipline, he insisted, could make the Russian Army a force to be reckoned with.

Nevertheless, Kerensky was obstinate. He would not consent to put Kornilov's program into action. A deadlock was reached which aroused Kornilov's temper. He blurted out:

"You are rushing the country to destruction. You know that the Allies regard us already with contempt. Should our front collapse they would consider Russia a traitor. You are under the delusion that the rank and file still believe in you. But almost all of them are Bolsheviki now. Another while, and you will find yourself overthrown, and your name will go down in history as the destroyer of the country. All your life you fought *Tsarism*. Now you are even worse than the *Tsar* was. Here you sit in the Winter Palace, unwilling to leave, too jealous to hand over the power to someone else. Although I knew the *Tsar* well, your distrust of me and belief that I am for *Tsarism* now is all false. How can I be for a *Tsar* when I love my country and the *moujik?* My whole aspiration is to build up a strong democratic nation, through a Constituent Assembly and a chosen leader. I want Russia to be powerful and advanced. Give me a free hand in the army and our motherland will be saved."

Kerensky heatedly rejected Kornilov's request.

"You will have to resign," he exclaimed, "and I will appoint Alexeiev to your place, and fight you in the event of your failure to obey me!"

"Scoundrel!" cried out Kornilov, and left Kerensky's study.

During the luncheon Kornilov told Rodzianko that if Kerensky carried out his threat he would lead the Savage Division, consisting of tribesmen loyal to him, against Kerensky. Rodzianko pleaded against such action, begging Kornilov not to war against the government as that would divide the country into several factions and lead to civil war. After a long, private conversation Kornilov was induced by the President of the *Duma* to stick it out as commander in chief for the sake of the peace of the nation.

At the table I also learned that General Alexeiev had been offered more than once the chief command, but declined to take it without the authority to exercise a free hand. It also appeared that Kerensky grew more and more self-opinionated and irritable, and was reluctant to see people and accept advice.

I parted from Rodzianko and Kornilov. The latter kissed me and pledged his friendship to me for my efforts to maintain discipline. I returned to the front while they went to Moscow to attend the Assembly.

My heart was heavy with sorrow. It was five months since freedom was born, only five months. But what a nightmare it had become. We were at war, but playing with the enemy. We were free, but disorder was on the increase. Our best men were happy and united five months ago. Now, they were divided and quarrelling among themselves. The people were divided, too. When the revolution first broke all were jubilating together, the soldier, the townsman, the peasant, the workman, the merchant. All were glad. All hoped for good and happiness. Now, there sprang up many parties that set one group of the people against the other. Each of them claimed to have the truth. All of them promised a blissful era, but what was good to one was evil to the other. They talked, argued, fought among themselves. And the minds of the people grew confused and their hearts divided. In the face of such a terrible foe as the Germans, how long could a disunited country last? I prayed to God for Russia.

CHAPTER 15

The Army Becomes a Savage Mob

My girls were enthusiastic over the return of their *Natchalnik*. I reported to the commander of the corps and was invited for luncheon with the staff. The officers were interested to know of events in the rear. I did not tell them the details of the quarrel between the prime minister and the commander in chief, but did indicate generally that a difference had developed.

Toward the end of the meal it was reported that the chairman of the corps committee had come to see the commander on important business. It appeared that the corps in the trenches was to be relieved at seven in the evening and orders were issued to the corps in reserve, some *versts* behind, to move toward the trenches at five in the morning. However, they did not move. The chairman now came to explain the cause of the delay. He was himself a patriotic and intelligent soldier and was treated to a seat by the general as he told the story.

"The rascals!" he said of the men who had elected him as their leader, "they wouldn't move. They are holding meetings all morning and refuse to go to relieve their comrades."

We were all shocked. The general became excited.

"What the devil!" he exclaimed angrily. "That's unheard-of! If the soldiers refuse to relieve the very men who had relieved them a couple of weeks ago, then it's no use continuing at the front, shamming war. It's a farce! It's no use staying here; let them lay down their arms and go home and save the government the bother of keeping up the semblance of an army. The villains! To shoot but a few of them, and they will know their duty! At seven o'clock the trenches will be empty. Go and tell them that I command that they move immediately!"

The chairman returned to the billets and told his soldiers that the general ordered them into the trenches under the penalty of death. This incensed the men.

"Aha, he is threatening to shoot!" cried one.

"He's of the old *régime*," joined another.

"He wants to practise on us the *Tsar's* methods!" shouted several voices.

"He is a blackguard!" suggested a voice.

"He ought to be killed! He would rule us with an iron fist!" the men roared, working themselves up to a fever.

Meanwhile, the news came from the trenches that the men were holding meetings there, proclaiming their determination not to remain in their positions after seven o'clock. The general was in great difficulty. He was faced with the probability of his section of the front being left entirely open to the enemy. He telephoned to the reserve billets and asked the chairman of the committee what was going on there.

Suddenly the general grew pale, dropped the receiver and said:

"They want to kill me."

Chief of Staff Kostayev took over the receiver and in a trembling voice inquired what the trouble was. I listened to the answer.

"They are in an ugly mood. They have mutinied and threaten to mob the general. The excitement is spreading, and some of them have already started out for headquarters."

The voice of the chairman at the other end of the wire was clearly one of alarm. In reply to questions what the general could do to calm the mob he said that the committee admired and respected the general, that its members tried their best to allay the aroused passions, but seemed helpless.

In a few minutes several officers and men ran into the house, greatly agitated.

"General, you are done for if you don't get away in time!" one of them said.

Shortly afterwards Colonel Belonogov, a man of sterling heart, beloved by his soldiers even before the Revolution, rushed in. He brought the same tidings, asking the general to hide. I joined in, pleading to the commander to conceal himself till the storm had passed. But he refused.

"I should hide?" he exclaimed. "What wrong have I done? Let them come and kill me! I have only performed my duty."

He went into his study and locked himself up. The mob was moving nearer and nearer. There was a deathly pallor on the faces of all those present. Every minute or so someone would dash in breathlessly, with eyes full of horror, to herald the approaching tempest.

The tide of tumultuous humanity reached the house. There were cries and howls. For a second we were all in suspense. Then Colonel Belonogov said he would go out and talk to them and try to reason the matter out. The colonel had a gentle voice and a gentle heart. He never addressed even his own orderly in the familiar form. When he sought sometime previous a transfer to another position, his own soldiers kept him by persuasion at his job.

In a word the colonel was a unique man. Without question there was no other officer in the corps as fit as he to undertake the task of mollifying an aroused mob. He went on the porch and faced calmly the constantly swelling crowd.

"Where is the general? Where is he? We want to kill him!" the savage chorus bawled.

"Boys, what are you doing?" the colonel began. "Come to your senses and consider the order. It was issued to relieve your own comrades, soldiers like yourselves. Now, you know that this was no more than right. The general simply wanted you to take the places of your brethren."

"But he threatened to shoot us!" interrupted the men. "You did not quite understand. He only said generally that to get obedience one must shoot. . . ."

"Shoot!" a hundred voices went up from every side, catching the word but not the meaning.

"Shoot! Aha, he wants to shoot! He's for the old *régime* himself!" a thousand mouths roared, without even giving the ashen-faced colonel a chance to explain.

"Kill him! Show him what shooting is!" raged the vast throng, while the speaker tried vainly to raise his voice and get a hearing.

Suddenly someone jerked the stool from under his feet. In an instant a hundred heavy heels squeezed all life out of that noble body. It was a horrible, terrifying scene. Several thousand men had turned into beasts. The lust of blood was in their eyes. They swayed back and forth as if intoxicated, crushing the last signs of animation from their victim, stamping on the corpse in a frenzy.

The mob's thirst for blood mounted. The officers realised that every moment was precious. Kostayev thought that the only way to save ourselves was to escape through the rear of the house.

"I will go out to them," I declared suddenly.

The remaining officers thought me mad and tried to dissuade me.

"Belonogov was the idol of his regiment, and see what's become of him. If you go it is sure death," they warned. Colonel Kostayev disappeared and several of the staff followed him.

I could not see how the situation would be saved by escaping. It might save a couple of lives, although even that was unlikely, but the mutiny would extend and might grow uncontrollable. "I will go out," I resolved, crossed myself and dashed into the infuriated mob.

"What is the matter?" I shouted at the top of my voice. "What's got you? Let me pass!"

The crowd split and made a way for me to the stool.

"Look at her!" railed some voices.

"Eh, eh, look at this bird!" echoed others.

"Your Excellency!" scoffed a man.

"Now," I began sharply, as soon as I jumped on the bench. "I am not 'your Excellency!' but plain Yashka! You can kill me right away, or you can kill me a little later, five, ten minutes later. But Yashka will not be afraid.

"I will have my say. Before you slay me, I must speak my mind. Do you know me? Do you know that I am one of you, a plain peasant soldier?"

"Yes, we do," the men answered.

"Well," I resumed, "why did you kill this man?" and I pointed at the disfigured body at my feet. "He was the kindest officer in the corps. He never beat, never punished a soldier. He always was courteous, to privates and officers alike. He never addressed a person in a derogatory manner. Only a month ago he wanted to be transferred and you insisted on keeping him. That was four weeks ago. Did he change, could he have changed, in such a brief time?

"He was like a father to his boys. Weren't you always proud of him? Didn't you always boast that in his regiment the food was good, the soldiers were well shod, the baths were regular? Didn't you, of your own impulse, reward him with a Soldiers' Cross, the highest honour that the free Russian Army has to offer?

"And now you killed, with your own hands, this noble soul, this rare example of human kindness. Why?

"Why did you do it?" I turned fiercely on the men.

"Because he was of the exploiting class," came one answer.

"They all suck our blood!" shouted some others.

"Why let her talk? Who is she anyhow, to question us?" somebody cried out.

"Kill her! Kill her, too! Kill them all! Enough have we bled! The *bourgeois!* The murderers! Kill her!" many voices rang.

"Scoundrels!" I screamed. "You will kill me yet, I am at your mercy, and I came out to be killed. You ask why let me talk, who am I anyhow, as if you don't know me! Who is Yashka Botchkareva?

"Who sent delegates to present icons to me, if not you? Who had me promoted to the rank of an officer, if not you? Who sent me this testimonial to Petrograd only a couple of weeks ago, if not you?"

Here I drew out from my breast pocket the resolution passed and signed by the corps committee and despatched to me while I was in the Petrograd Hospital. I had carried it with me. Pointing to the signatures, I cried:

"You see this? Who signed it, if not yourselves? It is the corps committee, your own representatives, whom you, yourselves, elected!"

The men were silent.

"Who suffered, fought with you, if not I? Who saved your skins under fire, if not Yashka? Don't you remember what I did for your brother at Narotch, when, to the armpits in mud, I dragged dozens of you to safety and life?"

Here, I turned abruptly on a gaping fellow, looked directly at him and asked:

"Suppose the rank and file were to elect their own officers. Now, what would you do in the commander's place, if you were chosen? You are a plain soldier, of the people. Tell me what you would do!" I thundered.

The chap looked stupid, making an effort to laugh.

"Ha, I would see," he said, "once I got there."

"This is no answer. You tell me what you would do if our corps were in the trenches and another one refused to relieve it. What would you do? What?" I demanded of the whole crowd.

"Would you hold the trenches indefinitely or leave? Answer me that!"

"Well, we would leave, anyhow," replied a number of men.

"But what are you here for," I shouted savagely, "to hold the trenches or not?"

"Yes, to hold," they answered.

"Then how could you leave them?" I fired back.

There was silence.

"That would be treason to Free Russia!" I continued.

The men bowed their heads in shame. Nobody spoke.

"Then why did you kill him?" I cried out in pain. "What did he want you to do but hold the trenches?"

"He wanted to shoot us!" several sullen voices replied.

"He never said anything of the sort. What he wanted to say was to explain that the general did not threaten you either, but remarked that in other circumstances your action would be punished by shooting. No sooner did Colonel Belonogov mention the word when you threw yourselves upon him without even giving the man an opportunity to finish his words."

"It was reported to us otherwise. We thought he threatened to shoot us," the men weakly defended themselves.

At this stage the orderlies and friends of the slain colonel rushed up. They raised such a woeful wail when they saw the mutilated corpse that all words were drowned out. They cursed and wept and threatened the mob, although they were few and the crowd was of thousands.

"Murderers! Bloodsuckers! Whom have you killed? Our little father! Did soldiers ever have a better friend than he? Was there ever a commander who took greater care of his boys? You are worse than the *Tsar* and his hangmen. Give you freedom, and you act like cut-throats. You devils!"

And the mourners broke out even in louder sobs. A cry went up that shook air. It gripped everybody's throat. Many in the mob wept. As the deceased's friends began to enumerate the various favours they had received from him, I could not choke down my tears and descended from the bench, convulsed with sobs.

Meanwhile, in response to calls for help, a division from a neighbouring sector arrived to quell the mutiny. The committee of the division came forward and demanded the surrender of the ringleaders of the movement that resulted in the soldiers' refusal to return to the trenches and in the mobbing of Colonel Belonogov. There were negotiations between the two committees, which finally ended in the surrender by the mob of twenty agitators, who were placed under arrest.

The officers who had fled and the general now reappeared, although the latter was still afraid to order the soldiers to relieve the corps in the trenches. He asked me to broach the subject.

I first addressed the men about the funeral.

"We must have a coffin made. Who will do it?" I asked.

Several volunteered to get some lumber and construct one.

"How about a grave? We want to bury him with full military honours," I suggested next. Some soldiers offered their services as grave-diggers.

An officer went to look for a priest. I sent a soldier to the woods to make a wreath. Then I turned and asked:

"Now, will you go to the trenches to relieve your comrades?"

"Yes," the men answered meekly.

It was an unforgettable scene. These thousands of men, all so docile and humble, some with tears still fresh on their cheeks, were like a forlorn flock of sheep that had lost its shepherd. One could never believe that these men were capable of murder. You could curse them now, you could even strike them, and they would bear it without protest. They were conscious, deeply conscious of a great crime. Quietly they stood, seldom exchanging a word of regret, engrossed in mourning. And yet these very lambs were ferocious beasts two hours ago. All the gentleness now mirrored in their faces was then swept away by a hurricane of savage passion. These obedient children had actually been inhuman a while ago. It was incredible, and still it was the truth.

Such is the character of the Russian people.

The coffin, an oblong box of unshaven boards, draped inside and out with a white sheet, was brought at four o'clock. The body had been washed, but it was impossible to restore the face to its normal appearance. It was disfigured beyond recognition. I, with the help of some men, wrapped the body in canvas and placed it in the coffin. Instead of one there were four green wreaths made. The priest began to read the services but could not contain himself and broke out sobbing. The general, the staff, and I, with candles in hand, sobbed too. Immediately behind the coffin, as the procession started, the dead officer's orderly wailed in a heart-rending voice, recalling aloud the virtues of his master. In our rear almost the whole corps marched, including the regiment commanded by the deceased. The weeping was general and grew with every step so that by the time the procession reached the grave the wailing could be heard for *versts* around. As the body was laid to rest everybody dropped a handful of sand into the grave. Prayers were on all lips.

The order was given that by seven o'clock the corps would be moved to relieve the soldiers at the fighting line. I went to my girls and gave the word for them to be ready too. They had heard of the disturbance and passed some anxious moments, and therefore gave me a hearty welcome. The general had telephoned to the front line that the corps was a few hours late and asked the soldiers there to remain in the trenches for the night. The distance that we had to cover was about fifteen *versts*, and we arrived at the front before dawn.

The battalion, now consisting of only some two hundred girls, occupied a small sector to itself, opposite the town of Kreva. There was no sign of actual warfare at the fighting line. Neither the Germans nor the Russians used their arms. Fraternisation was general. There was a virtual, if not formal, truce. The men met every day, indulged in long arguments and drank beer brought by the Germans.

I could not tolerate such war and ordered my girls to conduct themselves as if everything was as before. The men became very irritated by our militant attitude toward the enemy. A group of them, with the chairman of the Regimental Committee, came over to our trench to debate the matter.

"Who are our enemies?" began the chairman. "Surely, not the Germans who want peace. It's the *bourgeoisie*, the ruling class, that is the real enemy of the people. It's against them that we ought to wage war, for they would not listen to the German peace proposals. Why

179

does not Kerensky obtain peace for us? Because the Allies will not let him. Well, we will drive Kerensky out of his office mighty quick!"

"But I am not of the ruling class. I am a plain peasant woman," I objected. "I have been a soldier since the beginning of the war and fought in many battles. Don't agitate here against officers."

"Oh, I don't mean you," he replied, trying to win me over to the pacificists' viewpoint. Several German soldiers joined the Russian group. The discussion waxed hot. They repeated the old argument that the Germans had asked for peace and the Allies did not accept it. I replied that the Germans could have peace with Russia if they withdrew from the invaded parts of our country. So long as they kept our land, it was the duty of every Russian to fight and drive them out.

Thus, life dragged on. Nights and days passed in discussions. Kerensky had lost almost all of his hold on the men, who were drifting more and more toward Bolshevism. Finally, the feud between Kerensky and Kornilov reached a crisis. Kerensky asked the commander in chief by telephone to send to Petrograd some loyal troops, apparently realising that his days were numbered. Kornilov replied with a message through Alexeiev, requesting a written certificate from Kerensky, clothing the commander in chief with full authority to restore discipline in the army. It would seem that Kornilov was willing to save Kerensky, provided the latter allowed him to save the front.

But Kerensky evidently saw there an opportunity to restore his fallen prestige and secure his position. He therefore turned against Kornilov, publicly declaring that the latter sought sovereign power and appealed to the workmen and soldiers to rise against the commander of the army. The result was the brief encounter between the revolutionary masses and Kornilov's Savage Division. Kornilov was defeated. Kerensky triumphed and for the moment it looked as if he had attained his object. All the radical forces were united and Kerensky, as the saviour of the revolution from a counter-revolutionary assault, again became the idol of the soldiers and the labouring class.

The larger part of the army sided with Kerensky when he appealed for support against Kornilov. But this artificial state of mind did not last long. Kerensky little by little lost the suddenly acquired confidence of the masses, as he did not bring them the much-desired peace.

The soldier or officer who sided with Kornilov was nicknamed *Kornilovetz*. To call one by this name was equivalent to characterising one as a counter-revolutionary, advocate of the old regime, or enemy of the people. The inactivity of the trench life became wearisome.

One rainy day I sent out a listening party into No Man's Land, with instructions to shoot at the enemy in case of his approach. I watched the party go forward. Suddenly, a group of Germans, numbering about ten, came in the direction of our trenches. They walked nonchalantly, with hands in pocket, some whistling, others singing. I aimed my rifle at the leg of one of the group and wounded him.

The whole front was in an uproar in a second. It was scandalous. Who dared do such a thing! The Germans and the Russians were seething with rage. Several of my girls came running, greatly alarmed.

"*Natchalnik*, why did you do it?" they asked, seeing me with a smoking rifle in hand.

Many soldiers, friends of mine, hastened next into our trench to warn me of the men's ugly temper and threats. I told them that I saw the Germans approach my girls and make an effort at flirtation. But this defence did not appease the soldiers. They placed machine guns in the first trench and were going to wipe us all out. Fortunately, we were informed in time and hidden in a side trench. The machine guns raked our position, without causing any casualties. The firing was finally interrupted by the sharp orders of the chairman of the Regimental Committee. I was called before him for an explanation. I bade farewell to my girls, telling them that there would probably be a repetition of the episode of Colonel Belonogov's lynching.

I was met with threats and ugly words.

"Kill her!"

"She's a *Kornilovka!*"

"Make short shift of her!"

I was surrounded by the members of the committee, who held off the mob. Several speakers rose to my defence, but hardly succeeded in mollifying the crowd. Then an officer got up to talk in my behalf. He was a popular speaker. But this time his popularity failed. He said that I was right. He would have done the same thing had he been in my place. That was as far as he got.

"Aha, so you are a *Kornilovetz* too!" shouted the crowd. "Kill him! Kill him!"

In an instant the man was thrown off the chair and struck in the head. In another instant he was crushed to death under a thousand heels.

Then the mob swayed in my direction. But the committee seized me and carried me off to the rear, hiding me in a dugout. One of my girls, Medvedovskaya, was placed at the entrance to guard it.

Meanwhile, my girls heard of the happenings and hurried to my aid. The mob spread out to look for me and a part of it came to the dugout in which I was concealed.

"Where is Botchkareva? Let us in to see if she is there!" they shouted. The girl sentry said she had orders to shoot if they approached near her. They did. She fired, wounding one in the side.

The poor girl was bayoneted by the brutes.

The committee and my friends, numbering about one hundred, insisted that I be given a trial and not mobbed. My girls were ready to die to the last one for me right there. I was taken out from the dugout by my defenders, who made an effort to lead me to safety for an open trial.

The mob, now increased, pressed closer and closer. The two sides were fighting for me. It was agreed that no weapons were to be used in the scramble. The mass of humanity swayed back and forth, my girls fighting like enraged beasts to stave off the mob. Now and then a fellow would get close enough through the chain to land a blow at me. As the struggle progressed these blows multiplied till I was knocked unconscious. In that state my friends dragged me out of the tempestuous circle and spirited me away.

My life was saved, although I was badly beaten up. It cost the lives of a loyal girl and an innocent friend. I was sent to Molodechno, a couple of my girls going with me as attendants. The battalion was taken from the front to the reserve billets. But even there their lives were not safe. They were insulted, annoyed, called *Kornilovki*. There were daily scenes. The windows of their dugouts were broken. The officers were powerless and seldom showed their faces. My instructors did their best to defend me and the battalion, explaining that we were nonpartisan.

One morning a car came for me from headquarters at Molodechno. I met there a high officer of my corps, who described the intolerable surroundings in which my girls remained. They waited for me, refusing orders to go home, unless the *Natchalnik* disbanded them. He had sent them to dig reserve trenches in order to keep them away from the men. They did splendid work, he said, but as soon as they returned the men began to molest them. Only the preceding night a gang of soldiers made an assault on the dugouts in which my girls were billeted. They beat the sentry and broke in with the intention of attacking the women. There was a panic. Some of the girls seized their rifles and fired in the air. The noise attracted the attention of my instructors and many other soldiers, among whom there were numerous decent fellows. The situation was saved by the latter.

But what was to be done? Life for the battalion became absolutely unbearable, at least at this part of the front. It was difficult to understand the change undergone by the men in several months. How long ago was it that they almost worshipped me, and I loved them? Now they seemed to have turned wild.

The officer advised me to disband the Battalion. But that would amount to an acknowledgment of failure and the hopelessness of my country's condition. I was not ready to acknowledge these. No, I would not disband my unit. I would fight to the end. The visitor could not see it this way. Wasn't I at the end of the rope if the soldiers had turned machine guns on the battalion? Wouldn't I have been lynched if not for the desperate struggle of my girls and soldier friends?

I resolved to go to Petrograd and ask Kerensky to transfer me to a fighting sector. I went to see my girls before leaving for the capital. It was a pathetic meeting. They were glad to learn of my planned trip. They could not stand it much longer where they were. They were prepared to fight the Germans, to be tortured by them, to die at their hands or in prison camps. But they were not prepared for the torments and humiliation that they were made to suffer by our own boys. That never entered into our calculations at the time the battalion was formed.

I took my documents along and left the same evening, telling my soldiers that I would not stay away longer than a week, which was the limit that they set on their endurance. Upon my arrival in Petrograd I went to the quarters occupied by the battalion while in training. It took a very casual eye to observe that an oppressive atmosphere weighed heavily on the Russian capital. The joy, smiles and jubilation were gone from the streets of the city. There was gloom in the air and in everybody's eyes. Food was very scarce. Red Guards were plentiful. Bolshevism walked the streets openly and defiantly, as if its day had already come.

My friends, who had taken an interest in the battalion, were horrified to learn of conditions at the front. Their accounts of the state of affairs at the capital dejected me greatly. Kerensky, after his fight with Kornilov, cut himself off completely from his friends and acquaintances of the upper classes. I went to General Anosov, telling him of my mission. But he would not accompany me anywhere, although he placed his automobile at my disposal. I drove to the Commander of the Military District, then General Vasilkovsky, a Cossack who looked impressive and strong, but was actually a weakling. He received me cordially and asked for the purpose of my visit to the city. He had heard of the beating I got and expressed his sympathy.

"But," he added, "no one is sure these days. I, myself, expect to be cast out at any time. It is a matter of days, of hours, for the government. Another revolution is ripening and is at hand. Bolshevism is everywhere, in the factories and in the military barracks. And how is it at the front?"

"The same thing, even worse," I answered, and proceeded to tell him of all my trials and troubles, and the help I expected to obtain from him and the War Minister.

"Nothing can help you now," he said. "The authorities are powerless. Orders are not worth the paper on which they are issued. I am going now to Verkhovsky, the new War Minister. Would you like to go along?"

On the way we discussed Verkhovsky's appointment. He was the same man who, as commander of the Moscow Military District, had rescued me from the mob at Moscow some weeks before. He was a very popular leader and exerted great influence on the soldiers.

"Perhaps if he had been appointed some months ago he might have saved the army. But it is too late now," said Vasilkovsky.

When we arrived at the War Ministry, we found that Kerensky was in Verkhovsky's study. We were announced, and I was asked to come in first. As I opened the door I saw immediately that all was lost. The Prime Minister and the War Minister were both standing. They presented such a pathetic, heart-breaking sight! Kerensky looked like a corpse, literally. There was not a vestige of colour in his face. His eyes were red as if he had not slept for nights. Verkhovsky seemed to me like a man who is drowning, reaching for help. My heart sank. War had made me callous, and I was seldom shocked. But this time I was nearly crushed by the two agonised figures. It was the agony of Russia that was portrayed in their helpless faces.

They made an effort to smile, but it was a smile that pained more than a wail. The War Minister then inquired how things were at the front. "We heard you were badly mauled," he said.

I gave a detailed account of everything that I witnessed and experienced myself. I told in detail about the lynching of Colonel Belonogov, of the officer who tried to defend me, of the bayoneting of my girl, of the machine guns that were turned on me because I wounded one of the enemy.

Kerensky seized his head in his hands and cried out:

"Oh, horror! horror! We perish! We drown!"

There was a tense, painful pause.

I concluded my recital with the suggestion that action was urgently needed or all would be wrecked.

"Yes, action is needed, but what action? What is to be done now? What would you do if you were to be given the authority over the army? You are a common soldier, tell me what you would do?"

"It is too late now," I answered after some thinking. "Two months ago, I could have accomplished a great deal. Then they still respected me. Now they hate me."

"Ah!" exclaimed the War Minister. "Two months ago, I might have saved the situation myself, if I had only been here then!"

We then discussed the purpose of my trip. I asked for a transfer to a more active part of the front and for a certificate that the battalion was to be run without committees. This certificate I obtained from the War Minister without delay, and still have it in my possession. He also agreed to my first request and promised to look into the matter and issue orders for my transfer.

Kerensky was silent during the conversation. He stood like a ghost, the symbol of once mighty Russia. Four months before he was the idol of the nation. Now almost all had turned against him. As I looked at him, I felt I was in the presence of that immense tragedy which was rending my country into fragments. Something seemed to clutch my throat and shake me. I wanted to cry, to sob. My heart dripped blood for Mother-Russia. What would I not have done to avert that impending catastrophe! How many deaths wouldn't I have died at that moment!

Here was my country drifting toward an abyss. I could see it slide down, down. . . . And here were the heads of the Government powerless, helpless, clinging hopelessly to the doomed ship, despaired of salvation, abandoned, forlorn, stricken. . . .

"God only knows the future—shall we ever meet again?" I addressed the ministers in a stifled voice, bidding them farewell.

Kerensky, livid, motionless, replied in a hoarse whisper:

"Hardly."

PART FOUR TERROR

CHAPTER 16

Bolshevism on Top

I returned to the front. The trains were frightfully crowded, but fortunately I had accommodations in a first-class compartment. At Molodechno I reported to General Valuyev, commander of the Tenth Army, and lunched with the staff. The general was painfully surprised to learn of the punishment I had received at the hands of the soldiers.

"Did they beat *you?*" he asked incredulously, finding it hard to imagine soldiers maltreating Yashka.

"Yes, Gospodin General, they did," I answered.

"But why?"

I told him of the German I had wounded as he came over in the company of several comrades.

"God, what has become of my once glorious army!" he cried out.

As I unfolded to him the remaining phases of the episode, he punctuated my story with exclamations of surprise.

At the end of the meal General Valuyev informed me that I had been promoted to the rank of captain. He pinned an extra star on my epaulets and congratulated me.

I was provided with a car and driven to Corps Headquarters, where I reported to my commanding general. He and the officers of the corps staff were anxious to know of the latest developments in the rear. I conveyed to them the impression made upon me by Kerensky and Verkhovsky two days before.

"Their appearance is witness to the fact that all is lost," I said.

"And how about the transfer?" the general asked. "The battalion is waiting for you to come and take it to a more congenial sector."

I answered that orders would soon arrive for the transfer, and showed the certificate of my right to command without a committee. The general was glad for my sake.

Meanwhile, my girls learned of my arrival. They formed ranks, desiring to give me a cheerful welcome. My presence seemed to have buoyed up their depressed spirits. After commending the women on their reception, I went with them to mess. It was my custom to eat the same food as the girls. Only I seldom ate with them. Before eating, I usually supervised the mess, satisfying myself that everything was plentiful and in good order. I knew from experience that there is nothing like food to keep up a soldier's heart.

Was it the promotion that put me in a happy mood, or my return to the girls, to whom I had grown deeply attached? I don't know. But after dinner it occurred to me that it would be the right thing to let the girls have some fun. So, I suggested a game and my soldiers took it up joyously. As the game proceeded, many men gathered around the circle in which it was going on. They watched anxiously, clearly desirous to play too, but not daring to join in for fear lest I order the girls away. It was a great pleasure to observe how these grown-up children longed to participate in the sports. But I looked indifferent.

Finally, they sent several delegates to express their desire to me. "Gospodin Captain," the men said, not very boldly, "we want to speak to you."

"All right, go ahead!" I answered, "only don't address me as an officer. Call me plain Yashka or Botchkareva."

"May we be allowed to take part in the game?" they asked, encouraged by my words.

"Yes, but on condition that you do not molest my girls; consider them as fellow soldiers only," I declared.

The men swore that they would behave, and the girls were not at all displeased at the new arrangement. They played for two or three hours, and the men kept their pledge. When the game ended they left with quite a different feeling towards me. It was a feeling of respect and even love, instead of their former one of hostility.

The battalion remained in the reserve billets for several days. There developed, as a result of that game, a new attitude on the part of many soldiers toward us women. Companies of them would come over and join the battalion in sports or singing and various entertainments.

The expected order for a transfer did not come promptly. Meanwhile, the time arrived to relieve the corps in the trenches. I determined that we had had enough rest and upon our arrival at the fighting line I put my battalion on regular war footing. I sent out scouting parties, established observation posts and swept No Man's Land with my machine guns and rifles. The Germans were tremendously stirred up. Our own soldiers became excited too, but because of the friendly relations we had established in the rear, they contented themselves with sending delegates and committees to argue the matter with me.

"We have freedom now, you say," I debated. "You insist that you do not want to fight. Very well. I will not ask you to fight the Germans. But you have no right to ask me to act against my convictions. We came here not to fraternise but to war, to kill and get killed. It is my freedom to get killed, if I want to. Then let me fight the Germans at my sector. Let the Germans fight only against the battalion. We will leave you alone, and you leave us alone."

The soldiers reasoned that this was no more than fair and consented to such an arrangement. When they asked me why I was so

YASHKA WITH SOME OF THE BATALLION OF DEATH SOLDIERS

anxious to kill Germans I told them that I wanted to avenge my husband who was slain early in the war. For this invention I had only a slight foundation—a rumour that reached me of the death in battle of Afanasi Botchkarev. Of course, it was an absurd excuse. But I used it previously and afterwards on a number of occasions and it finally gained large circulation and wide credence.

It was exhilarating to be able to do some real fighting again. It is true, we were a mere handful, scarcely two hundred girls. But we raised quite a storm. Our machine guns rattled and No Man's Land was turned from a boulevard for promenading agitators and drunkards into No Man's Land truly. The news spread rapidly along the front of the activity of the Women's Battalion, and, I believe, that for hundreds of *versts* our little sector was the only fighting part of the line. I was naturally very proud of this distinction.

For several days this state of affairs continued. Finally, the Germans became so annoyed that they ordered their artillery to bombard my position. There had not been any artillery fire at our sector for some time and the opening of the big guns caused tremendous excitement. Many of the men were caught in the bombardment and were killed or wounded. The battalion's casualties were four dead and fifteen wounded. The whole corps was aroused to the highest degree and a stormy meeting took place immediately. The men demanded my instant execution.

"She wants war," they cried, "and we want peace. Kill her and make an end of it!"

But the members of the committee and my friends insisted that I acted in accordance with an agreement. "She only engages her own battalion in fighting," my defenders argued, "and leaves us alone. It is not her fault that the German artillery could not find the range quickly and killed some of our comrades."

When word reached me of the indignation and threats of the men I decided to organise an offensive of my own and die fighting. I requested our artillery to answer in kind the enemy's fire. The engagement developed into a regular little battle. We were firing furiously.

While this was going on and the soldiers in the rear were holding the meeting the news arrived of the overthrow of Kerensky and the Bolshevists' victory in Petrograd. It was announced to the men by the chairman and was hailed with such an outburst of enthusiasm that the shouts almost drowned the rattling of the machine guns.

"Peace! Peace!!" thundered through the air.

"We will leave the front now! We are going home! Hurrah for Lenine! Hurrah for Trotzky! Hurrah for Kolontay!"

"Land and freedom! Bread! Down with the *bourgeoisie!*"

As the celebration was attaining new climaxes, the ears of the multitude suddenly caught the sound of the shooting at my sector. The men were struck with frenzy.

"Kill her! Kill them all! We have peace now!" they raved, and stampeded in our direction.

Several girls dashed up to me to tell of the approach of the bloodthirsty mob. Almost simultaneously the commanding general rang up on the field wire.

"Run!" was his first word. "We are all lost. I am escaping myself. Go to Krasnoye Selo!"

I ordered my girls to seize their rifles and whatever belongings they could and run without stopping. To one of the men instructors I gave the direction in which we were to go, asking him to transmit the information to our supply detachment.

Meanwhile the mob was advancing. It encountered in the immediate rear about twenty of my girls, who were engaged in the supporting line.

These twenty girls were lynched by the maddened soldiers.

Four of the instructors, who made an attempt at defending these innocent women, were crushed under the heels of the savage mob.

For fifteen *versts* I and my remaining soldiers ran. Although we could see no sign of pursuers we took no chances. We stopped in the woods beside the road to Molodechno. It was dark. We drank tea for supper and prepared sleeping quarters under the trees. Our supply train came up during the night and was intercepted by one of the sentries.

We were up at four in the morning. I had a connection made with the telephone wire running to Army Headquarters at Molodechno, and talked to the officer in charge, telling him of our approach and asking for dugouts. The officer replied that Molodechno was overflowing with deserters and that it was as dangerous a place for the battalion as the front itself.

But what could I do? I had to go somewhere. I could not very well continue living in the forest. It was an awful situation. We had escaped from one mob, leaving twenty victims in its hands, and were running straight into the arms of another, perhaps even more bloodthirsty. So, we resumed our march. Within three *versts* of Molodechno I led the

YASHKA IN UNIFORM

battalion deep into the woods and left it there with the supply detachment, comprising twenty-five men. I went to Molodechno alone, having decided to go over the ground first and see what was to be done.

Groups of soldiers here and there, in the streets of Molodechno, stopped me with derisive exclamations:

"Ha, there goes the commander of the Women's Battalion. She demands iron discipline. Ha, ha!" they would laugh, turning to me, "What now?"

With smiles and conciliatory answers, I managed to get to headquarters. I made a report to the *commandant* and was assigned some dugouts for the battalion. There were crowds of soldiers everywhere as I walked to the billets. They began to harangue me.

"You were late with your battalion," they said. "It's peace now."

"I am always with you; I am myself a common peasant soldier," I answered. "If you make peace now I will abide by your decision. I am not going to fight against the people."

"Yes, you are for the people now, but where were you before?" they inquired. "You maintained the discipline of the old *régime* in your battalion."

"If I had had no discipline," I answered, "my battalion would have become an institution of shame. You would have derided it yourselves. Women are not like men. It is not customary for women to fight. Imagine what would have become of three hundred girls among thousands of men let loose without supervision and restraint. You will agree with me that I acted right."

The men liked my argument.

"We guess you are right about that," they nodded, and became more sympathetic.

I requested their help in cleaning out the dugouts for my girls, and they gave it cheerfully. I despatched an instructor for the battalion and by night my soldiers were comfortably quartered. Under the protection of sentinels picked from the men attached to my unit we passed a restful night. But our presence offered too good an opportunity for the agitators to let go by. So, in the morning after breakfast, as I started on my way to headquarters, a small group of insolent soldiers, not more than ten in number, cut my path, heaping insults upon me.

In a few minutes the ten ruffians were increased to twenty, thirty, fifty, a hundred. I tried to parry their scoffs and threats, but made no headway. In ten minutes, I was almost surrounded by several hundred of these uniformed rogues.

"What do you want with me?" I cried out, losing patience.

"We want to disband your battalion. We want you to surrender all the rifles to us."

Now there can hardly be a greater dishonour for a soldier than to surrender his arms without a fight. However, my girls knew that I hated to lose my life at the hands of a mob. When they heard of the demand of the crowd they all came out, with rifles in hand.

I made a couple of efforts to argue, but it was apparent that the men came with the purpose fixed in their minds by propagandists. They would not recede and finally cut me short by giving me three minutes to decide. One of the ringleaders stood there, with a watch in hand, counting the time. Those were indescribably agonising moments.

"I would rather advance against an entire German Army than surrender arms to these Bolshevik scoundrels," I thought. "But it is not my life only that is at stake. Everything is lost anyhow. They say that peace has been declared already. Have I a right to play with the lives of my girls? But, Holy Mother, how can I, a soldier true to my oath and loyal to my country, order the surrender of my battalion's arms without a fight?"

The three minutes were up. I had arrived at no decision. Still I mounted the speaker's bench. There was a general quiet. The crowd of course expected my capitulation. My girls waited in great tension for their *Natchalnik's* orders. My heart throbbed violently as my mind still groped for a solution.

"Shoot!" I suddenly shouted at the top of my voice to the girls.

The men were so surprised that for a moment they remained petrified. They were unarmed.

A volley from two hundred rifles went up into the air. The crowd dispersed in all directions. My order almost drove the men insane with rage. They ran for their barracks after weapons, threatening to return and wipe us all out.

The real crisis now arose. There was no question that the mob would return, several times stronger, and tear us to pieces. A decision had to be arrived at and carried out instantly. It would take not more than ten minutes for the men to come back. If we did not escape it was certain death.

"In five minutes, the battalion shall be ready to march!" I thundered. I sent one of my instructors to the barracks, to mix with the crowd, and later report to me in the woods on the mob's activity. Simultaneously I directed the supply detachment to follow the road in the direction of Krasnoye Selo. Then I called for a volunteer from among the instructors to take care of our battle flag under oath that he would defend it to his death. Accompanied by three other instructors, he was sent ahead with the flag.

All this was done in less than five minutes. It was no ordinary feat for a military unit to form in full marching formation in that space of time. But my girls did it. I sent one squad after another into the woods, leaving with the last squad myself.

I had as our destination a certain clearing in the woods, seven *versts* deep. This distance we covered at a neck-breaking pace. I knew that the infuriated men would take the road in pursuing us and I ordered the battalion through the thick of the woods. There were few of us who did not trip on the way several times. Our uniforms were torn by thorns and brambles, and many of us had lacerated legs and arms. There was little time for dressing the wounds.

A couple of hours later, after reaching the clearing, we heard a distant whistle, the signal of the instructor I had left behind. He was hilarious over his experience, and in spite of our precarious position we enjoyed his story immensely.

The mob, it appeared, returned, as we had anticipated, to our billets, armed to the teeth. It was in a ferocious mood and rushed into the dugouts. The men were thunderstruck upon discovering that the dugouts were deserted! They ran about like madmen, scouring the neighbourhood, but there was no sign of us. They could not realise that in such a brief space of time the battalion had been marched away with all the equipment.

"The witch!" they shouted. "She must have spirited them away."

But this did not seem a plausible explanation to the cooler heads. They telephoned to headquarters, but received an answer of complete astonishment. Nobody there knew of my sudden withdrawal. The mob started along the road to Krasnoye Selo and soon overtook my supply wagons, which were in charge of old soldiers. These said that they had received orders to leave for Krasnoye, and they left ignorant of the movements of the battalion. The mob decided that we were on the same road and sent a couple of horsemen to overtake us. The horsemen, of course, returned with empty hands.

"She is a witch!" many soldiers shook their heads with superstitious awe.

Camping in the Woods

"A witch, veritably!" confirmed others, with uneasiness.

The four men with our flag lost their way in the woods and seeing that they did not come up, I sent out about twenty girls and instructors to look for them. They were finally discovered. Next, we had to get in touch with the supply wagons, and managed to bring them to our camp. Once this was accomplished we were fairly well established behind the protection of the thickets. There was only one question confronting us: How to get away in safety.

Molodechno was not to be considered. The next station was also a dangerous place, as our pursuers had warned the garrison there of our approach and requested that we be dealt with swiftly. The prospects were far from cheerful. I decided to get into secret communication, through the instructors, with the *commandant* of Molodechno.

We camped in the forest for a couple of days, till the *commandant* found an opportunity to slip out and come to see us. We held a conference, seeking a way out of the dilemma.

It was agreed upon that the career of the battalion was ended and nothing remained but to disband it. The problem was, how? The *commandant* suggested that he procure women's garments for the girls and let them return home.

The plan did not strike me as practical. It was hardly possible to obtain nearly two hundred costumes for us in a day or two. It might, therefore, consume a couple of weeks to disband the battalion, which would not be advisable. I proposed a different scheme, namely, to discharge the girls singly and direct them to a score of scattered stations and villages. This plan was adopted, as it did not seem difficult for individual members of the Battalion to board trains or obtain vehicles in the neighbouring villages and get away.

It took a day or so for the *commandant* to provide the necessary documents and funds for all the girls. Then the leaving began. Every ten or fifteen minutes a girl was sent away, now in one direction, now in the opposite. It was a pitiful finale to an heroic chapter in the history of Russian womanhood. The battalion had struggled gallantly to stem the tide of destruction and ignorance. But the tide was too mighty. It had swamped all that was good and noble in Russia. Russia herself seemed wrecked forever in that maelstrom of unbridled passions. One did not want to live. There remained only the honour and satisfaction of going down with all that had been upright in the country. Everything seemed upside down. There was no friendship, only hatred. The unselfishness of the days when *Tsarism* was overthrown, now, after the fall of Kerensky, had given way to a wave of greed and revenge. Every soldier, every peasant and workman, saw red. They all hunted phantom *bourgeois*, bloodsuckers, exploiters. When freedom was first born there was universal brotherhood and joy. Now intolerance and petty covetousness reigned supreme.

As I kissed my girls goodbye, exchanging blessings, my heart quivered with emotion. What had I not hoped from this battalion! But as I searched my soul I could find little to regret. I had done my duty by my country. Perhaps it was too rash for me to imagine that this handful of women could save the army from disruption. And yet, I was not alone in that expectation. There was a time when even Rodzianko believed likewise, and Brusilov and Kerensky thought that self-sacrificing women would shame the men. But the men knew no shame.

My girls had departed. I alone remained of the battalion, with several of the instructors. In the evening I made my way to the road where an automobile was waiting to smuggle me away. The *commandant* had arranged for me to go to Petrograd under the personal convoy of two members of the Army Committee. They were to join me at the train. The peril lay in the journey to the station. Hidden on the bottom of the car, I was driven to the railway, where the two committeemen took me under their protection. I had decided to go home, to the village of Tutalsk, near Tomsk, where my people had moved during the war.

CHAPTER 17

Facing Lenine and Trotzky

Petrograd seemed populated by Red Guards. One could not make a step without encountering one. They kept a strict watch over the station and all the incoming and outgoing trains. My escorts left me on the station platform, as they were to return to the front immediately.

I had hardly emerged from the station, intending to look for a cabman, when a Red Guard commissary, accompanied by a private with a naked sabre, stopped me with the polite query:

"Madame Botchkareva?"

"Yes."

"Will you come with me, please?" he suggested.

"Where?" I asked.

"To the Smolny Institute."

"But why?"

"Because I have orders to detain all officers returning from the front," he replied.

"But I am only going home!" I tried to argue.

"Yes, I understand. But as an officer you will also understand that I must obey orders. They will probably release you."

He hailed a cabman and we drove to the Smolny Institute, the seat of the Bolshevik Government. It impressed me as a heavily beleaguered castle. There were armed sentries everywhere. Accompanied by Red Guards, I was led inside. There were guards at every desk. I was taken before a sailor. He was very rough and brusque.

"Where are you going?" he demanded curtly.

"I am going home, to a village near Tomsk," I replied.

"Then why are you armed?" he sneered.

"Because I am an officer, and this is my uniform," I answered.

He blazed up.

"An officer, eh? You will be an officer no more. Give me that pistol and sabre!" he ordered.

The arms were those given to me at the consecration of the battalion's flag. I prized them too much to hand them over like that to this rogue of a sailor, and refused his demand. He grew furious. It would have been futile to resist as the room was full of Red Guards. I declared that if he wanted my arms he could take them, but I would never surrender them myself.

He violently tore the pistol and sabre from me and pronounced me under arrest. There was a dark cellar in the Institute which was used as a place of detention, and I was sent down there and locked up. I was hungry but received no answer to all my calls and remained in the hole till the following morning. As soon as I was brought upstairs I began to demand my arms. The various chiefs, however, remained deaf to my pleas.

I was informed that I would be taken before Lenine and Trotzky, and was soon led into a large, light room where two men of contrasting appearance sat, apparently expecting my entrance. One had a typical Russian face. The other looked Jewish. The first was Nikolai Lenine, the second Leon Trotzky. Both arose as I stepped in and walked toward me a few steps, stretching out their hands and greeting me courteously.

Lenine apologised for my arrest, explaining that he had learned of it only that morning. Inviting me to a seat, the two Bolshevik chiefs complimented me upon my record of service and courage, and began to sketch to me the era of happiness that they sought to bring upon Russia. They talked simply, smoothly and very beautifully. It was for the common people, the slaving masses, the under-dog, that they were fighting. They wanted justice for all. Wasn't I of the labouring class myself? Yes, I was. Wouldn't I join them and cooperate with their party in bringing happiness to the oppressed peasant and workman? They wanted peasant women like myself; they appreciated such deeply.

"You will bring Russia not to happiness but to ruin," I said.

"Why?" they asked. "We seek only what is good and right. The people are with us. You saw for yourself that the army is behind us."

"I will tell you why," I replied. "I have no objection to your beautiful plans for the future of Russia. But as for the immediate situation, if you take the soldiers away from the front, you are destroying the country," I argued.

"But we want no war. We are going to conclude peace," the two leaders replied.

"How can you conclude peace without soldiers at the front? You are demobilising the army already. You have got to make peace first and then let the men go home. I myself want peace, but if I were in the trenches I would never leave before peace had been signed. What you are doing will ruin Russia."

"We are sending the soldiers away because the Germans will not advance against us anyhow. They do not want to fight either," was the reply.

It irritated me, this view of the Germans held by the men who now ran the government of my country.

"You don't know the Germans!" I cried out. "We have lost so many lives in this war, and now you would give everything away without a struggle! You don't know war! Take the soldiers away from the front and the Germans will come and grab everything within reach. This is war. I am a soldier and I know. But you don't. Why did you take it upon yourselves to rule the country? You will ruin it!" I exclaimed in anguish.

Lenine and Trotzky laughed. I could see the irony in their eyes. They were learned and worldly. They had written books and travelled in foreign lands. And who was I? An illiterate Russian peasant woman. My lecture amused them undoubtedly. They smiled condescendingly at my suggestion that they did not know what war was in reality.

I rejected their proposal to cooperate with them and asked if I were free to leave. One of them rang a bell and a Red Guard entered.

He was requested to accompany me out of the room and to provide me with a passport and a free ticket to Tomsk. Before leaving I asked for my arms but was refused. I explained that they were partly of gold and given to me on an occasion that rendered them almost priceless to me. They answered that I would receive them back as soon as order was restored. Of course, I never got them back.

I left the room without bidding goodbye. In the next room I was given a passport and proceeded by tramcar to the station. I decided not to tarry in Petrograd and to depart without even seeing any of my friends. On the way I was recognised everywhere, but was allowed to proceed unmolested. The same evening, I boarded one of the three cars attached to a train that went by the way of Vologda and Tcheliabinsk directly to Irkutsk. I was going home. With me I had some two thousand *rubles*, saved during my command of the battalion, when I received a salary of four hundred *rubles* a month.

The train was over-crowded with returning soldiers, almost all fervid Bolsheviks. I remained in the compartment for eight days, leaving it only occasionally at night. I sent a passenger companion out, at stations, to buy food. As we neared Tcheliabinsk, at the end of the eight days, the crowd had thinned out and I thought I would be safe in going out on the platform and getting off at the great terminal for a little walk. No sooner had I reached the platform when I was recognised by some soldiers.

"Ah, look who is here!" one exclaimed.

"It's Botchkareva! The harlot!" a couple of others echoed.

"She ought to be killed!" shouted somebody.

"Why?" I turned on them. "What harm have I done to you? Ah, you fools, fools!"

The train slowed down, approaching the station. I had scarcely turned my head away from the insolent fellows, when I was suddenly lifted by two pairs of arms, swung back and forth, once, twice, three times, and thrown off the moving train.

Fortunately, the momentum of the swinging was so great that I was thrown across the parallel tracks and landed in a bank of snow piled along the railroad. It was the end of November, 1917. It was all so sudden that the laughter of the brutes back of me still rang in my ears as I became conscious of pain in my right knee.

The train was halted before pulling into the station. In a few moments there was a big crowd around me, of passengers, railway officials and others. All were indignant at the outlawry of the soldiers. The *com-*

mandant of the station and members of the local committee hurried to the place. I was placed on a stretcher and taken to the hospital on the grounds. It was found that I had a dislocated knee and my leg was bandaged. I then declared that I desired to continue the journey and I was given a berth in a hospital coach, attached to a train going east. There were attendants and a medical assistant on the car.

My injured leg pained more and more as I proceeded homeward. It began to swell and the medical assistant telegraphed to the station-master of Tutalsk, the village in which my folks now lived, to provide a stretcher for me.

My sister, Arina, was employed at the station as attendant at the tea-kettle, which is always kept boiling at Russian railway stations. It was this employment of hers that had caused the family to move to Tutalsk from Tomsk, where they had no means of livelihood whatever. When the message from the interne in charge of the car reached my sister and through her my parents, there was an outburst of lamentation. It was three years since they had seen their Marusia and now she was apparently being brought to them on her death-bed!

On the fourth day of the journey from Tcheliabinsk the train stopped at Tutalsk. My leg was badly swollen and was as heavy as a log. The pains were agonizing. My face was pallid.

A stretcher was prepared for me at the station. My sisters, my mother and father and the station-master were at the door of the coach when I was carried out. My mother shrieked heartrendingly, "My Marusia! My Manka!" clasped her hands toward heaven and threw herself full length on me, mourning over me as if I were ready for burial.

Her prodigal daughter had returned, my mother wailed, but in what condition! She thought that I must have been wounded and asked to be sent home to die. I could not talk. I could only grasp her bony arms as a gush of tears and sobs choked my throat. Everybody was crying, my sisters calling me by caressing names, my white and bent father standing over me, and even the strange station-master. . . .

I became hysterical and the doctor was sent for. He had me removed home immediately, promising in response to my mother's pleas to do everything in his power for me. I remained ill for a month, passing Christmas and meeting the New Year, 1918, in bed.

The two thousand *rubles* I had saved I gave to my parents. But this sum, considered a fortune before the war, was barely sufficient for a few months' living. It cost nearly a hundred *rubles* to buy a pair of slippers for my youngest sister, Nadia, who went barefoot! It cost almost twice as much to buy her a second-hand jacket at the Tomsk *tolkutchka*. (Market of second-hand articles.) Manufactured goods sold at a premium when they were to be had, but it was much more difficult to find what one needed than to pay an exorbitant price for it. There was plenty of flour in the country. But the peasants would not sell it cheaply because they could get nothing in town for less than fifty or a hundred times its former price. The result was that flour sold at two *rubles* a pound. One can see how far two thousand *rubles* could carry one in Russia.

Tutalsk had also been swept by the hurricane of Bolshevism. There were many soldiers who had returned from the front, imbued with Bolshevik teachings. Just before my arrival the newly-made heretics even burned the village church, to the great horror of the older inhabitants. It was not an unusual case; it was typical of the time. Hundreds of thousands of blinded youths had returned from the trenches with the passion to destroy, to tear down everything that had existed before, the old system of government, the church, nay, God Himself, all in preparation for the new order of life they were going to erect.

But one institution—the scourge of the nation—they failed to wipe out. They did more. They resurrected it. The *Tsar* had abolished vodka. The prohibition was continued in force by the new regime, but only on paper. Nearly every returned soldier took to distilling vodka at home, and the old plague of the country was in sway again, contributing to the building of the Bolsheviki's new world.

Every town and village had its committee or Soviet, which was supposed to carry out orders from the Central Government. An order was issued to confiscate all articles of gold and silver. Committees searched every house for such belongings. There was, also, or was supposed to be, an order taxing furniture and clothes. When the arbitrarily demanded taxes were not paid, the furniture and clothes were taken away.

In the towns it was the townsmen who suffered, in the villages the peasants, all under the pretext of confiscating the riches of the bourgeoisie. It was sufficient for a peasant to buy a new overcoat, perhaps with his last savings, to be marked an exploiter and lose his precious garment. The peculiar thing about such cases was the fact that the confiscated article would almost invariably appear on the back of one of the Bolshevik ringleaders. It was simple looting, and the methods were of unadulterated terror, practised mostly by the returned soldiers.

I received some letters at Tutalsk. One was from my adjutant, Princess Tatuyeva, who had arrived safely in Tiflis, her home town.

One morning I went to the post office to ask for mail.

"There goes Botchkareva!" I heard a man cry out.

"Ah, Botchkareva! She is for the old *régime!*" another fellow replied, apparently one of the Bolshevik soldiers.

There were several of them and they flung threats and insults at me. I did not reply but returned home with a heavy heart. Even in my own town I was not safe.

"My Lord," I prayed, "what has come over the Russian people? Is this my reward for the sacrifices I have made for my country?"

I resolved not to leave the house again. Surely this craze would not last long, I thought. I spent most of the day reading the Bible and praying to Heaven for the awakening and enlightenment of my people.

On the 7th of January, 1918, I received a telegram from Petrograd, signed by General X. It read:

Come. You are needed.

The same day I bought a ticket for the capital, parted from my folks and started out. I removed the epaulets of my uniform, thus appearing in the garb of a private.

About this time the Germans, to the profound shock of the revolutionary masses, began their lightning-like advance into Russia. It had an almost miraculous effect on the Bolshevik followers. The train was as usual packed with soldiers, but there was a different air about their faces and conversation. All the *braggadocio* had been knocked out of them by the enemy's action. They had been lulled into the sweet belief that peace had come and that a golden age was about to open for them. They could not reconcile that with the swift movement of the *Kaiser's* soldiers toward Petrograd and Moscow.

It was refreshing, exhilarating to listen to some of the men.

"We have been sold out!" one heard here and there.

"We were told that the German soldiers would not advance if we left the front," was another frequent expression.

"It is not the common people, it is the German *bourgeoisie* that is fighting us now," was an argument ordinarily given in answer to the first opinions, "and there is nothing to be afraid of. There will soon be a revolution in Germany."

"Who knows," some would doubtfully remark, "but what Lenine and Trotzky have delivered us into the hands of the accursed Germans?"

There were always delegates from local committees going somewhere, and they talked to the soldiers, answering questions and explaining things. They could not very well explain away the German treachery, but they held out the promise of a revolution in Germany due almost any day. The men listened but were not swept off their feet by the assurances of the agitators. One felt that they were still groping in the dark, although the light was dawning on their minds. The awakening could not be long postponed.

I had a safe and comfortable journey to Petrograd. Nobody molested me, nobody threatened my life. I arrived at the capital on the 18th of January. The station was not as beleaguered as two months previous. Red Guards were not in such evidence in the streets, which appeared more normal. I went to one of my former patronesses and learned of the terror in which the capital lived.

The following day I called on General X, who greeted me cordially. Kiev, he told me, had just been captured by the Germans. They were threatening Petrograd and the opposition of the Red Guards would not prevent or even halt for a day its capture if the Germans were bent upon it.

Red Terror was rampant in the city. The river was full of corpses of slain and lynched officers. Those who were alive were in an awful condition, in fear of showing themselves in public because of the mob spirit, and therefore on the verge of death from starvation. Even more harrowing was the situation of the country. It was falling into the hands of the enemy so rapidly that some kind of immediate action was imperative.

A secret meeting of officers and sympathizers had been held at which it was decided to get in touch with General Kornilov, who was reported as operating in the Don region. There were so many conflicting reports concerning Kornilov that it had been suggested that a courier be sent to him to find out definitely his plans and condition. After a thorough canvass, General X proposed that I, as a woman, was the only person that could possibly get through the Bolshevik lines and reach Kornilov. Would I go?

"I would not join the officers here or Kornilov in the south to wage warfare against my own people," I replied. "I can't do it because every Russian is dear to my heart, whether he be a Bolshevik, a Menshevik, or Red Guard. But I will take it upon myself to get to Kornilov, for your as well as for my own information."

It was agreed that I dress as a Sister of Mercy. A costume was obtained for me, and I put it on over my uniform. My soldier's cap I tucked away in a back pocket and put on the sister's regulation headpiece, which showed only my eyes, nose, mouth and cheeks, and made me look like a matron of about forty-five.

A passport, bearing the name of Alexandra Leontievna Smirnova, was furnished to me and this was to be my name on the way. As I wore army boots there was no danger of my trousers showing under the skirt. I took with me a letter from Princess Tatuyeva, in which she invited me to visit her in her Caucasus home. A direct ticket from Petrograd to Kislovodsk, a Caucasian resort, within several hundred *versts* of Kornilov's whereabouts, was given me to be used only in an emergency. It was agreed that in case of danger I should discard my garb of a Sister of Mercy, appear as my real self, and claim, with the aid of the emergency ticket to Kislovodsk and the letter from Princess Tatuyeva, that I was on my way to take a cure at the resort. In addition, I was, of course, provided with money for expenses.

It was great fun suddenly to lose one's identity and appear as a complete stranger. I was no longer Maria Botchkareva, but Alexandra Smirnova. And as I glanced at myself in the mirror it seemed even to my own eyes that I had been reincarnated from a soldier into a Sister of Mercy.

Upon leaving Petrograd my destination was Nikitino, a station which one would ordinarily pass on the way to Kislovodsk. Nobody recognised me on the train. Sometimes a soldier asked:

"Where are you going, little sister?"

"Home, to Kislovodsk," was my usual answer.

The next question would be about the service I had seen at the front, and the sectors at which I worked. I would reply with facts from my actual experience as a soldier. There was nothing strange about a Sister of Mercy returning home, and as I preferred silence and seclusion to conversation, I reached Nikitino, at the end of several days, without any trouble.

From Nikitino all trains were switched by the authorities to other lines and sent to their destination by roundabout routes. The road running direct south from there was used for military purposes exclusively by the Bolshevik forces fighting Kornilov. Thirty *versts* beyond, at Zverevo, the so-called front began. Private passengers were therefore not allowed to go to Zverevo.

One could see that vast preparations were being made for a campaign against General Kornilov. There were many ammunition trains and large numbers of men concentrated there waiting transportation. There was apparently no lack of money. The discipline was one of iron, reminding one of the early days of the war. There was order everywhere.

The first problem confronting me was how to get to Zverevo. I went to the *commandant* of the station, complained that I was penniless, that I could not wait indefinitely for the end of the fighting to return home to Kislovodsk and urgently begged him to advise me what to do. I made such an appeal to him that he finally said:

"A munition train is just about to leave for Zverevo. Come, board it and go there. Perhaps they will pass you through the lines at the front. There is a second-class coach attached to the train."

He led me to the car, in which were only five soldiers, those in charge of the train. He introduced me to one of them, the chief, as a stranded Sister of Mercy and asked for their indulgence. I thanked the obliging *commandant* profusely and from the bottom of my heart.

The train moved out, and although satisfied with the first step I was by no means cheerful as to my prospects in Zverevo, the Bolshevik war zone. The head of the party sat down opposite me. He was an unclean, ugly *moujik*. I did not encourage him to engage me in conversation, but he evidently was totally unaware of my feelings in the matter.

After the preliminary questions, he expressed his surprise that I should have chosen such an inopportune moment to go to Kislovodsk.

"But my mother is ill there," I lied, "perhaps she is dying now. It broke her heart when I went to the front."

"Ah, that's different," he declared, moving over to my side. "They will pass you in that case."

From an expression of sympathy, it was not difficult for him to make an effort at flirtation. He moved up closer and even touched my arm. It was a delicate situation. I could not well afford to antagonise him, so I warded off his advances with a smile and a promising look. He treated me to a good meal, at which the conversation turned to general conditions. He was, of course, a rabid Bolshevik and a savage opponent of Kornilov and all officers. My part in the conversation was confined to brief expressions of acquiescence. Suddenly he asked:

"Have you heard of the Women's Death Battalion?"

My heart thumped violently.

"What battalion did you say?" I asked with an air of ignorance.

"Why, Botchkareva's Battalion!" he replied in a positive voice.

"Botchkareva's?" I asked reminiscently. "Oh, sure, Botchkareva, yes, I heard about her."

"The ——!She is a *Kornilovka!*" he exclaimed. "She is for the old *régime.*"

"How do you know?" I asked. "I thought she was non-partisan."

"We know them all, the counter-revolutionists! She is one of them," my companion declared emphatically.

"Well, there is no more Battalion of Death anyhow, and Botchkareva has apparently vanished," I suggested.

"Yes, we know how they vanish. Many of them have vanished like that. Kornilov had vanished too. Then they all pop up here and there and cause trouble," he enlightened me.

"Now what would you do to her if she showed up here?" I dared to inquire.

"Kill her. She would never leave here alive, you can bet," he assured me. "We have the photographs of all the leading counter-revolutionaries, so that they can't hide their identities if caught."

The conversation took a more satisfactory turn for me. I learned all about the plans of the Bolshevik force against Kornilov. The arrival of the train at Zverevo put an end to my association with the fellow. I thanked him very much for all his favours to me.

"You know, sister," he unexpectedly addressed me before parting, "I like you. Will you marry me?"

This I didn't anticipate. It rather took me aback. He was such an awful-looking, dirty creature, and the proposal was so ludicrous that it was with difficulty that I mastered my desire to laugh. This was no place for fun-making, however.

"Yes, with pleasure," I responded to his offer, with as much graciousness as I could command, "but after I see my mother."

He gave me his address and asked me to write to him, which I promised. Perhaps he is still waiting for a letter from me.

I left him at the train and went toward the station. There were Red Guards, sailors, soldiers, even Cossacks who had joined the Bolsheviki, on the platform and inside. But there were no private citizens in sight. I sat down in a corner and waited. Taken for a nurse attached to the Bolshevik Army, I was not molested. An hour, two, three, passed and still I could find no opening to proceed to my destination. A civilian, who somehow found himself in the station, was placed under arrest

207

before my eyes without any preliminaries. I, therefore, preferred to sit quietly in my corner than move about.

Finally, a pleasant-looking young soldier became interested in me. He walked up and asked:

"Why are you waiting here, sister?"

"I am waiting for a comrade," I answered.

"What is his name?" he inquired, interested.

"Oh, that is a secret," I replied in an intriguing manner.

He sat down near me, questioning if I had worked at the front. I said that unfortunately I had been detailed only to hospitals in the rear.

"Why was that man arrested?" I ventured to ask.

"Because he had no papers from the Soviet," was the reply. "He will be shot immediately."

"Do you execute everybody who has no papers?" I wanted to know.

"Everybody, without distinction."

"Even women?" I inquired.

"Yes, even women," came in answer. "This is a war zone."

"Holy Mother!" I exclaimed with horror. "How terrible! You slay them all, ah? Without a trial even?"

"There is little time for trials here. Once fallen here, there is no escape. Our firing squads finish all suspects on the spot," he informed me kindly. "Come, you want to see the execution grounds right near here?"

I followed him reluctantly. Several hundred feet away from the station we stopped. I could not go further. The field in front of us was covered with scores of mangled, half-naked corpses. It made my flesh creep.

"There are about two hundred of them here, mostly officers who had joined or sought to join Kornilov," he explained. I could not help shivering. The dreadful scene nearly shattered my nerves and I had to strain all my energies not to collapse.

"Ah, you women, women," my escort nodded sympathetically. "You are all weak. You don't know what war is. Still," he admitted, "there are some who can compare with men. Take Botchkareva, for instance, she would not shudder at sights like this."

"Who is she, this Botchkareva?" I was curious.

"Haven't you heard of her?" he asked in surprise. "Why, she was a soldier of the old *régime* and organised the Women's Battalion of Death. She is for Kornilov and the *bourgeoisie*. They gave her an officer's rank and bought her over to their side, although she is of peasant blood."

It was all very interesting, this theory of my corruption. I had heard it before, but not in such clear-cut form. At the same time the picture of those mangled bodies occupied my vision, and the thought rankled in my mind of the treacherous Bolsheviki who had opposed capital punishment in the war against Germany but introduced it in a most beastly fashion in the war against their own brothers.

I then told my friend of the trouble in which I found myself, that I was moneyless, had to get home to Kislovodsk and did not know how to get through the front. He explained to me that the so-called front was not a continuous line but a series of posts, maintained on this side by the Bolsheviki and on the opposite side by Kornilov.

"Sometimes," he added, "the peasants of the neighbouring villages are allowed by both sides to pass through to Novotcherkask, Kornilov's headquarters. If you take that road," and he pointed at it, "you will get to a village four *versts* from here. One of the peasants may agree to carry you across."

I thanked him for the valuable information, and we parted friends. The walk to the village was uneventful. At the edge of it I saw an old *moujik* working outside of his cabin. There was a stable and horses on the grounds.

"Good day, *diedushka!*" (Grandfather!) I greeted the old man.

"Good day, little sister," he answered.

"Would you drive me to the city?" I asked.

"Great God! How is it possible? The Bolsheviks are warring before the city, and they don't pass anybody," he said.

"But people do go sometimes, don't they?"

"Yes, sometimes they do."

"Well, I will give you fifty *rubles* for driving me to the city," I offered.

The *moujik* scratched his neck, reconsidering the matter.

"But aren't you a *politichkaf*" (woman political) he inquired cautiously.

"No," I assured him, "I am not."

He went into the cabin to talk it over with his *baba*. It was a lucrative job and her consent was apparently quickly obtained, for he soon returned and said:

"All right, we will go. Come into the house. We will have tea and something to eat."

The invitation was welcome indeed, as I had grown hungry during my long wait at the station and the walk to the village. When we finished with the samovar and lunch and the peasant harnessed his horse, I asked for a large apron, which I put on top of my clothes. I then asked for the *baba's* winter shawl and wrapped my head and shoulders, almost covering my face completely, so that I no longer appeared as a Sister of Mercy, but a *baba* of the neighbourhood.

Praying to God for a safe passage, I seated myself in the vehicle. The horse started off along the road.

The Bolshevik front was still ahead of me. But I was making progress. . . . .

CHAPTER 18

Caught in a Bolshevik Death-Trap

What shall I say to the guards?" the *moujik* asked me as we approached the front positions.

"Tell them that you are carrying your sick *baba* to a hospital in the city, as she is suffering from high fever," I answered, requesting him to wrap me in the huge fur overcoat that was under him. I was warm enough without it, but I thought that it would raise my temperature even more, and was not wrong. Under all the covers I resembled more a heap than a human form. When the battle positions were reached I began to moan as if in pain.

"Where are you going?" I heard a voice ask my driver sharply, as the horse stopped.

"To a hospital in the city," was the answer.

"What are you carrying?"

"My *baba*. She is dying. I am taking her to a doctor," the peasant replied. Here I groaned louder than ever. I was suffocating. My heart hammered from fear of sudden exposure and discovery. Every particle of time seemed an age.

The sentry who halted us apparently talked the case over with some of his comrades, to the accompaniment of my exuberant moans. Without uncovering my face, he issued a pass to the *moujik*.

My heart thumped with joy as the horse started off at a rapid pace. For a while I still held my breath, hardly believing my senses that I had left Bolshevik territory behind me with so little difficulty.

After some time, we arrived at the Kornilov front. The posts along it were held by officers, of whom his force consisted almost exclusively. At one such post we were stopped by a commanding "Halt!"

The driver was starting to rehearse the yarn about his feverish *baba* when I surprised him by throwing off the fur topcoat, then the shawl, and jumping out of the vehicle, issuing a deep sigh of relief. I could not help laughing.

The *moujik* must have thought me mad at first. The officers at the post could not understand it either.

"What the devil!" a couple of them muttered under their breath. I proceeded very coolly to pay out the fifty *rubles* to the peasant, discharging him there, to his great amazement.

"I will get to the city from here all right," I informed him.

"Like hell you will!" the officer in charge blurted out. "Who are you?"

"Why, can't you see, I am a Sister of Mercy," I answered testily.

"Where are you going?"

"I am going to see General Kornilov," I giggled.

The officers were getting furious.

"You will not go a step further," the chief ordered.

"Oh, yes, I will too," I announced emphatically.

"You are arrested!" the examiner commanded.

I broke out in a fit of laughter, bringing the officers to white anger. "Don't you recognize me? I am Botchkareva," and I threw off the head-dress of the Sister of Mercy. The officers gasped, immediately crowding around me with congratulations and hand-shakes. Kornilov was notified by telephone of my arrival and the joke I had played on the sentries.

"How do you do, little sister?" he greeted me laughingly when I was brought to his headquarters. My arrival and the way I got through the lines amused him very much. He looked very thin and somewhat aged, but as energetic as ever.

I reported to him that I was sent from Petrograd by General X and other officers, for the purpose of ascertaining his plans and exact condition. I also informed him that the Bolsheviki were making big preparations for an attack against him, that I had seen eleven cars with ammunition at Zverevo, and that the blow was due in a couple of days.

Kornilov replied that he knew of the impending offensive and that his condition was precarious. He had no money and no food, while the Bolsheviki were amply supplied with both. His soldiers were deserting him one by one. He was cut off from his friends and surrounded by enemies.

"Did you wish to remain with me and join my force?" he asked me.

"No," I said, "I could not fight against my own people. The Russian soldier is dear to me, although he has been led astray for the present."

"It is also very hard for me to fight the boys that I loved so much," he declared. "But they have turned beasts now. We are fighting for our lives, for our uniforms. The life of every Russian officer is at the mercy of the mob. It is a question of organising for self-defence. One can expect to do little for the country, if the Bolsheviks are waging civil war when the Germans are advancing into Russia. This is a time for peace and union among all classes. It is a time for presenting a united front to the enemy of the motherland.

But Bolshevism has clouded the minds of the people. What is necessary, therefore, is to enlighten the masses. We can't hope to enlighten them by fighting. If it were possible to organise a counterpropaganda, to convince the Russian peasants that the Bolsheviks are speeding our country to complete destruction, then they would rise and put an end to Lenine and Trotzky, elect a new government, and drive the Germans out of Russia. This is the only solution that I can see, unless the Allies aid us in conciliating our soldiers and re-establishing a front against Germany."

This, in substance, was Kornilov's view of conditions in Russia, when I saw him in February, 1918. I remained only one day at his headquarters. From conversations with the men attached to his staff, I learned that Kornilov's force comprised only about three thousand fighters. The Bolshevik army opposing it was perhaps twenty times its strength. I left Novotcherkask in the evening, after an affectionate parting from Kornilov. He kissed me farewell and I wished him success for the good of the country. But there was no success in prospect. We both knew it only too well. A heavy darkness had settled on Russia, stifling all that was still noble and righteous.

Encouraged by my success in reaching there, I determined to return by myself. I was taken to the battle positions by a group of officers, and from there, accompanied by their blessings, I started out through the battle zone alone. I crawled on all fours as if through No Man's Land, making a couple of *versts* without any mishap. The experience gained at the front came in handy. I scented the approach of a patrol and hid just in time to escape being observed. The patrol turned out to be of Kornilov's force, but I remained hidden. After some more crawling I caught the sound of voices coming from the direction of a coal mine and judged the place to be one of the front positions.

Exercising extreme caution, I managed to pass beyond it safely. Some distance away, dimly standing out against the horizon, was a wood.

A Bolshevik force got wind of the patrol I had encountered and went out to capture it by a flank operation. I decided to conceal myself behind a pile of coal and wait till quiet was restored. On my right and left were dumps of coal, too.

Hugging the chunks of coal, I breathlessly awaited the outcome of the manoeuvre. In a short while the Bolsheviks returned with their prey. They had captured the patrol! There were twenty captives, fifteen officers and five cadets, I learned. They were led to a place only a score or so feet away from the coal pile that hid me.

The hundred Bolshevik soldiers surrounded the officers, cursed them, beat them with the butts of their rifles, tore off their epaulets and handled them like dogs. The five youthful cadets must have suddenly discovered an opportunity to slip away, for they dashed off a few minutes afterwards. But they failed to escape. They were caught within several hundred feet and brought back.

The Bolshevik soldiers then decided to gouge out the eyes of the five youths in punishment for their attempt to run away. Each of the marked victims was held by a couple of men in such a position as to allow the bloody torturers to do their frightful work. In all my experiences of horror this was the most horrible crime I ever witnessed.

One of the officers could not contain himself and shrieked:

"Murderers! Beasts! Kill me!"

He was struck with a bayonet, but only wounded. All the fifteen officers begged to be killed right there. But their request would not be granted.

"You have to be taken before the staff first," was the answer. Soon they were led away.

The five martyrs were left to expire in agony where they were.

My heart was petrified. My blood congealed. I thought I was going insane, that in a second I would not be able to control myself and would jump out, inviting death or perhaps similar torture.

I finally collected strength to turn about and crawl away, in the opposite direction, toward the woods. At a distance of several hundred feet from the forest it seemed to me safe to rise and run for it. But I was noticed from the mine.

"A spy!" went up in a chorus from several throats, and a number of soldiers were after me, shooting as they ran.

Nearer and nearer the pursuers came. I raced faster than I ever did before in my life. Within another hundred feet or so were the woods. There I might still hope to hide. I prayed for strength to get there. Bullets whistled by me, but firing on the run, the men could not take aim.

The woods, the woods, to them my whole being was swept forward. Louder and louder grew the shouts behind me:

"A she-spy! A she-spy!"

The woods were within my reach. Another bound, and I was in them. Onward I dashed like a wild deer. Was it because there were only several soldiers left at the post and they could not desert it to engage in a hunt, or because the men decided that I could not escape from the forest anyhow, that my pursuers did not follow me into the woods? I know only that they were satisfied with sending a stream of bullets into the forest and left me alone.

I concealed myself in a burrow till absolute calm was restored. Then I got out and tried to figure out the right direction, but I fell into an error at first and returned to the edge at which I entered. I then walked to the opposite side, struck a path and before taking it, I threw off my costume of a Sister of Mercy and hid it in a bush, drew out my soldier's cap, destroyed the passport of Smirnova, and appeared again in my own uniform. I realised that reports must have been sent out by my pursuers of a spy in the dress of a nurse and determined that as Botchkareva I might still stand a chance for life, but as Smirnova I was done for.

Day was breaking, but it was still dark in the woods. I met a soldier, who greeted me. I answered gruffly, and he passed on, evidently taking me for a comrade. A little later I encountered two or three other soldiers but again passed them without being suspected. I pulled out my direct ticket to Kislovodsk and the letter from Princess Tatuyeva. These were my two chief reliances. After walking for almost twenty *versts* I came in view of the station at Zverevo. A decision had to be adopted without delay. Loitering would surely land me in trouble, I considered, and so I made up my mind to go straight to the station, announce my identity, claim that I had lost my way and surrender myself.

When I opened the door of the station, filled with Red Guards, and appeared on the threshold, the men gaped at me as if I were an apparition.

"Botchkareva!" they gasped.

Without stopping to hear them, I walked up to the first soldier, with my legs trembling and my heart in my mouth, and said:

"Where is the *commandant?* Take me to the *commandant!*"

He looked at me hastily, but obeyed the order and led me to an office, also packed with Red Guards, where a young chap, not more than nineteen or twenty, was introduced to me as the head of the investigation committee, who was acting as chief in the absence of the *commandant.* Again, everybody emitted ejaculations of surprise at my unexpected appearance.

"Are you Botchkareva?" the young fellow inquired, showing me to a seat. I was pale, weak and travel-worn, and sank into the chair thankfully. Looking at the chief, hope kindled in my breast. He had a noble, winning face.

"Yes, I am Botchkareva," I answered. "I am going to Kislovodsk, to cure my wound in the spine, and I lost my way."

"What has come over you? Are you in your senses? We are preparing for an offensive against Kornilov just now. How could you ever take this route at this time? Didn't you know that your appearance here would mean your certain death?" the young man asked, greatly agitated over my fatal blunder.

"Why," he continued, "I just had a telephone call telling that a woman-spy had crossed from Kornilov's side early this morning. They are looking for her now. You see the quandary into which you have fallen!"

The youthful chief was apparently inclined toward me. I thought it worth trying to win him over completely.

"But I came myself," I broke out in tears, punctuating them with sobs. "I am innocent. I am just a sick woman, going to seek a cure at the springs. Here is my ticket to Kislovodsk and here is a letter from a friend of mine, my former adjutant, inviting me to come to the Caucasus. Surely you will not murder a poor, sick woman, if not for my own sake, at least for the sake of my forlorn parents."

Several of the Red Guards present cut short my pleading with angry cries:

"Kill her! What is the use of letting her talk! Kill her, and there will be one slut less in the world!"

"Now wait a minute!" the acting *commandant* interrupted. "She has come to us of her own volition and is not one of the officers that are opposing us. There will be an investigation first and we will ascertain whether she is guilty or innocent. If she be guilty, we will shoot her."

The words of the chairman of the investigation committee gave me courage. One could see that he was an educated, humane chap.

Subsequently I learned that he was a university student. His name was Ivan Ivanovitch Petrukhin.

As he was still discoursing, a man dashed in like a whirlwind, puffing, perspiring, but rubbing his hands in satisfaction.

"Ah, I just finished a good job! Fifteen of them, all officers! The boys got them like that," and he bowed and made a sign across the legs. "The first volley peppered their legs and threw them in a heap on the ground. Then they were bayoneted and slashed to pieces. Ho, ho, ho! There were five others captured with them, cadets. They tried to escape and the good fellows gouged their eyes out!"

I was petrified. The newcomer was of middle height, heavily built, and dressed in an officer's uniform but without the epaulets. He looked savage, and his hideous laughter sent shudders up my spine. The bloodthirsty brute! Even Petrukhin's face grew pale at his entrance. He was no less a person than the assistant to the Commander in Chief of the Bolshevik Army. His name was Pugatchov.

He did not notice me at first, so absorbed was he in the story of the slaughter of the fifteen officers.

"And here we have a celebrity," Petrukhin said, pointing at me.

The assistant commander made a step forward in military fashion, stared at me for an instant and then cried out in a terrifying voice:

"Botchkareva!"

He was beside himself with joy.

"Ho, ho, ho!" he laughed diabolically. "Under the old *régime* I would have gotten an award of the first class for capturing such a spy! I will run out and tell the soldiers and sailors the good news. They will know how to take care of her. Ho, ho, ho!"

I arose thunder-stricken. I wanted to say something but was speechless. Petrukhin was deeply horrified too. He ran after Pugatchov, seized him by the arm, and shouted:

"What is the matter; have you gone insane? Madame Botchkareva came here herself. Nobody captured her. She is going to Kislovodsk for a cure. She is a sick woman. She claims that she lost her way. Anyhow, she never fought against us. She returned home after we took over the power."

"Ah, you don't know her!" exclaimed Pugatchov. "She is a Kornilovka, the right hand of Kornilov."

"Well, we are not releasing her, are we?" parried Petrukhin. "I am going to call the committee together and have an investigation of her story made."

"An investigation!" scoffed Pugatchov. "And if you don't find any evidence against her, will you let her go? You don't know her? She is a dangerous character! How could we afford to save her? I wouldn't even waste bullets on her. I would call the men and they would make a fine *kasha* of her!"

He made a motion toward the door. Petrukhin held on to him.

"But consider, she is a sick woman!" he pleaded. "What is the investigation committee for if not to investigate before punishing? Let the committee look into the matter and take whatever action it considers best."

At this point the *commandant* of the station arrived. He supported Petrukhin. "You can't act like that in such a case," he said; "this is clearly a matter for the investigation committee. If she is found guilty, we will execute her."

Petrukhin went to summon the members of the investigation committee, who were all, twelve in number, common soldiers. As soon as he broached the news to each juror, he later told me, the man became threatening, talking of the good fortune that brought me into their hands. But Petrukhin argued with each of them in my favour, as he was convinced of the genuineness of my alibi. In such a manner he won some of them over to my side.

Meanwhile Pugatchov paced the room like a caged lion, thirsting for my blood.

"Ah, if I had only known it before, I would have had you shot in company with those fifteen officers!" he addressed me.

"I would not have the heart to shoot at my own brothers, soldier or officer," I remarked.

"Eh, you are singing already," he turned on me. "We know your kind."

"All in all," I declared, "you are not better than the officers of the old *régime*."

"Silence!" he commanded angrily.

Petrukhin came in with the committee at that instant.

"I beg you not to yell," he turned to Pugatchov, feeling more confident with the committeemen at his back. "She is in our hands now, and we will do justice. It is for us to decide if she is guilty. Leave her alone."

There were only ten jurors within reach. The other two members were absent and the ten, being in the majority, decided to go on with the work.

217

"Whether you find her guilty or not, I will not let her get out of here alive!" Pugatchov declared. "What am I?" he added. "I am no enemy either."

However, this threat worked in my favour, as it touched the committee's pride. They were not to be overridden like that. Pugatchov demanded that I be searched.

"Please, I am at your disposal," I said, "but before you go ahead I want to hand over to you this package of money. There are ten thousand *rubles* in it, sent to me by Princess Tatuyeva, my former adjutant, to enable me to take the cure at the springs. I kept this money intact, because I hoped to return it to her upon reaching the Caucasus."

The money had in reality been given to me by Kornilov, to secure my parents and myself from starvation in the future.

The valuable package was taken away, without much questioning. I was then ordered to undress completely. Petrukhin protested against it, but Pugatchov insisted. The dispute was settled by a vote, the majority being for my undressing.

The search was painstaking but yielded nothing. There was the ticket to Kislovodsk, the letter from Princess Tatuyeva, a little bottle of holy water, given to me by my sister Nadia, and a scapula, presented to me before leaving for the front by one of the patronesses of the battalion.

"Ah, now we have got it!" exclaimed Pugatchov, seizing the hallowed bag. "There is the letter from Kornilov!"

The bag was ripped open and a scroll of paper was taken out on which a psalm had been written in a woman's hand. I declared that the sin of tearing it open would fall on their heads and that I would not sew it up again. One of the soldiers obtained a needle and thread and sewed the bag together.

The members of the committee excused themselves for being constrained to have me searched in such a manner.

"What will you do with me now?" I asked.

"We will have you shot!" answered Pugatchov.

"What for?" I demanded in despair.

The beast did not reply. He smiled.

Petrukhin was afraid to defend me too much, lest he be suspected of giving aid to a spy. He preferred to work indirectly for me, by influencing the committeemen individually. It was decided that the case be submitted to the commander in chief, Sablin, for review and sentence, I believe, on the motion of Petrukhin. This was just a trick to stave off immediate execution, but the expectation among the men was that my death was certain. Nevertheless, I was profoundly grateful to Petrukhin for his humane attitude. He was a man of rare qualities, and among Bolsheviks he was almost unique.

I was ordered to a railway carriage used as a jail for captured officers and other prisoners. It was a death chamber. Nobody escaped alive from there. When I was led inside, there went up a cry:

"Botchkareva! How did you get here? Coming from Kornilov?"

"No," I answered, "I was on my way to Kislovodsk."

There were about forty men in the car, the larger part officers. Among the latter were two generals. They were terribly shocked at my appearance among them. When my convoys left, the prisoners talked more freely. To some of them I even told the truth, that I had actually been to Kornilov. None of them gave me any hope. All were resigned to death.

One of the generals was an old man. He beckoned to me and I sat down beside him.

"I have a daughter like you," he said sadly, putting his arm around my shoulders. "I had heard of your brave deeds and came to love you as much as my own girl. But I never expected to meet you here, in this death-trap. Isn't it dreadful? Here we are, all of us, the best men of the country, being executed, tormented, crushed by the savage mob. If it were only for the good of Russia! But Russia is perishing at this very moment. Perhaps God will save you yet. Then you will avenge us. . . ."

I broke down, convulsed with sobs, and leaned against the general's shoulder. The old warrior could not restrain himself either and wept with me. . . .

The other officers suddenly sang out in a chorus. They sang from despair, in an effort to keep from collapsing.

I cried long and bitterly. I prayed for my mother.

"Who would sustain her?" I appealed to Heaven. "She will be forced to go begging in her old age if I am put to death." Life became very precious to me, the same life that I had exposed to a hundred perils. I did not want to die an infamous death, to lie on the field unburied, food for carrion crows.

"Why haven't you allowed me to die from an enemy's bullet?" I asked of God. "How have I deserved being butchered by the hands of my own people?"

The door swung open. About forty soldiers filed in. Their leader had a list of names in his hand.

"Botchkareva!" he called out first.

Somehow my heart leaped with joy. I thought I would be released. But the officers immediately disillusioned me with the statement that it was a call for execution. I stepped forward and answered:

"I am here!"

"*Razdievaysia!*" (Undress.)

The order stupefied me. I remained motionless.

Some soldiers came up, pushed me forward and repeated the order several times. I awoke at last and began to undress.

The old general's name was read off the list next. Then a number of other officers were called out. Each of them was ordered to cast off his uniform and remain in his undergarments.

The Bolsheviks needed all the uniforms they could get, and this was such an inexpensive way of obtaining them! Tears streamed down my cheeks.

The old general was near me.

"Don't cry!" he urged me. "We will die together."

Not all the prisoners were in our group. Those remaining kissed me farewell. The parting among the men was alone sufficient to pierce one's heart.

"Well, we will follow you in an hour or two," those who were left behind said bravely.

After I took my boots off, I removed the icon from my neck and fell before it on my knees.

"Why should I die such a death?" I cried. "For three years I have suffered for my country. Is this shameful end to be my reward? Have mercy, Holy Mother! If not for the sake of humble Maria, then for the sake of my destitute old mother and my aged father! Have mercy!"

Here I collapsed completely and became hysterical.

After a few moments an officer approached me, put his hand on my shoulder, and said:

"You are a Russian officer. We are dying for a righteous cause. Be strong and die as it behoves an officer to die!"

I made a superhuman effort to control myself. The tears stopped. I arose and announced to the guards:

"I am ready."

We were led out from the car, all of us in our undergarments. A few hundred feet away was the field of slaughter. There were hundreds upon hundreds of human bodies heaped there. As we approached the place, the figure of Pugatchov, marching about with a triumphant face, came into sight. He was in charge of the firing squad, composed of about one hundred men, some of whom were sailors, others soldiers, and others dressed as Red Guards.

We were surrounded and taken toward a slight elevation of ground, and placed in a line with our backs toward the hill. There were corpses behind us, in front of us, to our left, to our right, at our very feet. There were at least a thousand of them. The scene was a horror of horrors. The poisonous odours were choking us. The executioners did not seem to mind it so much. They were used to them.

I was placed at the extreme right of the line. Next to me was the old general. There were twenty of us altogether.

"We are waiting for the committee," Pugatchov explained the delay in the proceedings.

"What a pleasure!" he rubbed his hands, laughing. "We have a woman today."

"Ah, yes," he added, turning to us all, "you can write letters home and ask that your bodies be sent there for burial, if you wish. Or you can ask for other favours."

The suspense of waiting was as cruel as anything else about the place. Every officer's face wore an expression of implacable hatred for that brute of a man, Pugatchov. Never have I seen a more bloodthirsty pervert. I did not think that such a man was to be found in Russia.

The waiting wore me out soon and I fell again on my knees, praying to the little icon, and crying to Heaven:

"God, when have I sinned to earn such a death? Why should I die like a dog, without burial, without a priest, with no funeral? And who will take care of my mother? She will expire when she learns of my end."

The Bolshevik soldiers broke out laughing. My pleading touched their sense of humour. They joked and made merry.

"Don't cry, my child," the general bent over me, patting me. "They are savages. Their hearts are of stone. They would not even let us receive the last sacrament. Let us die like heroes, nevertheless."

His words gave me strength. I got up, straightened myself out and said:

"All right, I will die as a hero."

Then, for about ten minutes I gazed at the faces of our executioners, scrutinising their features. It was hard to distinguish in them signs of humanity. They were Russian soldiers turned inhuman. The lines in their faces were those of brutal apes.

221

"My God! What hast Thou done to Thy children?" I prayed.

In a long file the numerous events of my life passed before me. My childhood, those years of hard labour in the little grocery store of Nastasia Leontievna; the affair with Lazov; my marriage to Botchkarev; Yasha; the three years of war; they all passed through my imagination, some incidents strangely gripping my interest for a moment or two, others flitting by hastily. Somehow that episode of my early life, when I quarrelled with the little boy placed in my charge and the undeserved spanking I got from his mother stood out very prominently in my mind. It was my first act of self-assertion. I rebelled and escaped. . . . . .Then there was that jump into the Ob. It almost seemed that it was not I who sought relief in its cold, deep waters from the ugly Afanasi. But I wished that I had been drowned then, rather than die such a death. . . .

CHAPTER 19

Saved by a Miracle

The investigation committee finally appeared in the distance. Petrukhin was leading them. There were twelve members present, the two absentees apparently having joined the other ten.

"You see how kind we are," some of the soldiers said. "We are having the committee present at your execution."

None of us answered.

"We were all to see Sablin, the commander in chief," Petrukhin announced as soon as he approached near enough to Pugatchov. "He said that Botchkareva would have to be shot, but not necessarily now and with this group."

A ray of hope was lit in my soul.

"Nothing of the sort!" Pugatchov bawled angrily. "What is the matter here? Why this postponement? The list is already made up."

The soldiers supported Pugatchov.

"Shoot her! Finish her now! What's the use of bothering with her again!" cried the men.

But just as Pugatchov sensed that Petrukhin had obtained the delay hoping to save me, so the latter realised that words would not be sufficient to carry his argument. He had provided himself with a note from Sablin.

"Here is an order from the commander in chief," Petrukhin declared, pulling out a paper. "It says that Botchkareva shall be taken to my compartment in the railway carriage and kept there under guard."

Pugatchov jumped up as if bitten. But the committee here rallied to the support of Petrukhin, arguing that orders were orders, and that I would be executed later.

Not the least interested spectator of the heated discussion was myself. The officers followed the argument breathlessly, too. The soldiers grumbled. The forces of life and death struggled within me. Now the first would triumph, now the second, depending on the turn of the quarrel.

"Nothing doing!" shouted Pugatchov, thrusting aside the order of the commander in chief. "It's too late for orders like that! We will shoot her! Enough words!"

At this moment I became aware of one of the two newly arrived committeemen staring at me intently. He took a couple of steps toward me, bent his head on the side and nailed his eyes on me. There was something about that look that electrified me. As the man, who was a common soldier, craned his neck forward and stepped out of the group, a strange silence gripped everybody, so affected were all by the painful expression on his face.

"A-r-e y-o-u Y-a-s-h-k-a?" he sang out slowly.

"How do you know me?" I asked quickly, almost overpowered by a premonition of salvation.

"Don't you remember how you saved my life in that March offensive, when I was wounded in the leg and you dragged me out of the mud under fire? My name is Peter. I would have perished there, in the water, and many others like me, if not for you. Why do they want to shoot you now?"

"Because I am an officer," I replied.

"What conversations are you holding here?" Pugatchov thundered. "She will have to be shot, and no arguments!"

"And I won't allow her to be shot!" my God-appointed saviour answered back firmly, and walked up to me, seized my arm, pulled me out of my place, occupying it himself.

"You will shoot me first!" he exclaimed. "She saved my life. She saved many of our lives. The entire Fifth Corps knows Yashka. She is a common peasant like myself, and understands no politics. If you shoot her, you will have to shoot me first!"

This tirade had a remarkably wholesome effect on me. It also struck home in the hearts of many in the crowd.

Petrukhin went up, took a place beside Peter and me, and declared: "You will shoot me, too, before you execute an innocent, sick woman!"

The soldiers were now divided. Some shouted, "Let's shoot her and make an end of this squabble! What's the use of arguments?"

Others were more human. "She is not of the *bourgeoisie*, but a common peasant like ourselves," they argued. "And she does not understand politics. Perhaps she really was going to seek a cure. She was not captured, but came to us herself, we must not forget."

For some time, the place turned into a meeting-ground. It was a weird situation for a debate. There were the hundreds of bodies scattered around us. There were the twenty of us in our under-garments awaiting death. Of the twenty only I had a chance for life. The remaining nineteen stoically kept themselves on their feet. No hope heaved their breasts. No miracle could save them. And amidst all this a hundred Russian soldiers, a quarter of an hour before all savages, now half of them with a spark of humanity in their veins, were deliberating!

The committee finally found their wits and took charge of the situation. Turning to Pugatchov, they declared:

"Now, we have an order here from the commander in chief, and it shall be obeyed. We will take her away."

They closed about me and I was marched out of the line and off the field. Pugatchov was in a white rage, raving like a madman, grinding his teeth. As we walked away, his inhuman voice roared:

"Fire at the knees!"

A volley rang out. Immediately cries and groans filled the air. Turning my head about, I saw the savages rush the heap of victims with their bayonets, digging them deep into the bodies of my companions of a few minutes previous, and crushing the last signs of life out of them with their heels.

It was frightful, indescribably frightful. The moans were penetrating, blood-curdling. I staggered, fell to the ground my full length, and swooned.

For four hours I remained unconscious. When I came to, I was in a compartment of a railway coach. Petrukhin sat near me, holding my hands, and weeping.

As I thought of the circumstances that led to my fainting, the figure of Pugatchov swam up before my eyes, and I took an oath there and then to kill him at the first opportunity, if I escaped from the Bolshevik trap.

Petrukhin then told me that Peter had aroused the investigation committee to such a state of compassion for me that the members agreed to go with him to Sablin, and petition the commander in chief to send me to Moscow for trial by a military tribunal. About fifty soldiers were also won over to my side by Peter's accounts of Yashka's work in the trenches and No Man's Land, and my reputation among all men. Petrukhin had remained at my bedside till I recovered consciousness, but he now desired to join the deputation. I gratefully thanked him for his humane attitude toward me and his desperate efforts to save my life.

Before he left, word reached him that Pugatchov had incited some of the men against me, threatening to kidnap me from my friends and lynch me. Petrukhin placed five of his loyal friends at my compartment, with orders not to surrender me at any cost.

I prayed to God for Petrukhin, and hearing my prayer, he said: "Now, I, too, believe in God. The appearance of this man, Peter, was truly miraculous. In spite of all my efforts, you would have been executed but for him."

"And how are my chances of escaping death now?" I asked.

"They are still very small," he answered. "Your record is against you. You do not deny being a friend of Kornilov's. Your strict discipline in the Battalion and your fighting the Germans at a time when the whole front was fraternizing, are known here. Besides, the death penalty has become so customary here that it would be very unusual for one to escape it. Only the other day a physician and his wife, on their way to Kislovodsk to the springs, somehow landed in Zverevo. They were arrested, attached to a party ready for shooting, and without any investigation were executed. Afterwards there were found in their clothes papers from their local Soviet, certifying that they were actually ill, the physician suffering from a cancer, and requesting that they be passed to Kislovodsk."

Petrukhin kissed my hand, and left, warning me:

"Wait here till I return. Nobody will harm you in my absence."

He locked the door behind him. I took out the little bottle of holy water, given to me by my youngest sister, Nadia, and drank it. On my knees before the little icon, I prayed long and devoutly to God, Jesus, and the Holy Mother. My cars caught a noise outside the car: it came from several menacing soldiers who wanted to get in and kill me on the spot. I prayed with greater fervour than before, begging for my life in the name of my mother, father and my little sister. My heart was heavy with sorrow and despair.

As I was hugging the little icon, tears streaming from my eyes, I suddenly heard a voice, a very tender voice, say to me:

"Your life will be saved."

I was alone in the compartment. I realise that it is an audacious statement to make. I do not seek to make any one believe it. One may accept it or not. But I am satisfied that I did hear the voice of a divine messenger. It was soothing, elevating. Suddenly I felt happy and calm. I thanked the Almighty for his boundless kindness and vowed to have a public prayer offered at the Moscow Cathedral of Christ the Saviour at the first opportunity, in commemoration of His miraculous message to me.

Then I fell asleep, and rested calmly till the arrival of Petrukhin. His face was wreathed in smiles, he clasped my hand joyously, saying:

"Thank God! Thank God! You are at least saved from the mob. Sablin ordered you sent to Moscow. The necessary papers are being prepared now."

At this point Peter came in, followed by some members of the investigation committee. All were happy. It was such a wonderful moment. How an act of humanity does transform men's countenances! Peter and his comrades congratulated me, and I was too overcome to express all the gratefulness that I felt toward these men.

Petrukhin then narrated how he had disposed of the incited soldiers, who clamoured for my life. He told them that I was being led away to Moscow in the hope that I would deliver there several counter-revolutionary generals, associated with Kornilov.

"Will she be shot afterwards?" they inquired.

"Sure," Petrukhin declared. The lynchers went away satisfied.

I was curious to know what would be done to me in Moscow. Petrukhin, in reply to my inquiries, said that among the papers relating to my case, which my convoys would take to Moscow, the chief document was the protocol. That protocol had been drawn up by himself, in the capacity of chairman of the investigation committee. He described in it how I had lost my way while going to Kislovodsk, getting stranded at Zverevo and how I had reported of my own free will to the authorities, adding that I had with me a ticket to Kislovodsk, an invitation from Princess Tatuyeva to come to the Caucasus, *and a statement from a physician certifying to my ill health.* The latter was, of course, an invention. Petrukhin sent along the ticket and the letter from Tiflis, adding that he had misplaced the physician's certificate and would send it on later.

"It is unlikely," he said to me, "that you would be punished with death on the strength of such evidence. I should expect your release, sooner or later. But in any event, here is a poison pill. I prepared it for you originally to take in case the mob got the upper hand, so that you could escape torture at the hands of these savages. I hope you will not have to resort to it in Moscow."

I still carry with me that pill of poison wherever I go. . . .

Petrukhin gave me forty *rubles* for expenses, as I was penniless. I thanked him and asked him to write a letter to my people, telling them of my whereabouts. We then took leave of one another. Petrukhin and Peter exchanged kisses with me, and I again and again reiterated how much I owed to them, swearing that in any future emergency, whatever happened, I would always be ready to do everything within my power for them. We all realised that many changes were still in store for Russia, till she settled down to peaceful pursuits.

Accompanied by my friends and surrounded by four armed guards, my convoy, I was led to an empty railway coach, attached to an engine. On this train, consisting of cattle-cars and my coach, I was taken to Nikitino. There I was brought before the *commandant*, with a request to provide accommodations for the party on a regular train. It was the same *commandant* who had helped me so generously to get to Zverevo on the munition train. Of course, he did not recognize the Sister of Mercy in Botchkareva.

On the platform I had another striking encounter. The word that Botchkareva had been seized and was being taken to Moscow had gone around the station and a number of Red Guards and soldiers gathered about me, showering insults, curses and threats. Among these, in the foremost rank, was that ugly creature of a man who had been in charge of the train on which I rode to Zverevo and who had proposed marriage to me!

The beast did not recognise me now. He scoffed straight into my face, repeated my name syllable by syllable, taking a peculiar joy in distorting it and railing generally at my appearance and reputation.

"The slut! We have got her, the harlot!" he raved. "Only I can't understand why they didn't shoot her there. Why bother with such a one!"

I could not help laughing. I laughed long, without restraint. It was so amusing. I almost had a desire to disclose to him how I had duped him. He still has no idea that Alexandra Smirnova, whose fictitious address at Kislovodsk he, in all probability, cherishes yet, was Maria

Botchkareva!

For three days I travelled with my convoy from Nikitino to Moscow. I was treated with consideration, but always as a prisoner. The guards would get food for me and themselves at the stations on the way. Upon our arrival at Moscow I was taken in an automobile to the Soldiers' Section of the Soviet, housed in what was formerly the governor's mansion. My guards delivered me to a civilian, with all the documents of the case, and left.

"What, coming from Kornilov?" the official asked me gruffly.

"No, I was going to take the cure at Kislovodsk," I replied.

"Ah, yes, we know those cures! What about the epaulets? Why did you take them off?"

"Because I am a plain peasant woman. I have defended my country bravely for three years. I am not guilty."

"Well, we will see about that later," he interrupted and ordered me led away to prison.

I was locked up in a small cell, in which there were already about twenty prisoners, officers and civilians, all arrested by agents who had overheard them talk against the Bolshevik regime! A fine reincarnation of the worst methods of *Tsarism*.

The cell was in a frightful condition. There was no lavatory in it, and the inmates were not permitted to leave the room! The stench was indescribable. The men smoked incessantly. The prisoners were not even allowed to take the short, daily promenade outside, which was granted by the old *régime*.

Apparently in order to make me confess, I was subjected to a new form of torture, never practised by the *Tsar's* jailers. I was denied food! For three days I did not receive even the niggardly ration given to the other prisoners. My companions were very nice to me, but the portions that they received were barely enough to sustain life in their own bodies. So, for three days and three nights I lay on the bunk, in a heap under a cover, on the point of suffocation, starved, feverish, and thirsty, as not even water was allowed me.

During these days the *commandant* of the prison, a sailor, came in several times daily to torment me with his tongue.

"What are you going to do to me?" I asked.

"What? You will be shot!" was his answer.

"Why?"

"Ha, ha. Because you are a friend of Kornilov's."

Those were the hours when I hugged the pill given me by

Petrukhin, in anticipation of a momentary order to face a firing squad.

Soon one of the arrested officers, who had been heard cursing Bolshevism while drunk, was set free. Before going some of his fellows intrusted him with messages to their relatives. I thought of the Vasilievs, who so kindly took me from the hospital to their home in the fall of 1916, and begged the officer to visit them and tell of my plight. He promised to do so and carried out the errand. I sent them a message that I expected to be executed and asked their help.

When Daria Maximovna got the message, she was shocked and immediately set out to get permission to see me. But when she called at the Soldiers' Section for a pass to see Botchkareva, she was taken for a friend of Kornilov's and would have been badly mauled but for the fact that her son Stepan, the very fellow who belonged to my company and who had brought about the friendship between his mother and me, was now one of the Bolshevik chiefs. Daria Maximovna raised the cry that she was the mother of Stepan Vasiliev, of such and such a department, and he was brought to identify her.

This saved her from severe punishment. She then appealed to her son to intervene in my behalf, but he refused, claiming that he could not come to the aid of an open friend of Kornilov. He, however, obtained a pass to my cell for his mother. Later he responded to her entreaties and did say a few good words for me, telling the proper authorities that I was a simple peasant woman with no understanding of politics.

On the fourth day of my imprisonment I received a quarter of a pound of bread, some tea and two cubes of sugar. The bread was too black for description, consisting partly of straw. I could not even touch it and had to satisfy myself with three cups of tea. Later in the day a sailor came in, addressing me as comrade, and informed me that one Vasilieva was waiting to see me. I was weak, so weak that I could not move a few feet without assistance. As soon as I got up and made a step, I sank back on the bunk, helpless.

"Are you sick?" the sailor asked.

"Yes," I murmured. He took me by the arm and led me to a chair in the office. I was all in perspiration after the little walk and was unable to see anything from dizziness. When Daria Maximovna saw me, she fell on my neck and wept. Turning to the officials, she cried out bitterly:

"How could you ever have such a woman arrested and subjected to torture? She was so kind to the soldiers, she suffered so much for your own brothers!"

She then opened a package, took out some bread and butter, and handed them to me, saying:

"Manka, here is a quarter of a pound of bread. All we got today was three-eighths of a pound. And this is a quarter of a pound of butter, our entire ration."

I was immensely grateful to this dear woman and her children, who had sacrificed their own portions for me. The bread was good. The difficulty was, according to Daria Maximovna, to get enough for all mouths. Even this meagre ration was not always obtainable.

I then told her my troubles and the punishment I faced, begging her to write to my mother in case of my execution.

Two weeks I spent in that abominable cell until I was taken before, the tribunal. I was marched along the Tverskaya, Moscow's chief thoroughfare, and was recognised by the crowds. The tribunal was quartered in the Kremlin. For a couple of hours, I waited there, at the end of which time I was surprised to see Stepan Vasiliev come in and approach me.

"Marusia, how did you ever get into this?" he asked me, shaking my hand and inviting me to sit down.

I told him the story of my going to Kislovodsk to take the cure.

"But how did you ever get to Zverevo?" he inquired.

"I had a ticket to Kislovodsk. I did not know that Zverevo was such a forbidden place. Once they sold me a ticket, I thought it all right to follow the regular route," I answered heatedly.

"I spent a couple of hours yesterday examining your case and the documents pertaining to it, but could not quite understand how you got to Zverevo," Stepan said. "Perhaps you really did go to see Kornilov?"

"I do not deny my friendship for Kornilov," I declared, glad at heart that Stepan turned up in such a position of authority. "But you know that I am almost illiterate and understand no politics and do not mix with any party. I fought in the trenches for Russia and it is Mother-Russia alone that interests me. All Russians are my brothers."

Stepan answered that he knew of my ignorance of political matters. He then went out to report to the tribunal, and soon afterwards I was called in. There were six men, all common soldiers, seated at a long table covered with a green cloth, in the middle of a large hall, richly finished. I was asked to sit down and tell my story, and how I ever got into Zverevo. The six judges were all young men, not one of them over thirty.

I started to rise from the chair to tell my yarn, but was very courteously asked to remain seated. I then told of my wound in the back, of the operation that I still needed for the extraction of a piece of shell, and of my consulting a Petrograd physician who advised me to go to the springs in Kislovodsk. I said that I had heard of fighting between Kornilov and the Bolsheviki, at Novotcherkask, but had no idea what a civil war was like and never thought of a front in such a struggle. I, therefore, continued to Nikitino, where the *commandant* had sent me on to Zverevo. Of course, I failed to mention the fact that the *commandant* had sent on to Zverevo not Botchkareva but Smirnova, a Sister of Mercy. I concluded with the statement that as soon as I reached Zverevo I realised that I was in a bad situation, and surrendered to the local authorities.

I was informed that it would take a week for my case to be cleared up and a decision reached. Instead of sending me to the Butirka, the prison in which I had been the last two weeks, I was taken to the military guardhouse, opposite the Soldiers' Section. Drunken sailors and Red Guards were kept there as a rule. The room in which I was confined was narrow and long, the windows were large but closely grated. There were about ten prisoners in it.

"Ah, look who's here! Botchkareva!"

With these words I was met as soon as I crossed the threshold. They quickly turned into phrases of abuse and ridicule. I was quiet, and sought seclusion and rest in a corner, but in vain. The inmates were Bolsheviks of the lowest sort, degenerates and former criminals. I was the object of their constant ill-treatment, so that day and night torturing me became their diversion. If I tried to sleep, I soon found someone near me. When I ate or drank, the beasts were around me, showering insults and playing dirty tricks. Weeping did not touch them. For nights and nights, I was forced to stay awake, sometimes throwing myself upon an intruder with my teeth in an effort to drive him away. I prayed the warden for a solitary cell.

"Let it be a cold, dingy hole. Give me no food. But take me away from these drunken brutes!" I pleaded.

"We will take you away soon—to shoot you!" the warden would joke in reply, to the uproarious merriment of my tormentors.

The promised week elapsed and still there was no decision in my case. Days—long, torturous, agonising days—passed slowly by. Above all, the inability to sleep was so excruciating that it drove me to a state actually bordering on insanity. Two and a half weeks I lived in that inferno, seventeen days without a single full night's sleep!

Then one morning the warden, who had delighted daily in telling me stories of what would be done to me, very vivid stories of frightfulness, came in with some papers in his hand.

"Botchkareva!" he called me out. "You are free." And he opened the door before me.

I was so surprised that I thought at first that this was another trick to torture me.

"Free?" I asked. "Why? I had grown to believe the warden's tales of what awaited me, and I could not imagine him as the carrier of such tidings.

"Am I free for good?" I asked.

"Yes," was the answer. "You will go with a guard to the Soldiers' Section, where you will get the necessary papers."

I bade farewell, with a sigh of relief, to the chamber of horrors, and went immediately to get the document from the tribunal, which stated that I had been arrested but found innocent of the charge and, being a sick woman, was to be allowed full freedom of movement in the country. With this passport in my pocket I was turned loose to go.

CHAPTER 20

Bearing a Message from My People

The Vasilievs were the only people I could go to in Moscow. They lived on the outskirts of the city. I made an attempt to walk to their house, but was too weak to proceed more than two blocks. There was a cabman at the curb, but he wanted twenty-five *rubles* to take me to my friends. I tried to bargain, offering fifteen, and he would not hear of it. As I had no money, I finally hired the cab in the hope that Daria Maximovna would pay for it. The alternative was to remain on the curb.

Madame Vasilieva received me as if I were her own daughter. She was overwhelmed with joy at my release. I was too emaciated and worn out to react fully to my miraculous deliverance from the clutches of torture and death. I was served some light food, and Daria Maximovna went about preparing a bath for me. I had not changed my undergarments for several weeks, and my body was blacker than it ever had been during my life in the trenches. My skin was in a terrible condition from vermin. The bath was a greater deliverance at the moment than my release itself. And the long hours of sleep following it were even more welcome. I doubt if sleep ever tasted sweeter to me.

One could not remain long as a guest in Moscow in those early days of March, 1918. Stepan lived away from his home, as his parents differed sharply with him on the political situation. The family consisted of Daria Maximovna, her husband and the younger son. The daughter, Tonetchka, was married and lived apart. The three Vasilievs received daily a pound and one-eighth of bread! The weekly meat ration was a pound and a half. I therefore promptly realised what a burden I was bound to be. But I could not make up my mind where to go and what to do. The Vasilievs offered to buy me a ticket home, but the document I had from the Soldiers' Section was in itself a ticket.

I recalled that some of my maimed girls had been sent to Moscow, to be quartered in the House of Invalids, and thought of looking them up. I took a walk to the city. When I approached the block in which the Home for Invalids was situated, I saw several crowds, largely composed of soldiers, in the street, holding meetings of indignation. As I reached the place I found a number of maimed soldiers, some of them without legs or arms, scattered about the front grounds.

On inquiry I learned that the Bolshevist authorities had turned the hundreds of crippled inmates into the street. Many of them, including my girls, had already disappeared, some undoubtedly spreading out to beg, others gathered up by charitable people and societies. But still a goodly number remained, crying, cursing Lenine and Trotzky, and asking passers-by for food and shelter. It was a pathetic sight. The cruelty of the order made one's blood boil. It was an order apparently promulgated just for the sake of cruelty. The excuse that the government needed the building certainly did not justify the wanton act.

There were about two hundred soldiers in the crowd, and I stopped to listen to their conversation. All of them had been attracted to the place by the complaints of the evicted invalids. Their talk came as a revelation to me. They were in a mutinous state, aroused against Lenine and Trotzky's *régime*. For several hours I lingered about the various groups, sometimes participating in the discussions.

"See what you have brought on by your own acts. You have atrociously beaten and killed your officers. You have abandoned God and destroyed the Church. Now, this is the result of your deeds."

In some such manner I addressed the men, and they answered something like this:

"We believed that by overthrowing our officers and the wealthy class, we would have plenty of bread and land. But now the factories are demolished and there is no work. We are terrorised by the Red

Guard, which is composed mostly of drunkards and criminals. If there are any honest soldiers in it, it is because hunger and poverty force them to enlist in order to escape starvation. If we demand justice and a square deal, we are shot down by the Red hangmen. And all the while the Germans are advancing into Russia, and nobody is sent to fight them, our real enemies."

At these words I crossed myself, thanking the Almighty for the deep change He had wrought in the minds of the people. The crowd became so demonstrative that the authorities were notified and a Red Guard detachment was sent to suppress it. It arrived suddenly and by firing a volley into the air warned us to disperse. The gathering split up and vanished from the street. A group of about ten soldiers, including myself, rushed into a neighbouring courtyard and continued the conversation there behind the gates.

"See, what you get now! If you were armed, they would not dare to treat you like that. They made you surrender your arms and now oppress you worse than the *Tsar*. Who ever heard of a thousand invalids thrown out into the street under the old *régime*?" I asked.

"Yes, we have been sold out. It is clear now. The Germans are taking away all our bread, occupying our land, destroying our country, demanding all our capital and possessions. We have been sold out," nodded several men.

"Ah, so you are beginning to see the light!"

"Yes, we are," declared one fellow. "A month ago, I wouldn't have talked to you. I was then the chairman of a local Soviet. But I see what it all means now. We are being arrested, searched, robbed, terrorised by the Red Guard mercenaries. I would, myself, shoot Lenine and Trotzky for this outrageous treatment of the invalids. A month ago, I was a fool, but I see now that I was all wrong in my ideas about you and other opponents of the Bolsheviki. You are not an enemy of the people, but a friend."

Accompanied by a couple of soldiers, I walked away. One of them told me he had seen a girl of mine, thrown out of the Home, begin begging. My heart pained at the thought, but I was absolutely without means. What could I have done for her? We reached the Cathedral of Christ the Saviour and I remembered the vow I had made to have a public mass served in commemoration of my miraculous escape from death.

I took leave of my companions and entered the church. There were about five or six hundred people there. On that very day, I believe, the order was promulgated separating the Church from the State. All the devout members of the Cathedral went to the Communion service that afternoon.

I went to see the deacon in the vestry and told him of the miracle that was vouchsafed me and the vow I had made. I did not fail to mention the fact that I was penniless and could not pay for the service. At the conclusion of the Communion, the priest announced:

> There has just come here a Christian woman who had suffered greatly for the country and whose name is known throughout the land. A miracle saved her in a desperate moment. God listened to her prayers and sent her an old friend, whose life she had once saved, on the eve of her execution. The execution was postponed. She then prayed to God again, and a divine voice informed her that her life would be spared. She vowed to offer public prayers in this Cathedral in the event of her release. The Lord mercifully granted her freedom, and she is now here to fulfil the vow.

The priest then asked the deacon to bring me up to the altar. When I was led there, a murmur went through the assembly:

"Lord! It's Botchkareva!"

Candles were lit and for fifteen minutes prayers of praise to the Lord were read, glorifying His name.

I returned to the Vasilievs by trolley. On the car there were many soldiers, and again their conversation cheered me up.

"A fine end we have come to! The Germans are moving nearer and nearer, and here they are shooting and arresting the people!" the men said to one another. "Why don't they send the Red Guard to resist the enemy? We are being sold to the Germans."

This was my second encounter with sober-thinking soldiers in one day. I arrived at Daria Maximovna's in high spirits. The awakening of the Russian soldier had begun!

I had left my medals and crosses in Petrograd before starting out on the fateful errand. Borrowing some money from Madame Vasilieva, I went for them to Petrograd. The railway carriage in which I travelled was packed with about a hundred and fifty soldiers. But they were no longer the cut-throats, the incensed and revengeful ruffians of two months ago. They did not threaten. They did not brag. The kindness of their real souls had again asserted itself. They even made a place for me, inviting me to sit down.

"Please, Madame Botchkareva," they said, "take this seat."

"Thank you, comrades," I answered.

"No, don't call us comrades any more. It's disgraceful now. The comrades are at present fleeing from the front, when the Germans threaten Moscow," some of them remarked.

One felt among friends. This comradeship was what endeared the Russian soldier to my heart. Not the comradeship of the agitators, not the comradeship so loudly proclaimed in the Bolshevik manifestoes and proclamations, but the true comradeship that made the three years in the trenches the happiest of my life. That old spirit again filled the air. It was almost too good to be real. After the nightmare of revolution and terror, it felt like a dream. The soldiers were actually cursing Bolshevism, denouncing Lenine and Trotzky!

"How does it happen that you all talk so sanely?" I asked.

"Because the Germans are moving on Moscow, and Lenine and Trotzky don't even snap their fingers," came in answer. "A soldier has escaped from Kiev and just telegraphed that the Germans are seizing Russians and sending them to Germany to help fight the Allies. Lenine and Trotzky told us that the Allies were our enemies. We now see that they are our friends."

Another soldier, who had been home on leave, told of an armed Red Guard detachment that descended on his village one fair day and robbed the peasants of all the bread they had, the product of their sweat and blood, exposing them to starvation.

"The people are hungry, that's why they join the Red Guard," one of the men remarked. "At least then they get food and arms with which to plunder. It is getting so that one is not safe unless he belongs to the Red Guard."

"But why don't you do something?" I addressed myself to them. "Everywhere I see the people are aroused, but they do nothing to overthrow the yoke."

"We have demanded more than once the resignation of Lenine and Trotzky. There were large majorities against them at several elections. But they lean on the Red Guard and keep themselves in power in spite of the will of the people. The peasants are almost to a man against them."

"The more reason why you should act," I said. "Something ought to be done!"

"What? Tell us what!" several wanted to know.

"Even to get together, for instance, and re-establish the front!" I suggested.

"We would, but we have nobody we can trust to lead us. All our good people are fighting among themselves," they argued. "Besides, we would need arms and food."

"You just said that the Allies were our friends. Suppose we asked them to send us arms and food and help us to reorganise the front, would you be willing to fight the Germans again?" I inquired.

"Yes," answered some, "we would."

"No," replied others, "what if the Allies got into Russia and wanted to take advantage of us, like the Germans?"

"Well, you must elect your own leader to cooperate with the Allies only on condition that we fight till we defeat the enemy and finish the war," I proposed.

"But whom could we choose as our leader?" the men persisted. "All our chiefs are divided. Some are reputed to be monarchists. Others are said to be exploiters of the poor labouring people. Still others are declared to be German agents. Where could we find a man that would not belong to one of these or other parties?"

"What if I, for instance, took charge, and became your leader?" I made bold to ask. "Would you follow me?"

"Yes, yes!" they cried. "We could trust you. You are a peasant yourself. But what could you do?"

"What could I do? You know that these scoundrels are destroying Russia. The Germans are grasping everything they can lay hold on. I would try to restore the front!"

"But how?" they quizzed.

Here the idea of going to America originated in my mind. We had all heard that America was now one of the Allies.

"What if I should go to America to ask there for help?" I ventured.

My companions all burst out laughing. America is so remote and so unreal to the Russian peasant. It did not sound like a practical proposition to the soldiers. But they raised only one objection.

"How would you ever get there? The Bolsheviks and Red Guards will never let you out of the country," they said.

"But if I did get there and to the other Allies," I insisted, "and came back with an army and equipment, would you join me then, and would you have all your friends come with you?"

"Yes, we would! Yes! We know that you could not be bought. You are one of us!" they shouted.

"In that event, I will go to America!" I announced resolutely, there

237

and then making up my mind to go. The soldiers wouldn't believe me. When we reached Petrograd and I parted from them affectionately, with their blessings following me, I did not forget to warn them to remember their pledge upon hearing of my arrival from foreign lands with troops.

I spent only several hours in Petrograd and did not go to see General X. I got my war decorations from the woman friend with whom I had left them, and saw only a few of my acquaintances. I told all of them of the great change in the soldiers' state of mind, and they rejoiced.

"Thank God!" they exclaimed. "If the soldiers are waking up, then Russia will yet be saved."

After dinner I took a train back to Moscow. As usual, soldiers formed the larger part of the passengers. I listened to their discussions attentively, although this time I took no part in them, as there were a few Bolsheviks among the men, and I did not wish to divulge my plans. I heard many curse Lenine and Trotzky, and all expressed their willingness to go to fight the Germans. One fellow asked:

"How could you fight them, without leaders and organisation?"

"Ah, that's the trouble," answered several at once. "We have no leaders. If some appeared and only called on us, we would make short work of the Bolsheviks and drive the Germans out of Russia."

I said nothing, but remembered the words well. The people were groping for light. It strengthened my determination to go to the Allied countries in search of help for Russia. But it was necessary to evolve some plan whereby I could get out of the country. A happy thought then occurred to me: I would make my destination the home of my valued friend, Mrs. Emmeline Pankhurst, London.

Upon my arrival at Moscow, I announced to the Vasilievs my decision to go to London. It was explained to me that the only way out of Russia lay through Vladivostok, and that I would have to cross America before reaching England. That suited me exactly.

Before taking the necessary steps for the departure I resolved to look up my girls and visited a clinic in which my poor little soldiers were said to be located. When I arrived at the address I found the building closed and was referred to a certain professor, whom I finally found. He told me that those of the girls who were not severely wounded had left for their native places. Only about thirty invalids remained. Five of these suffered from shell shock and were either hysterical or idiotic. Many of the others were nervous wrecks. He had tried hard to have them quartered in the Home for Invalids, but hardly had they got there when the building was requisitioned by the Bolsheviks and the inmates turned out into the streets.

Vera Michailovna, a wealthy woman, had picked them up from the streets and sheltered them in her house, but just before my call she had telephoned to him that the Bolsheviks had requisitioned her own house, and she was in a quandary as to how to dispose of the girls. He concluded with the suggestion that both of us go over to Vera Michailovna.

With a heavy heart I entered the large building in which my unfortunate girls, momentarily awaiting the word to get out, were kept. I came as a complete surprise to them. But there was no joy in my heart as I crossed the threshold of their room. It was not a happy re-union. I had no means with which to help them, no power, no influential friends.

"The *Natchalnik! Natchalnik!*" the women exclaimed joyously as soon as they perceived me, rushing toward me, throwing themselves upon my neck, kissing me, hugging me.

"The *Natchalnik* has come! She will save us! She will get us money, bread, a home!"

They danced and pranced about me in a spirit of jubilation, making me feel even more bitter and miserable.

"Girls dear!" I tried to disillusion them early, "I am myself penniless and hungry. You mustn't expect any help of me now."

"*Nitchevo!* You know how to get everything!" they answered with confidence. "You will take us to fight the Bolsheviks as we fought the Germans!"

There was a conference between Vera Michailovna, the professor, and myself on the problem facing us. Vera Michailovna suggested that I take the girls with me to my home village. I rejected the idea at first, both because I did not intend to remain at Tutalsk but continue on to Vladivostok and because of my lack of funds.

Vera Michailovna, however, insisted that the wisest thing in the circumstances would be to take them away from Moscow. She told me that several of the girls had been lured away and maltreated by the Bolshevik soldiers and that the result of leaving them in Moscow would be their ruin. She offered to provide tickets for them all to my village and a thousand *rubles* in ready money. I finally consented to take my invalids with me, hoping to obtain sufficient funds in America to insure them a life of peace and comfort.

I had resolved to go to America, but I had no funds. As my destination was to be London, for the reasons mentioned, I thought of seeking assistance from the British Consul in Moscow. With the aid of the Vasilievs I succeeded in locating the consul's offices and went to see him. There were many people waiting to see the consul, and I was informed that he could not be seen. His secretary came out and asked me for the purpose of my call. I gave him my name, told him of my plight and of my decision to go to London, to visit Mrs. Pankhurst, and asked for aid on the ground that I had fought and sacrificed much for the cause of Russia and the Allies. He reported my presence to the consul, who received me almost immediately.

The consul was very courteous. He met me with a smile and a cordial handshake, said that he had read in the papers of my arrest at Zverevo and inquired what he could do for me. I showed him the document from the Soviet, but did not reveal to him the fact of my mission to Kornilov, adding:

"Gospodin Consul, as you see, this paper allows me freedom of movement. I want to take advantage of it and go to London, to visit my friend, Mrs. Pankhurst. But I am without means. I came to ask you to send me, as a soldier, who had fought for the Allied cause, to England. If Russia should awake, I will eagerly resume my service to this cause."

The consul explained that the Bolsheviks would not allow him to draw on the consulate's deposits in the banks but, in view of my circumstances, he could supply me with some money for expenses. As to my visit to London, he said, there were great difficulties in the way, even for his own countrymen, let alone Russians.

But I would not alter my mind, and persisted in begging him to send me to his country. He promised to consider the matter and give a definite answer that night. He then invited me to dine with him at eight o'clock that evening.

When I returned for dinner the consul informed me that he had already telegraphed to the British Consul at Vladivostok of my going to London by way of America, requesting him to aid me in every way he could. At dinner I told the consul how Mrs. Pankhurst came to know me, but kept to myself the real purpose of my trip, as I feared that the consul would not want to antagonise the Bolsheviks by extending his protection to me. He gave me five hundred *rubles*, and I decided to leave immediately. A Siberian Express was leaving at 12.40 the same night. I had a few hours left to get my girls started to the station and to bid farewell to the Vasilievs.

My immediate destination was Tutalsk, on the Great Siberian Line. I was uneasy about the treatment our party might get from the soldiers filling three-quarters of the space on the train. But here again the mental transformation was obvious. The passengers discussed affairs sanely. There were many officers aboard but they were not molested. The soldiers were friendly to them and to us. The all-absorbing topic was the advance of the Germans. Lenine and Trotzky were cursed and denounced as despots worse even than the *Tsar*. There were many refugees from the newly invaded provinces and their tales added fuel to the mutinous spirit of the men.

"We were promised bread and land. Now the Germans are taking both away."

"We wanted an end to the war but Lenine got us into a worse position than before."

"We went to the Bolshevist bureaus and told of our hunger, and they advised us to enlist in the Red Guard."

"One can't find work; all the factories are shut down or disorganised."

These and similar sentiments were expressed on every side. Underlying them all was a greater hatred for the Germans than ever. There was no question in my mind that those men were ready to follow any trusted leader, with arms and food, against the Germans.

In Tcheliabinsk the train stopped for a couple of hours. There were two regiments stationed there, and there were several hundred soldiers aboard the express. A meeting was quickly organised right near the station, within a short distance of the place where I had been thrown off the train some three months previous. But how different was the mood of the masses now! There were thousands at the meeting. A refugee addressed the crowd. He made a stirring, sarcastic speech.

"Every one of us," he began, "has something at stake in Russia. We all went to defend our country. We all made our sacrifices. For three years I fought in this war. Then I was set free to return home. But I found my home in the hands of the Germans. I could not return. I lost my parents, my wife, my sisters! What do I now get for all my sacrifices? "Liberty! "I came to Petrograd. For three days I went hungry. I was not alone. There were many other soldiers who suffered the same fate. They gave us no bread. What do we get to satisfy our needs? "Liberty! "I went to see the chief of the Government in Petrograd. But I was never admitted to him. I was nearly beaten to death and thrown out of the building. Why?

"Liberty!

"The Germans are taking everything they can and at the same time the Red Guard is being increased to fight—whom, the Germans?—no, the so-called *bourgeoisie!* But are they not our own brethren, our own blood? In the name of what are we urged to slaughter our own people while the Germans ravish our land?

"In the name of Liberty!

"Our country has been disgraced and ruined and still we are being called upon to destroy our own educated and intelligent classes.

"Is this Liberty?

"I hear that in Moscow a thousand invalids were thrown out into the street. These invalids are soldiers like yourselves and myself, only maimed and crippled for life. Why were they thrown out?

"For the sake of Liberty!"

We were all deeply impressed by this speech of the soldier. Not a single voice was raised in protest. Every heart felt that the liberty we had received was not the kind of liberty we had dreamed about. We wanted peace, happiness, brotherhood, not civil war, foreign invasions, strife, starvation and disease.

Another speaker said:

"The comrade is right. We have been deceived and disgraced. We do go hungry and no one cares. But how can we get out of this shameful situation? We would have to overthrow the present leaders, and re-establish the front. The Japanese are already moving into Siberia, and the Germans are occupying Russia, all because we are divided. We will be under some foreign yoke if we don't get together. We quarrelled with our officers, but how can we ever hope to do anything without officers? We might make peace with them, but where can we get arms to overthrow our present leaders, who have surrounded themselves with bands of Red Guards?"

For a moment the vast gathering remained silent. It was a pathetic calm. Somehow one felt poignantly that our much-cherished freedom had turned into an oppressive bondage.

Suddenly a couple of men raised their voices in protest, denouncing the speaker, even threatening him. They were promptly seized and placed under arrest, and quiet was restored.

"Allow me to answer the question!" I shouted to the chairman from the distant place I occupied.

"Botchkareva! It's Botchkareva!" a number of voices passed the word to the platform, and immediately I was picked up and carried to the speaker's stand.

"It's a pleasure to speak to you now," I began, "only a few weeks ago you would have torn me to pieces."

"Yes, it's true! We killed many!" several men interrupted. "But we were told that the officers wanted to enslave us, that's why we killed them. We now see that our real enemies are not the officers, but the Germans."

"Before I answer the question put by the preceding speaker, let me ask you what your attitude is toward the Allies," I said.

"America, England and France we trust. They are our friends. They are free countries. But we distrust Japan. Japan wants Siberia," came in reply from many corners.

Here a soldier requested permission to ask a question. It was granted.

"I can't understand why our Allies do not defend us," he said. "Not one of them has come to our succour at a time when Germany is eating us up. The Allied envoys are running away from Russia, and those that remain do not listen to the voice of the masses, but to the representatives of Lenine and Trotzky. At Moscow I saw an official of the Soviet escort an Englishman to a train. I was hungry. There were hundreds of soldiers like me at the station. Our hearts were aching. We wanted to give him a message, but he did not even turn to us. Instead, he pressed heartily the hand of the Soviet official."

"What if we should appeal to the Allies, to America, England and France, to furnish us bread, arms and money for the reconstruction of the front?" I resumed.

"How can we trust them?" I was interrupted again. "They will come here and work together with Lenine and his band of bloodsuckers."

"Why not get together and elect a Constituent Assembly, and let your own leaders cooperate with the Allies?" I suggested.

"But whom could we choose?"

"That we would decide later. There are plenty of good men still left in Russia," I answered. "But what if I, for instance, should want to do something, would you trust me?"

"Yes, yes! We know you! You are of the people!" hundreds of throats cried.

"Well, let me tell you then, I am going to America and England. If I should get through and come back with an Allied force, would you come to aid me in saving Russia?"

"Yes! We will! Yes, yes!" the crowd roared.

With this the meeting ended. The train was made up and we hurried toward it, singing on the way. I felt happy and hopeful. Several thousand soldiers were not to be disregarded. They were almost unanimous in their new view of the country's condition. With my observations in Moscow and on the way to Petrograd, this meeting added enthusiasm to my hopes for Russia's salvation. It was obviously a country-wide phenomenon, this awakening of the soldiery.

My mother had received Petrukhin's letter, and for six weeks had mourned me as dead. She was overwhelmed with joy upon my return, but became a little uneasy as she perceived a long line of girls, many of them almost barefoot, file behind me into the little cabin. She took me aside and asked what it meant, confiding that she had only fifty *rubles* left of the money I had given her before. I begged her to be patient and assured her that I would arrange matters promptly. I immediately went to the owner of the cabin and several other leading peasants of the community, got them together, explained to them the situation, informed them that I had only one thousand *rubles* to spend toward the support of the girls, and asked if they would undertake to feed and house them on credit till my return from America.

"I swear that I will pay every *kopeck* due to you. I will get enough money to pay not only the debts, but to insure for them sustenance and shelter to the end of their lives. Now I want you to keep a record of all your expenses. Will you trust me?"

"Yes," replied the peasants. "We know that you have done a great deal for Russia, and we have confidence in you."

This was the arrangement under which the thirty invalids of my Battalion of Death were left by me in the village of Tutalsk in March, 1918. The thousand *rubles* I gave to my mother with instructions to buy shoes for the neediest of the girls. Of the five hundred *rubles* given to me by the consul, I left three hundred to my mother. I decided to take my youngest sister, Nadia, along with me to America. Accompanied to the station by my parents, the thirty girls, and half the community, I started eastward, for Irkutsk and Vladivostok, dressed once more as a woman.

At the station in Irkutsk I noticed a young girl, with two tiny children in her arms. Somehow her face looked familiar to me, but I could not place her. She was evidently in trouble, poor and ragged. For a while she stared at me. Then she ran up and cried out breathlessly:

"Mania!"

She was the younger daughter of the woman Kitova who accompanied her husband, who had killed the dogcatcher, into exile when I went there with Yasha. Then she was not more than eleven or twelve years old. Now she was the mother of two children.

For three days, she told me, her mother and herself lived on the floor of the station. They had only seventy *kopecks* left in their possession. With this money the mother had gone to the town to find a lodging! More than three months they had been traveling from Yakutsk, where this girl had been married to a political. All the money in my purse was two hundred *rubles*. I gave forty and then another twenty to the poor girl.

While I was cuddling one of the two babies, a *commissary* approached me.

"Are you Botchkareva?" he asked.

"Yes," I answered.

He wanted to detain me, but several soldiers who had travelled on the same train with me hurried to my defence. There was a hot argument. I drew out my pass from the Soviet and claimed the freedom to go wherever I pleased. I was finally left alone.

I waited for the return of the old Kitova to the last minute, desiring to see her and especially to learn about Yasha and other friends in North Siberia. Her daughter could only tell me that Yasha had married, after the native fashion, a Yakut woman and was still in Amga when she last heard. . . .

We resumed the journey eastward. At Khabarovsk, seven hundred *versts* from Vladivostok, we changed trains and had to accommodate ourselves for the night at the station in the women's rest-room. When I was about to turn in, the door opened and a voice behind me called out sharply:

"Commander Botchkareva?"

"Yes," I replied, alarmed at this form of address.

"Are you going to England?" was the next question.

"No."

"Where, then, are you going?"

"To Valdivostok, to stay with relatives."

The *commissary* then demanded my baggage for a search. He found a letter from the Moscow Consul to his Vladivostok colleague. I explained that the consul had supported me in Moscow and now asked the English representative at Vladivostok to help me out also. The commissary told me whisperingly that he was only fulfilling orders, but did not sympathise any longer with Lenine's *régime*. He had left four soldiers outside of the room in order to facilitate matters for me. His eyes fell on a photograph of mine in the trunk, which showed me in full uniform and was the last copy in my possession. He asked for it and my autograph, and to win his favour I gave it to him without delay. He then advised me to conceal the letter from the consul, and I sent it through Nadia to Ivanov, one of my fellow travellers outside. One of these was a member of a provincial Soviet, an ex-Bolshevik. He and other soldiers aided me while aboard the train to evade the Red Guards who searched it daily, at various stations, for officers going to join General Semenov. More than once I was covered under their overcoats in an emergency. When the searchers asked:

"Who's there?"

"A sick comrade," would be the answer, and the Red Guards passed on.

The *commissary* had orders to take me to town and hold me. Convoyed by the four Guards, Nadia and I were taken to the police-station. I was locked up while the commissary went to call a meeting of the local Soviet. Nadia remained outside of the cell, and I suddenly heard her cry for help. Rushing to the door, I saw through the key-hole that the Red Guards were annoying her. I banged at the door, shouting to the rascals to leave her alone, appealing to their sense of shame, but they jeered and kept pestering her. My helplessness behind the locked door infuriated me. I don't like to think of what the ruffians would have done to Nadia had not my friend Ivanov come in with two other soldiers to plead for me.

They found Nadia crying and me banging at the door in a white rage. I told them of the behaviour of the four Red Guards toward my sister and a sharp quarrel ensued. Presently the chairman of the local Soviet and a majority of its members arrived. My case was taken up. It appeared that orders had been received from Moscow or Irkutsk to detain me. As the search had netted nothing incriminating against me, my claim that I was going to Vladivostok could not be refuted.

Ivanov and the two soldiers put up a valiant defence, arguing that I was a sick woman, that they had come to know me during our companionship on the train as a real friend of the people, and that it would be a disgrace to arrest me and send me back with no evidence against me. If not for these three defenders, I would in all probability have been despatched under convoy to Moscow or Tutalsk. With their aid,

I was able to make such a favourable impression on the Khabarovsk Soviet that I was permitted to proceed to Vladivostok, where I arrived early in April, 1918, with five *rubles* and seventy *kopecks* in my purse.

The Soviet in Valdivostok kept a very close watch over all arrivals and departures. As soon as Nadia and I reached a lodging house, our documents were demanded to be sent to the Soviet for inspection. Nadia had a regular passport, while I made use of the paper from the Moscow Soldiers' Section. It is usual for such documents to be returned to their owners with the stamp of the local Soviet on their backs. But ours were somehow slow in arriving—not a good omen.

I went to the English Consul and was received in his office by an elderly Russian colonel, who served there in the capacity of secretarial interpreter. He recognised me at once, as a telegram from Moscow announcing my coming had preceded me. The consul was very kind and cordial when I was shown into his study, but declared that his position was such that he could not take it upon himself to obtain a passport for me from the Soviet, as he was suspected of counter-revolutionary activities.

Without revealing to the consul, the real purpose of my trip, I explained to him that my journey to London was undertaken not merely as a social visit to Mrs. Pankhurst, but as an avenue of escape from the terror of Bolshevism, which made life for me perilous anywhere in Russia. He advised me to go to the local Soviet, tell there of my desire to go to Mrs. Pankhurst, of whom the Bolsheviks had certainly heard, and ask for passports. The Consul thought that the Soviet could find nothing dangerous about my journey to his country, and would allow me to proceed unmolested. I replied with an account of some of the things I had endured at the hands of Lenine's government and said I was very certain that my formal application for a passport would be the end of my venture. He then called up the American Consul at Vladivostok, informed him of my arrival and my plight, and enlisted his interest.

I returned to the hotel, with three hundred *rubles* given me by the consul in my purse. The place was dirty and without conveniences, but it was almost impossible to obtain decent accommodations in the city. However, the proprietor of the inn was very helpful and later saved me from trouble. The following day the consul told me that all efforts to win the good-will of the Soviet toward me not only failed, but were met with threats at my address. The Bolsheviks might even send me back, I learned. I redoubled my plea to the consul to send me away, even without the Soviet's passport. He would not promise to do so, but under the pressure of my appeals finally showed an inclination to consider the matter.

Upon leaving the consulate I was stopped in the street by a soldier. "Botchkareva?" he asked.

"Yes," I answered.

"Why did you come here to tramp the streets?" was the next question.

"I came to visit my relatives, but found that they had moved, so I am going back soon."

He let me go my way. As soon as I arrived at the hotel, the proprietor took me aside to tell me that representatives of the Soviet had called in my absence, and inquired as to my doings and my plans. He had informed them that I came to look up some relatives, but was unable to locate them. They left with the threat that they would return to arrest me. It was not in my plan to wait for their arrival and allow myself to be detained and sent back. I called up the consul and told him of the latest development. Fortunately, he had some good news for me. An American transport was to touch at Vladivostok two days later!

Nadia and I hurried to the consulate. The consul declared that the Bolsheviks had threatened him if he should be found aiding me to get away. Meanwhile he proceeded to have all the necessary foreign passports prepared for us, and we were photographed for that purpose. The difficulty of leaving Vladivostok without a pass from the Soviet still confronted us. The harbour was under strict control, and the boats used to ferry passengers from the shore to the steamships were manned and inspected by Bolsheviks.

For nearly two days I remained in my room, in constant dread of the appearance of Red Guards to arrest me. They did not come, however, apparently sure that I could not escape their net anyway. They had ample reason afterwards to change their minds about it. I then went to the consul again. The American transport *Sheridan* was due that night, he said, but he was not sure yet if the captain would be willing to take me on.

Meanwhile we sought a means to elude the inspectors at the port. A large traveling basket was tried, and I managed to accommodate myself in it, but the consul decided that I might be suffocated should the basket be left at the pier for a couple of hours. I got out of the basket.

The transport arrived in the evening and the captain expressed his willingness to carry me across the Pacific. At the request of the consul I remained in his house while my sister, accompanied by an officer, went to the hotel to get my things, and with them left for the vessel. Two hours later I called up the hotel to find out whether Nadia had been there with the officer. The proprietor informed me that about fifty Red Guards had just been there looking for me, and were painfully surprised to learn that I had departed.

"Where did she go?" they asked the proprietor.

"To the railroad station, to take a train," he lied.

"What train?" they shouted indignantly. "There are no trains leaving tonight."

With that they went away, presumably to search for me. I communicated to the consul what I had learned on the wire, and he hid me in a closet. Soon afterwards several Red Guards arrived, asking for Botchkareva. The consul denied knowledge of my whereabouts, declared that I had come to him only once, as a result of which he had applied to the Soviet for a passport for me, but since he was refused he washed his hands of my case. The Red Guards said that I had been observed entering the consulate, but was not seen leaving it. They looked about for me and left, after the consul's denial of my visit.

The officer returned, after taking Nadia aboard the transport, with the news that I would have company on the way, as eight Russian officers were to be passengers on the same vessel. Hundreds of Russian officers had arrived in Vladivostok in the belief that they could join the British Army there and be transported to France. Unfortunately, the Allies would not accept their services and they found themselves in troubled circumstances, without means to return to European Russia and with no desire to do so, as long as Bolshevism was still rampant there. Some of them succeeded by various means in going to the United States or Canada.

The colonel asked me if I wanted to meet my fellow-travellers. I answered in the affirmative, and as they were at the moment at the Consulate, he took me into the room in which they were waiting. Scarcely had I crossed the threshold, when, glancing at the small group of officers, my eyes suddenly fell on Leonid Grigorievitch Filippov, my former battle adjutant, who had carried me unconscious under German fire to safety in that unhappy advance of the battalion.

"What are you doing here?" both of us asked each other simultaneously, astonished at the unexpected meeting.

I had always felt that I owed my life to Lieutenant Filippov after I was shocked by a shell and contused when running from the enemy at the end of the abortive offensive launched by the Battalion. He had taken charge of the battalion upon my despatch to the Petrograd hospital, and later left for Odessa to train as an aviator.

From a short private conversation, I learned that Lieutenant Filippov was in the same plight as all the other officers who had come to Vladivostok under the impression that they would be accepted by the Allies. I decided to ask the consul to allow him to assume his former post of adjutant to me and let him become a member of my party. The consul graciously consented, and I was happy at the thought of journeying to foreign lands in the company of an educated friend, with a knowledge of languages, peoples and geography, who was also devoted to Russia with all his heart.

After another conference with the consul, it was decided that I should dress as an Englishwoman and then make an effort to get to the American transport. The necessary clothes were obtained and in fifteen minutes I appeared no longer as a soldier, but as a veiled foreign woman who did not understand a word of Russian. Accompanied by the colonel, I left for the harbour, after having expressed my deepest thanks to the consul for his sacrifices in my behalf.

I was supposed to play a dumb role and leave everything to my escort. This I did, although more than once my heart jumped when a guard seemed to scrutinise me closely, and now and then I had to suppress an impulse to laugh when the colonel, in reply to questions, said that I was an Englishwoman returning home. It was dark when I was ferried to the transport and passed without mishap. But that was not the end of the adventure.

The transport had to remain for another day in the harbour and it was expected that the Soviet would search it for me. To baffle all attempts to discover me I was placed in a cabin, the entrance and all approaches to which were guarded. Nobody was allowed to come near the room, all inquirers being told that an important German general was detained there on his way to an American prison camp. Even Lieutenant Filippov did not know of the trick and was greatly worried over my non-arrival as the hour for the departure of the ship drew near. If any Bolshevik emissary was sent aboard the vessel to look for me, he undoubtedly was halted in front of a certain cabin by American soldiers and informed that no one would be permitted to get within so many feet of the imprisoned enemy general.

When the anchors of the *Sheridan* were raised and the ship began to move, I came out of the cabin, to the liveliest merriment of eve-rybody who expected to see a gruff Teuton general emerge from the door.

I was free!

It was April 18, 1918, when I left Russian soil for the first time in my life. Under the American flag, on an American transport, I was headed for that fantastic land—America—carrying in my breast the message of the Russian peasant-soldier to the Allies:

Help Russia release herself from the German yoke and become free—in return for the five million lives that she has sacrificed for your safety, the security of your liberties, the preservation of your own homes and lives!

LEONAUR

ALSO FROM LEONAUR

AVAILABLE IN SOFTCOVER OR HARDCOVER WITH DUST JACKET

THE WOMAN IN BATTLE *by Loreta Janeta Velazquez*—Soldier, Spy and Secret Service Agent for the Confederacy During the American Civil War.

BOOTS AND SADDLES *by Elizabeth B. Custer*—The experiences of General Custer's Wife on the Western Plains.

FANNIE BEERS' CIVIL WAR *by Fannie A. Beers*—A Confederate Lady's Experiences of Nursing During the Campaigns & Battles of the American Civil War.

LADY SALE'S AFGHANISTAN *by Florentia Sale*—An Indomitable Victorian Lady's Account of the Retreat from Kabul During the First Afghan War.

THE TWO WARS OF MRS DUBERLY *by Frances Isabella Duberly*—An Intrepid Victorian Lady's Experience of the Crimea and Indian Mutiny.

THE REBELLIOUS DUCHESS *by Paul F. S. Dermoncourt*—The Adventures of the Duchess of Berri and Her Attempt to Overthrow French Monarchy.

LADIES OF WATERLOO *by Charlotte A. Eaton, Magdalene de Lancey & Juana Smith*—The Experiences of Three Women During the Campaign of 1815: Waterloo Days by Charlotte A. Eaton, A Week at Waterloo by Magdalene de Lancey & Juana's Story by Juana Smith.

NURSE AND SPY IN THE UNION ARMY *by Sarah Emma Evelyn Edmonds*—During the American Civil War

WIFE NO. 19 *by Ann Eliza Young*—The Life & Ordeals of a Mormon Woman During the 19th Century

DIARY OF A NURSE IN SOUTH AFRICA *by Alice Bron*—With the Dutch-Belgian Red Cross During the Boer War

MARIE ANTOINETTE AND THE DOWNFALL OF ROYALTY *by Imbert de Saint-Amand*—The Queen of France and the French Revolution

THE MEMSAHIB & THE MUTINY *by R. M. Coopland*—An English lady's ordeals in Gwalior and Agra duringthe Indian Mutiny 1857

MY CAPTIVITY AMONG THE SIOUX INDIANS *by Fanny Kelly*—The ordeal of a pioneer woman crossing the Western Plains in 1864

WITH MAXIMILIAN IN MEXICO *by Sara Yorke Stevenson*—A Lady's experience of the French Adventure

AVAILABLE ONLINE AT **www.leonaur.com**
AND FROM ALL GOOD BOOK STORES
07/09

LEONAUR

ALSO FROM LEONAUR
AVAILABLE IN SOFTCOVER OR HARDCOVER WITH DUST JACKET

A DIARY FROM DIXIE *by Mary Boykin Chesnut*—A Lady's Account of the Confederacy During the American Civil War

FOLLOWING THE DRUM *by Teresa Griffin Vielé*—A U. S. Infantry Officer's Wife on the Texas frontier in the Early 1850's

FOLLOWING THE GUIDON *by Elizabeth B. Custer*—The Experiences of General Custer's Wife with the U. S. 7th Cavalry.

LADIES OF LUCKNOW *by G. Harris & Adelaide Case*—The Experiences of Two British Women During the Indian Mutiny 1857. A Lady's Diary of the Siege of Lucknow by G. Harris, Day by Day at Lucknow by Adelaide Case

MARIE-LOUISE AND THE INVASION OF 1814 *by Imbert de Saint-Amand*—The Empress and the Fall of the First Empire

SAPPER DOROTHY *by Dorothy Lawrence*—The only English Woman Soldier in the Royal Engineers 51st Division, 79th Tunnelling Co. during the First World War

ARMY LETTERS FROM AN OFFICER'S WIFE 1871-1888 *by Frances M. A. Roe*—Experiences On the Western Frontier With the United States Army

NAPOLEON'S LETTERS TO JOSEPHINE *by Henry Foljambe Hall*—Correspondence of War, Politics, Family and Love 1796-1814

MEMOIRS OF SARAH DUCHESS OF MARLBOROUGH, AND OF THE COURT OF QUEEN ANNE VOLUME 1 by A. T. Thomson

MEMOIRS OF SARAH DUCHESS OF MARLBOROUGH, AND OF THE COURT OF QUEEN ANNE VOLUME 2 by A. T. Thomson

MARY PORTER GAMEWELL AND THE SIEGE OF PEKING *by A. H. Tuttle*—An American Lady's Experiences of the Boxer Uprising, China 1900

VANISHING ARIZONA *by Martha Summerhayes*—A young wife of an officer of the U.S. 8th Infantry in Apacheria during the 1870's

THE RIFLEMAN'S WIFE *by Mrs. Fitz Maurice*—*The Experiences of an Officer's Wife and Chronicles of the Old 95th During the Napoleonic Wars*

THE OATMAN GIRLS *by Royal B. Stratton*—The Capture & Captivity of Two Young American Women in the 1850's by the Apache Indians

LEONAUR

ALSO FROM LEONAUR

AVAILABLE IN SOFTCOVER OR HARDCOVER WITH DUST JACKET

ZULU:1879 *by D.C.F. Moodie & the Leonaur Editors*—The Anglo-Zulu War of 1879 from contemporary sources: First Hand Accounts, Interviews, Dispatches, Official Documents & Newspaper Reports.

THE RED DRAGOON *by W.J. Adams*—With the 7th Dragoon Guards in the Cape of Good Hope against the Boers & the Kaffir tribes during the 'war of the axe' 1843-48'.

THE RECOLLECTIONS OF SKINNER OF SKINNER'S HORSE *by James Skinner*—James Skinner and his 'Yellow Boys' Irregular cavalry in the wars of India between the British, Mahratta, Rajput, Mogul, Sikh & Pindarree Forces.

A CAVALRY OFFICER DURING THE SEPOY REVOLT *by A. R. D. Mackenzie*—Experiences with the 3rd Bengal Light Cavalry, the Guides and Sikh Irregular Cavalry from the outbreak to Delhi and Lucknow.

A NORFOLK SOLDIER IN THE FIRST SIKH WAR *by J W Baldwin*—Experiences of a private of H.M. 9th Regiment of Foot in the battles for the Punjab, India 1845-6.

TOMMY ATKINS' WAR STORIES: 14 FIRST HAND ACCOUNTS—Fourteen first hand accounts from the ranks of the British Army during Queen Victoria's Empire.

THE WATERLOO LETTERS *by H. T. Siborne*—Accounts of the Battle by British Officers for its Foremost Historian.

NEY: GENERAL OF CAVALRY VOLUME 1—1769-1799 *by Antoine Bulos*—The Early Career of a Marshal of the First Empire.

NEY: MARSHAL OF FRANCE VOLUME 2—1799-1805 *by Antoine Bulos*—The Early Career of a Marshal of the First Empire.

AIDE-DE-CAMP TO NAPOLEON *by Philippe-Paul de Ségur*—For anyone interested in the Napoleonic Wars this book, written by one who was intimate with the strategies and machinations of the Emperor, will be essential reading.

TWILIGHT OF EMPIRE *by Sir Thomas Ussher & Sir George Cockburn*—Two accounts of Napoleon's Journeys in Exile to Elba and St. Helena: Narrative of Events by Sir Thomas Ussher & Napoleon's Last Voyage: Extract of a diary by Sir George Cockburn.

PRIVATE WHEELER *by William Wheeler*—The letters of a soldier of the 51st Light Infantry during the Peninsular War & at Waterloo.